1989 The Berlin Wall

My Part in Its Downfall

PETER MILLAR

ARCADIA BOOKS

Arcadia Books Ltd
15–16 Nassau Street
London W1W 7AB

www.arcadiabooks.com

First published by Arcadia Books 2009

A catalogue record for this book is available from the British Library.

ISBN 978-1-906413-47-7

Typeset in Minion by MacGuru Ltd
Printed in Finland by WS Bookwell

Arcadia Books gratefully acknowledges the financial support of Arts Council England.

The article by Peter Millar on page 10 has been printed with kind permission from

Arcadia Books is a member of English PEN, the fellowship of writers who work together to promote literature and its understanding. English PEN upholds writers' freedoms in Britain and around the world, challenging political and cultural limits on free expression.

Chicago, IL 60610

in Australia:
Tower Books
PO Box 213
Brookvale, NSW 2100

in New Zealand:
Addenda
PO Box 78224
Grey Lynn
Auckland

in South Africa:
Quartet Sales and Marketing
PO Box 1218
Northcliffe
Johannesburg 2115

Arcadia Books is the *Sunday Times* Small Publisher of the Year 2002/03

Contents

Acknowledgements

I have to thank my wife Jackie, who lived through so many of these experiences with me, and put up with my, often prolonged, absence during so many more of them. Also my sons, Patrick and Oscar, who had me dip in and out of their early lives, in particular during the tempestuous year that was 1989. At one stage Patrick, then four, used 'Budapest' as the name of a nook behind the sofa where he hid his toy cars: when things suddenly disappeared they had 'gone to Budapest'.

I also have to thank my great friends from East Berlin, some of them now sadly deceased, in particular the Falkner-Margan family: Bärbel, Alex, Alexandra, Horst and Sylvia. And also everyone else who was a regular at the wonderful little East Berlin corner bar, Metzer Eck, during the 1980s. It is still there, run by Sylvie Falkner, substantially unchanged, and remains the best bar in Berlin.

And finally I must acknowledge a huge debt of gratitude to my late mother who throughout that hectic period never failed to cut out her son's clippings from whichever newspaper I was working for at the time, and to preserve them in a scrapbook for me. Her efforts have made the burden on my memory so much lighter.

Foreword

One thing needs saying before anything else, at least for those unfamiliar with the autobiographical works of Spike Milligan: I make no claim whatsoever to having been instrumental in the fall of the Berlin Wall any more than any other of the millions of people who experienced life behind it and the tremendous exhilaration of seeing its ugly scar removed from the face of a much-loved city. And a tumour excised from the heart of Europe.

From 1981 until 1989 – and beyond – I was an eyewitness, albeit a highly involved one, to the events that shook the communist Soviet empire to its foundations, eventually toppling it, bringing down the Iron Curtain and leaving the way open for a fresh start in a new century. Like Milligan's account of his World War II soldiering in the wonderful *Adolf Hitler, My Part in His Downfall*, I have tried to take the reader from my own version of 'square bashing' (in the boozers of Fleet Street) to the trenches of the Cold War, where I was, if not exactly a foot soldier, then a front-line reporter.

I am not a comic writer in the vein of the late, great goon, and this is not primarily a funny story, although it does have more than a few comic moments. I have always firmly believed that, to the appreciative eye, history has a sense of humour, even if it is sometimes black humour.

This is not primarily a history book but the story of the curious love-hate relationship between events and journalists, a relationship that ends up as history. It is in particular the story of this journalist and this story is one which I did not so much report as *live*. East Berlin wasn't just a place I went to write about, but an inseparable part of my life. The people whose lives were forever changed by the events of November 9th, 1989 were not interviewees, but close personal friends, people I considered almost part of my family.

East Berlin was where my wife and I made our first home together as a married couple, a home we had to share with a secretary and a housekeeper, one of them possibly in the employ of the secret police, with microphones in the walls, and men in unmarked cars on our tails as we went about our daily business. It was where we learned the difference between acquaintance and friendship, about the value of freedom and the curious sweet-and-sour taste of life when it is limited, about how the tide of history can all of a sudden sweep over people and places. And how all that really matters is to keep standing when it does. This is a story in which the politicians take a back seat and everyday life springs to the forefront, for even journalists have everyday lives. And the people they meet – especially in totalitarian societies – are often more interesting than the events they are sent to report on.

In these pages, I have tried to introduce you to some of those people and convey a taste of the lives they led, in many ways so foreign to those of Britons or Americans in the second half of the twentieth century, yet every bit as typical of those decades. Between the affluence of 'the West' and the poverty of 'the Third World', was a second world, rarely referred to as such. Even those who lived there dared not speak its name: a world of making do, getting by, of living with the shadow of the past, a darkness in the present and little hope for the future. A world that shattered like a glass ceiling in those chaotic days of the autumn of 1989.

I have tried also to answer at least in part one of those questions journalists are so often asked: how do you get the news? And another one that should be asked more often: what do you do with it when you get it? This is a short ride on a rollercoaster of a profession that many people wish they could get into and a good many others wish they could get out of. An insider's look at the [frequent] nuts and [often missing] bolts of the news business, in particular the ups and downs of being a foreign correspondent in the pre-internet days: from shouting, 'No love, it's the Warsaw Pact, not the Walsall Pact,' over a crackly phone line to *Sunday Times* copytakers recently moved from the *News of the World*, to the joys of punching endless seemingly identical rows of holes in telex tape, of vandalising hotel telephone sockets to fit 'crocodile clips' to bare wires, and standing in phone boxes in the rain with 'acoustic couplers' clamped in an armpit.

The only message of my story is that people make the world. For better or worse. And that accidents happen. All the time.

The fact that the twenty-first century has so far failed to live up to the promise of the end of the twentieth is a depressing reality. All the more reason why we should look back on the events of 1989, the road that led up to them, and savour once again the taste of those moments of euphoria when it seemed the problems of the world were over once and for all.

Because the taste of hope is one none of us dare lose.

Peter Millar, London and Berlin, 2009

East Germany and West Germany plus the exclave of West Berlin

Oh, What a Night!

My wife sat at home in floods of tears in front of the television, the uncomprehending toddlers hugging her knees. I was hanging out on a chaotic street corner hundreds of miles away pouring three nineteen-year-old waitresses into a taxi to take them to the biggest party the world had seen in four decades.

My wife's tears were tears of joy. The night was November 9th, 1989, and the Berlin Wall was coming down. For the first time in a century it seemed the whole world was empathising with the Germans. But for me, on that street corner in Berlin in the midst of the biggest story of my career, the predominant thing on my mind as a Sunday newspaper reporter on a Thursday night was: 'Damn, this is all happening twenty-four hours too early.'

But then nobody had known it would happen at all. Least of all the intelligence agencies of the West, caught napping on the eve of their greatest 'victory', as they would be again on September 11th, 2001, their greatest embarrassment. Not even the men who gave the orders in East Berlin knew it would happen. Not even as they gave them. They had intended something else. Something else entirely. The fall of the Berlin Wall was the triumphant vindication of the 'cock-up' theory of history, of what happens when those seemingly immovable objects of political inertia and the status quo get swept away by two irresistible forces: accident and emotion.

I had been a hundred miles away on East Germany's Baltic coast when the first checkpoint on the Wall that for a generation had severed one half of Berlin from the other was suddenly, unexpectedly thrown open. Driving a rented – and I was about to discover lamentably underpowered – Mercedes I rammed the accelerator to the floor and headed like a lunatic for Berlin. At Checkpoint Charlie, already awash with East Berliners clamouring to be let through, I had entrusted my less than impressive symbol of the capitalist car industry to the tender mercies of East Germany's border troops and crossed the border into the West to have a beer can thrust into my hand with the joyful shout: 'Welcome to freedom!'

Was it really happening? Could the most concrete manifestation of the Iron Curtain really be crumbling? Was this really a sea change in global politics? Or just a moment of madness? Would the story by Sunday be of a crackdown and the restoration of the Cold War status quo, or would we be welcoming a brave new world?

My three waitresses had been working in an East Berlin hotel all evening, while outside the world turned upside down. They had heard the news that the Wall had opened while they served pork and dumplings to Russian tourists, but with typical Prussian thoroughness they had worked to the end of their shift, after midnight, before one winked at the others and said, 'Anyone for the Ku'damm?' They burst out giggling, spraying cheap *ersatz* champagne through the gates at Checkpoint Charlie, and as we headed for West Berlin's most famous boulevard, I realised they were just what I was looking for: a bright young element of human colour to enliven the momentous news story breaking over my head. A story that was already on television screens around the world and would have been in the newspapers for two days before my own version of events hit the streets on Sunday morning.

Yet at that precise moment I was less concerned about what I would write than soaking up the intoxicating atmosphere of a once-in-a-lifetime experience. This wasn't just a news story, this was personal. For that one delirious night most of East Berlin took a walk on the wild side: two-stroke 'Trabbies', the fibreglass midget cars soon to become an accidental symbol of a revolution based on middle-class values, raced Porsches along the glitzy avenues of the West, littered with broken bottles beneath a sky ablaze with fireworks; it was as if a long-awaited marriage had occurred; Berlin embraced Berlin. Policemen (West) kissed bus conductresses (East). 'Berlin is again Berlin. Germany weeps with joy' screamed the headlines on special edition tabloids, rushed off the presses and handed out free on the streets of the West.

On the Ku'damm itself, awash with people hugging one another, spreading across the wide avenue in a vast, uproariously happy drunken party I let my waitresses vanish into the throng, when I found myself suddenly grabbed and embraced by friends who were practically family. And for them it really was a family reunion: Kerstin Falkner and her husband Andreas had only weeks before fled their home in East Berlin, via the West German Embassy in Poland, thinking it would be years before they saw the rest of their family again, if ever. Now she was standing arm in arm with her brother Horst and his wife Sylvia, who had only hours before walked through a gap in the Wall they thought would keep them apart forever.

If for the world at large the fall of the Berlin Wall was theatre on a grand stage, for me it was as first-hand as a family wedding. Eight years earlier my wife and I had made a decrepit flat in a run-down corner of East Berlin our first family home. I had passed my driving test there. We had made friendships that would last a lifetime, lived alongside the natives in a world of grimy buildings pockmarked by bullet holes, of grey cobbled streets and the tiny Trabant cars with fibreglass bodies in fluorescent orange and apple green that rattled over them. We had held conversations in whispers in the kitchen with the taps running and the radio on because there were micro-phones in the walls. Even in the bedroom. We had sat and gossiped with the locals in the pub and exchanged knowing wary glances when somebody new walked in. 'Just in case.' Friendships mattered more than anywhere I had lived before or have lived since. Friends could help you get your hands on things you couldn't find in the sparsely stocked shops. Friends could tell one another jokes, even about the government. As long as you were sure they were really friends.

We were sure about most of them. There was Manne, the obese thirty-something who smuggled disco tapes and hardcore porn from the West in his outsize underpants. Kurtl the fading music hall musician with his comic specs, repertoire of old-fashioned tunes and memories of the Berlin blitz and his father's death at Stalin-grad. Uschi with her broad Saxon vowels and her lust for imported fashion-plate clothes. And her husband Bernd the classical musi-cian whose life was made a misery trying to provide them. Big, bearded Busch who ran a hostel for young print workers and paid lip service to the Communist Party because he had to belong to it to hold down his job. Jochen, a stage designer of ambiguous sexuality whom nobody quite trusted. Bärbel, the cackling good-natured landlady of a corner pub that had managed to swim against the tide of enforced nationalisation and remain in family hands. And Alex, her partner, worldly-wise cynic, wit and raconteur who transformed Metzer Eck into an oasis of bonhomie, free speech and free-flowing beer that made life in a dictatorship better than just bearable. For all of them the events of that night in November 1989 changed their lives.

Even when we had lived in their midst, we were not, of course, in exactly the same position as they were. We could travel. We could cross into the other half of their city. The border guards, who even on the night of November 9th, 1989, were portrayed on the television screens of the West as scowling faces in communist uniforms, had over the years become for us no longer sinister ciphers but familiar – if nameless – faces. Nor were they all male: there was an attractive dark-haired woman we referred to privately as 'Lovely Rita' (from the Beatles' song: 'Lovely Rita, meter maid'). Another guard, a big grinning bear of a bloke who always smiled – so many of his colleagues presented only blank stares – and exchanged a few words. I nicknamed him 'Yogi Bear'. I would get to know his real name only when we shared a beer in a bar just a few yards west of Checkpoint Charlie, the border he had defended for so long, on the night he was finally out of a job.

When the idea of going to Berlin as a foreign correspondent for Reuters news agency was first put to me back in 1981, it was inconceivable that the Berlin Wall could ever fall. Hanging on my wall at home I had a big map of Europe, showing the split in the world that everyone thought would never heal: the invisible scar down the middle of a continent. On one side was what was then still called the EEC, the European Economic Community, on the other Comecon, the Soviet trading block; on the one side Nato, on the other the Warsaw Pact, one tucked under the protective wing of the American eagle, the other under the threatening paw of the Russian bear. East versus West, with the old continent of Europe in the middle, the fault line running through the heart of Germany.

The nineteenth-century German military philosopher Clausenburg had famously declared politics to be the 'continuation of war by other means'. By the mid-twentieth century the Cold War had become the new definition of those 'other means'. Everyone assumed it would last forever. Some – primarily on the Western side – were even thankful for it. Peace was assured by the policy of Mutual Assured Destruction, which had the pleasing acronym MAD: whichever side started a nuclear conflict would assure its own annihilation. Retaliation was inevitable, therefore war was unthinkable. The Cold War was a stalemate that had once been known as the Balance of Power.

That balance had not been achieved easily. The Germany of the immediate post-war years was a country in ruins and under occupation. Vast swathes of its territory in the East had been carved off forever, most given to the new communist-dominated Poland which had literally been shifted several hundred miles westward. The old eastern Polish territories had been grabbed by Stalin as the result of the Molotov-Ribbentrop pact in 1939.

The remainder of Germany was divided into three occupation zones: between the Soviets, British and Americans. The Russians reckoned that as France had technically lost the war it wasn't entitled to any of the spoils. A French zone had to be carved out of the British and American share. The same happened in Berlin, which had once occupied a relatively central position in the country but now lay in the far north-east. The idea was for Germany to be disarmed and declared perpetually neutral; the problem was that neither side in the emerging Cold War hostility trusted the other to assure that.

In June 1948 the three Western powers introduced a new currency, the Deutsche Mark or D-Mark, to replace the old Reichsmark. The Soviet Union, convinced it was a plan by Wall Street to create a new capitalist puppet state, introduced a separate Mark in the East. It also tried to seize all of Berlin with a blockade barring access to the Western sectors. Only a remarkable and highly risky British and American policy of supplying the city with food and fuel by air ensured that the tactic failed. In May 1949 the three Western zones united to become the Federal Republic of Germany (West Germany) and announced that, pending unification, their provisional capital would be the little university town of Bonn, birthplace of Beethoven.

Five months later on October 7th the Soviet-controlled communists in the East responded by declaring their own German Democratic Republic (East Germany). West Germans would, for years, joke that it was neither German, nor democratic nor a proper republic (Berliners still called the territory around them 'the zone'). But another German concept said it was *Realpolitik*.

Berlin remained theoretically under the control of the four victorious 'Allies', even if by this time the Soviets and Westerners were hardly on speaking terms. Berliners, East and West, came and went in the city and the surrounding countryside much as they had always done, using whichever currency anyone would accept. But with better living conditions in the West, the Soviet 'zone' kept haemorrhaging people. In 1952 at Stalin's behest, the East Germans built a fortified fence along the border with West Germany and equipped it with watchtowers, armed guards, dogs and eventually automatically triggered machine guns. But there was still nothing to stop people wandering into the Western sectors of Berlin and not coming back. By 1960 the working-age population of East Germany had dropped from seventy to sixty per cent of the total. Before long it would be empty of all but geriatrics and the disabled. People denied a genuine vote at the ballot box were voting with their feet.

On June 15th, 1961 Walter Ulbricht, the general secretary of the East German Communist Party (officially the Socialist Unity Party since a forced merger with the Social Democrats in 1946) gave a speech in which he famously said: '*Niemand hat die Absicht, eine Mauer zu errichten.* (Nobody has any intention of building a wall.)' He obviously woke up next morning and said to himself, 'Now there's a thought!'

At midnight on August 12th, armed guards began to roll out barbed wire along the border between the sectors that ran through the middle of Berlin. And not just along the forty-three kilometres that actually lay within the city limits but out in the country too, all along the 156 kilometres that formed the rest of the border between the Western half of Berlin and the landscape around it. Within hours, especially in the middle of the city itself, they were digging up the road alongside the barbed wire and cementing concrete blocks into a wall that would be the first of several incarnations, each one more intimidating and permanent than the last, over the next two and a half decades. All the work was done, standing firmly on ground that was in the Eastern sector, by labourers watched over by armed guards. One guard, a young soldier of nineteen called Conrad Schuman, made himself famous just two days later by jumping over the barbed wire within range of a Western photographer's lens.

Because the sectors had been drawn up along old postcode lines, in some places the boundary itself ran along the line of the buildings. This meant that in Bernauer Strasse to the north of the city centre, the houses were in the East, but the pavement they opened onto was in the West. The closing of the border meant that armed guards marched into people's apartments and began bricking up their windows. Western photographers captured images of people dropping from upper windows as the troops bricked up the lower ones. Within months the houses were evacuated and in 1963 the last of them was demolished.

On the Western side, the Wall changed over the years from a basic, breeze-block structure topped with barbed wire to a uniform curtain of concrete slabs three metres high topped with a cylindrical concrete drum with a circumference designed to make it impossible to get a grip on, though it was only ever envisaged that anyone trying to climb it would be coming from the other side.

In the East, paradoxically, the Wall was less intimidating, as if the authorities wanted to achieve the impossible and make it disappear. The frontier retreated often by as much as ten to fifteen metres and the Wall as seen by ordinary East Berliners more closely resembled that of a factory compound, just under three metres high and still built of breeze blocks or in places even brick. It bore simple signs that said *Frontier area, strictly no admittance* or *Trespassers will be prosecuted*. The difference lay in what everyone knew separated the two walls, the 'death strip' of tank trap obstacles, barbed wire and armed guards patrolling with dogs and orders to shoot to kill. At more isolated spots watchtowers sprouted on concrete stalks manned by men with night-vision binoculars and automatic weapons. Over the nearly three decades of its existence at least 136 people died (that is the official figure), but including those dragged back bleeding whose bodies were never recovered, there were certainly substantially more than 200. In the East everyone knew someone who knew one of them.

The East German hope was that for West Berliners, faced with a blank wall, the other half of their city would eventually be forgotten. And gradually it was. West Germans, whom the logic behind the 'two German states' doctrine insisted were as foreign as British or French, were consequently just as free to visit East Germany (that is they could apply for a visa, which would not always be granted). But until 1971 the same regulations did not apply to West Berliners (a remnant of the blockade mentality that hoped one day all of Berlin would be capital of the GDR) who were only allowed occasional visits. The West Berlin city senate erected wooden viewing platforms at strategic locations – the Brandenburg Gate, Bernauer Strasse – where you could climb up and peer across at what had once been the continuation of the same street, even perhaps to wave. Few East Berliners dared wave back. Later only tourists climbed the platforms, while the grey expanse of the Wall itself became the world's biggest blank canvas for graffiti artists. Early examples were political: *Shit Wall*; *Last one to leave, turn out the lights!*, then tourists with no traumatised memories and their own trivial axes to grind joined in: *Geoff Boycott rules*, and *Leeds United AFC* are but two typical examples from the early eighties. In the end the abstract artists took over dabbing broad swathes of colour. Parts of the Wall attained such a cultural significance in their own right that there would be some who complained of 'vandalism' when they were torn down.

But on that night of Thursday, November 9th, 1989, the prospect of the bulldozers moving in went from fantasy to possibility to probability and finally reality within just a few hours. The scenes that most people around the world would have imprinted on their retinas were those from the Brandenburg Gate. That too was one of those accidents of history. There was no crossing point at the Gate, but precisely because it was where foreign leaders were brought to see the 'inhumanity' of the Wall, this was the spot where the East Germans had tried to make it least threatening. Here the Wall was lower, and flat-topped, without the cylindrical 'anti-climb' drum on top, not least because the Gate itself, as a historical monument, was manned twenty-four hours by East German troops in full ceremonial dress. In true 'bizzaro world' form, the East German government also brought visitors to the Gate, to show off the effectiveness of the 'anti-fascist protection wall'. When faced with concrete proof of an unpalatable reality they chose simply to turn interpretation of it on its head.

But the flat surface meant that on that fateful night, drunk West Berliners could do the unthinkable: climb onto the Wall. And dance. Bewildered East German guards ordered them to get down, then called up reinforcements, but what were they to do? Shoot? Almost uniquely among border guards the world over, their 'shoot to kill' orders applied to their own citizens trying to leave rather than others who might try to get in. And in any case they weren't doing that, were they? They were just dancing, and waving beer bottles. By the time someone had the bright – if just possibly fatal – decision to take a pickaxe to part of it, nobody really knew what the rules were anymore.

One pickaxe of course was never going to do serious harm to a structure as solid as the Berlin Wall. At least not physically. But the images that went round the world – and more importantly back into East Germany where millions also sat glued to their screens, albeit in ever dwindling numbers as they piled into cars or trains and headed for Berlin – were devastating. Yet that too was more circumstance than foresight. The world's cameramen had gathered at that spot simply because it was the most photogenic – most of the reporters who hurriedly jetted in over the twenty-four hours after the first crossing point was opened spoke little or no German. All they wanted were images. And tipsy West Berliners – goaded on by their presence – provided them. As Canadian philosopher Marshall McLuhan had prophesied a decade earlier, the medium had become the message.

For those of us on the ground, swept up and carried away by the euphoria it was also difficult not to see philosophy, if not theology, in the tide of history. I could not help but recall that November 9th, 1989 was to the day exactly fifty years plus one after Kristallnacht, Joseph Goebbels' orchestrated pogrom of violence against the Jews. It was also the anniversary of the defeat of Adolf Hitler's 'beer hall putsch' in 1923. Even for a convinced atheist it was hard not to feel a shiver down the spine.

THE SUNDAY TIMES, 12 NOVEMBER 1989

A MILLION MARCH TO FREEDOM
By Peter Millar

More than one million Germans from East and West held the world's biggest non-stop party in Berlin yesterday as their sober leaders tried in vain to dampen euphoria by warning that a united Germany was not yet on the political agenda.

East Berliners poured into West Berlin to celebrate their liberty on free beer and wine and queues of East German cars stretched back forty miles from the border. Berlin was a city reborn. The party clogged the streets as the barriers that divided Germany melted like the ice of the Cold War. Officials revealed that well over a million people had passed the frontier from East Germany into West Berlin and West Germany in only a matter of hours.

As the leaders of East and West Germany spoke on the phone, young people from the West tried to speed up history by ripping down parts of the wall by the Brandenburg Gate, long the symbol of division, not just of Berlin but of the European continent. East German border guards dispersed the crowds with water cannon and rebuilt it.

But elsewhere parts of the wall were coming down for good. In East Berlin concrete blocks were being removed from the entrance to an underground station. For the past twenty-eight years West Berlin trains have trundled without stopping through unlit stations beneath the eastern half of the city. Now they will carry East Berliners into the West.

The first new border crossing point came into use just after dawn after a night of activity by workmen with bulldozers, and East Berliners filed on foot from Bernauer Strasse into the West. On Potsdamer Platz, once the Piccadilly Circus of the German empire and a hundred yards from the unmarked underground site of Hitler's bunker, the bulldozers were creating another crossing to be opened this morning.

Elsewhere official teams were knocking down the wall to create eighteen new crossing points. At one site East Berlin engineers shook hands with their Western counterparts through the gap they had created in the six-inch thick, steel-reinforced concrete.

Tourists watched in amazement, their cameras recording the historic moments. One American borrowed a hammer from a Berliner and told his wife: 'Get one of me hitting the Wall, honey.'

That was the story that appeared on the front page. My waitresses, my friends and the whole mad mix-up that led to the fall of the Wall, were reserved for the lengthy colour/analysis piece on the Focus pages inside. But even that was not the whole of the story.

The Berlin Wall was not just a concrete manifestation of the Iron Curtain, it was its most potent symbol. Almost its soul. Its fall was to bring in its wake the end of the Cold War, the collapse like dominoes of Moscow's satellite dictatorships in Eastern Europe and finally the implosion of the Soviet Union itself. The year of miracles, 1989, would give the world a new chance, which surely only fools would throw away.

2

The Street of Shame

The long and winding road that led me to Checkpoint Charlie on the night the Berlin Wall came down began improbably enough thirteen years earlier on the outskirts of Paris where I was trying to hitch a lift to the Côte d'Azur. That was when I learned my first journalistic trick: know how the story is going to end before you start writing it.

I have to give a little context here. I was in the third year of a modern languages degree at Magdalen College, Oxford, reading French and Russian, and spending it, as linguists were supposed to do, abroad. Rather than appreciating a paid job with free accommodation in one of the world's most glamorous cities, I regarded my 'year out' as purgatory away from the hedonistic delights of seventies studenthood.

Theoretically I had landed on my feet, with a position as an '*assistant*' – you have to pronounce it the French way '*ass-eees-t'ahn*' – a sort of guinea-pig native speaker for the locals learning English to laugh at – in the posh Lycée Lakanal in the southern Parisian suburbs. I say 'posh' because it had a formidable academic record and boasted famous old boys such as André Gide and was housed in its own magnificent parkland in the leafy suburb of Sceaux, which is more or less to Paris what Hampstead is to London. But in the stark reality of a cold wintry day in October with the leaves ripped from the trees by a biting wind, Lakanal's imposing old brick buildings, seen from the street, looked to me more like a maximum security state penitentiary.

This was not helped when I announced my presence and immediately felt both the immense pressure of French bureaucracy and my own linguistic inadequacy as I was asked to fill in a sheaf of forms with my personal details. I fell at almost the first hurdle. Age, date of birth, sex were no problem but, '*État civil*'? I knew what this meant:

was I married or single? I simply had no idea what the French for 'single' was. We had learned about people being *'marié'* but no one had ever taught me the opposite. *'Simple'* didn't sound right, nor did *'unique'* or *'seul'* or any of the other random words my panicky brain flirted with. Eventually a kindly – if somewhat exasperated – secretary smiled tartly at me and said she presumed, at my age, I was *'célibataire'.* I was horrified. Even as I realised instinctively that that had to be the right word, just the fact that it contained the concept of 'celibacy' was so far removed from anything I had hoped for from a year in Paris.

Things did not get better when I was eventually shown to my room, up long echoing wooden-floored corridors and into a bare space with an iron bed, a clunking radiator and fantastically high ceilings. These would have given the room a feeling of lightness and airiness if it weren't for the fact that the windows were so high up, that at a compact five-foot-six I couldn't quite see out of them without standing on a chair. Luckily I did have a chair: just one, an old wooden classroom chair which stood next to an old wooden classroom desk, inscribed with the initials – and possibly the teeth marks – of countless generations of bored French adolescents. As they closed the door on me – thankfully without the sound of a key in the lock – I looked around dolefully at my spartan cube, with its walls painted hospital green, obliquely up at the white overcast sky and directly up at the solitary light bulb dangling yards above my head. I reflected that if it ever needed changing I'd be in trouble. Luckily it never did.

Inevitably my last year at Lakanal didn't turn out to be as bad as it had first seemed. I have bittersweet memories – perhaps as lonely boys sent to English boarding schools do – of pre-dawn starts with steaming bowls of hot milk left to warm on the radiators in the canteen ready for mixing with strong, piping-hot coffee to form your own blend of *café au lait*; of twenty-five-centilitre bottles of red wine served with lunch to the teaching staff and the university students who in return for free accommodation kept order in the boarders' dormitories at night; of school lunches that – unlike anything I had ever experienced back home – would creep onto my menus for life: *'lapin aux pruneaux',* rabbit with red wine and prune sauce.

And one ridiculously romantic vision that – more ridiculous than romantic – was somehow quintessentially French: a bright blue-skyed freezing winter morning beneath the coppiced plane trees in the still empty playground watching the steam rise from the newly-rinsed open-air *pissoirs*. Monet could have worked miracles with it.

Over time I managed to brighten up my room, most significantly covering one wall with a full-size cinema poster, picked up at *Les Puces*, the sprawling flea market held each weekend at *Porte de Clignancourt*. The film: *Cabaret*, with Liza Minelli, posing large-as-life on my wall in her stockings and bowler hat against the Brandenburg Gate and the film's French subtitle, *Adieu Berlin*. It had to be fate.

Which leads me back to that fateful hitchhiking journey south. For all that I had got used to Lakanal and life in the Parisian suburbs, as soon as the weather started warming up – and there was a break in the school timetable – the idea of a few days soaking up the sun in St Tropez, or wherever I could get a lift to, seemed irresistible. That was why I was standing with my thumb out on one of the southern slip roads off the Paris *périphérique*, only to find that the first car to stop and offer me a lift anywhere in the general direction of the sun happened to be driven by an Englishman.

His name was Terry Williams and he was a journalist. He told me he worked in the Paris bureau of Reuters News Agency. Had I, he asked, as a linguist, ever thought of going into journalism? Well, yes, maybe, sort of, I replied. As much as I had thought about going into anything other than a student bar. The world 'beyond university' was unimaginably far away, and didn't bear thinking about. I was thinking about getting back there. Not leaving for good. It's only a year away, you know, he told me as we headed south on the *autoroute*, the warm wind from the Midi flowing in through the open windows of his sports car. It'll go fast. He meant the year. I hated him for it. But it was true, I knew. In little over fifteen months I would be out there in the real world. I would have to do something. Maybe even get a job.

It was then that Terry made up for everything with what I now know to be one of the oldest saws in the book: 'The thing about journalism,' he said with a grin, 'is that it's the worst job in the world.' And he paused before the punchline: 'But it's better than working.'

He didn't take me very far along my road south, but he did give me a card and told me his brother also ran a newly opened journalism school in Cardiff. A few weeks later I took him up on the invitation to drop in and take a look at the Reuters office in Paris. It wasn't particularly impressive. Terry was 'minding the desk' which meant sitting there with his feet up watching the television news, with a printer from the French news agency AFP (Agence France-Presse) chuntering away next to him, feeding out screeds of paper which he glanced at occasionally and now and then tore off, and attached to a growing pile fixed to a clipboard. 'Slow news day,' he said. 'Might nip out for a beer later.' The job didn't seem particularly exciting but it didn't seem particularly strenuous either. Before I left, however, he did something which is the reason for this little Parisian interlude in a story otherwise primarily concerned with Germany: he told me a secret. 'If you should ever think of applying to Reuters,' he said, 'you should know there's one question they always ask, and there's only one right answer.'

That was how I found myself, barely thirteen months later – in the last stages of my final year at Oxford with the prospect of finals still to come and unemployment beckoning unless I found myself a job – sitting in a room on the fourth floor of No. 85 Fleet Street in front of an intimidating audience of mostly middle-aged men with clipboards.

I had just about survived some thirty minutes or so of grilling on international affairs: 'What did I know about Charter 77?' (the then recently formed movement dedicated to human rights in Czechoslovakia). I answered most of them on a wing and a prayer. And then a severe-looking man who couldn't have been older than his mid-forties despite a shock of snow-white hair and thick glasses leaned back thoughtfully, chewed the end of his ballpoint pen for a second or two, then flicked the chewed end towards me and in a clipped Scottish accent posed a question it seemed he had only just come up with.

'Say we were to send you somewhere to cover a breaking news story,' he intoned ominously, 'what do you think would be the first thing you might do when you got there?' I bit my lip and let my head drop as I ummed and ahhed a bit as if trying to mull over such a difficult question. In fact I was desperate not to let him see the smile I was having immense difficulty suppressing. 'We-ell,' I began. And in my head I was playing over my Parisian mentor's words: 'There's any number of sensible things you might do of course, find a hotel, have a shit and a shower, hit the sack or get yourself a stiff drink.' But that wasn't the answer he wanted to hear.

So I furled my brow and gave a vintage performance. 'I suppose,' I said slowly, as if I was just working this out, and looking for some sign of reassurance, which was decidedly not forthcoming from the man with the white hair and impenetrable glasses, 'I suppose it might be sensible to find a phone or a telex, some way of getting in contact with London to be sure I can get the story back.' (Mobile phones were still something you saw on *Star Trek*.) The white-haired man, who I would later learn was Reuters Chief News Editor Ian McDowell (more frequently referred to as Ian McDour) looked at me for a second, and then nodded slowly, as if he thought that wasn't necessarily the stupidest thing he'd ever heard. There were a couple more questions, but somehow they seemed like an anti-climax, to me at least, and maybe they were to them too. I'd come through the big one, and as I walked out of the office with a nod to the other candidates sitting nervously on chairs outside, I had a sneaking hunch the job might be mine. And it was.

I have no misgivings about the 'sneaking' either. All's fair in love and journalism, not that the two mix much. Two other colleagues of mine – both of whom came through the Reuters training process – have publicly identified the main characteristics of a successful journalist as, and I quote, 'ratlike cunning' and 'intelligent guile'. One has been a successful Reuters bureau chief on most continents and the other is the editor of an esteemed British national newspaper. There is also one other element, which had been on my side that day back on the *périphérique* in Paris, one which editors prize in their journalists as much as Napoleon prized in his generals: luck.

Knowing the answer to the $64,000 question was not, of course, the only thing that got me the job, even if it was probably the clincher. All ten of us who got hired – with another to be taken on twelve months later after a sponsored year at the new Cardiff journalism school – had been tested on our basic mastery of the English language, our ability to marshal facts and our command of one other language fluently and a second at a basic level of competence. I had had no difficulty proving the first in French – after a year living with students in the Parisian suburbs I had acquired a facility with the current *argot* that mystified some of my Oxford tutors but would have let me pass for any *mec* on the *métro*. My Russian, despite my degree, was at an altogether different level: I could read (if not exactly race through) Gogol and Dostoevsky but with the Soviet Union still a difficult destination, my experience of the vernacular on the ground had been limited to a two-week holiday course. But it was good enough to be my 'banker'. The signal absence, you will have noticed, was the language that would eventually become more important to me than any other: German.

In the meantime we all had a more basic linguistic function to master: typing. None of us could. Not properly anyhow. I had spent an hour or two a week during the summer before starting the job in September, bashing away on an ancient Remington typewriter of my mother's, but it weighed a tonne and had been ill-maintained. It would all be different when I got to the real world of journalism and super modern equipment, I told myself.

It wasn't. The trainees were dumped not even in the hallowed 85 Fleet Street headquarters but in a draughty building belonging to British Telecom around the corner in Seacoal Lane. And our equipment was – yes – heavy, old, ill-maintained typewriters. Not necessarily Remingtons: anything that came to hand, it seemed. I would later discover to my surprised dismay that it was little different in the newsroom itself. We weren't taught to type properly. I discovered later very few journalists could 'touch-type', even though some were lightning fast with two fingers alone and in at least one instance, with just one. We were given news stories to analyse and rewrite; we played through scenarios of being fed reports from police, firemen, army, and told to 'type it up' and make 'a story' out of it. Typed. We got sore fingers.

Our training was undertaken by a variety of senior journalists from 'across the road' but supervised by a genial, grinning, expansive-waisted West Country man called George Short*, who saw to it straight away that we understood the most important duty of a trainee journalist: buying his betters a beer. Fleet Street was tribal in those days. And each tribe had its watering hole. Printers and journalists on the newspapers hardly spoke to one another – there were literally demarcation lines on the floor in the print works which no journalist dared cross for fear of triggering a walkout. But the journalists too all drank in different places. It wasn't that they didn't mix with one another, just that if you weren't in the office it was a good idea to be in the office pub: that way in a crisis all hands could get, however unsteadily, to the deck.

The *Daily Telegraph*, for example, drank in the King and Keys, right next door, while the *Daily Express* drank in The Popinjay, which had virtually been incorporated into an extension to their art deco black glass palace. The *Daily Mirror*, up Fetter Lane, drank in The White Hart opposite, though no one ever called it anything other than The Stab (short for The Stab in The Back, an enduring testimony to how what was said in the pub could make or break careers). The *Daily Mail* drank in The Harrow in Whitefriars Street. The Press Association, Britain's national news agency which shared 85 Fleet Street with Reuters, drank in The Olde Bell, on the street itself. El Vino, the legendary wine bar opposite the law courts, attracted a wider variety of leader writers and columnists, the types who blended more easily with the barristers and solicitors who formed the rest of its clientele, and were happy with its insistence on jacket and tie at all times, though there were already rumblings against its insistence that women were not allowed in unless they wore skirts and even then could not be served at the bar.

Reuters men – and the increasing band of women – used to working in the background, their names usually removed from copy before a national newspaper printed it, chose a suitably subterranean locale. It was called, at least as far as I knew in the early days of

---

* George retired from Reuters and passed away in the nineties, but his spirit lives on: he is remembered by former friends and colleagues who meet up from time to time to reminisce about the 'Good Old Days'. In his honour these occasions are known as 'short lunches'. They aren't.

my introduction to 'the Street', Mrs Moon's, bizarrely located underneath a branch of Pizza Hut. Older, wiser heads would eventually inform me that its real name was The Falstaff and it had once been a pub on several stories, but for one reason or another – it seemed hard to imagine it had been for lack of custom – the owners had sold off most of it for offices and the fast food franchise. It had no visible signage anywhere and precious little indication of its existence at ground level. Unless you knew it was there you would only have come across it if you were about to go into Pizza Hut and looked left in the doorway to where a staircase led to an underground room with an old paraffin heater on the linoleum floor and a long mahogany bar propped up by hordes of beer-drinking hacks.

It was called Mrs Moon's because, quite literally, the landlady's name was Mrs Moon. She ran the place with her son, Billy Moon, and a rod of iron that frequently extended to throwing out almost anybody who came in shortly after nine p.m. This was not because she favoured early closing but because nine p.m. was throwing-out time across the road at The Cheshire Cheese, a celebrated seventeenth-century pub and famous tourist haunt. Mrs Moon's was not the sort of place that would have attracted many tourists – even if they had somehow managed to find it – but it did occasionally pull in senior executive types, including those from Reuters, and Mrs Moon wasn't having them treat her gaffe as second best.

It was in Mrs Moon's that George Short taught me one of the lessons that has stayed with me all my life and really ought to be included in school lessons for British kids and all who value what remains of the most traditional British institution: bar space management. This is the technique essential to making sure the maximum number of people desired can take part in the main activity for which a proper English pub is designed. No, not sinking pints, that is merely the lubrication. Banter. Chitchat. Talking to one another, in a group, not merely in a little cluster of introspective twosomes.

'It's all right when there's just two or three of you nattering away,' said George in his broad West Country accent while trying to marshal his gaggle of keen young wannabes up to the bar. 'Two of you can lean on the bar and the one in between can face either of them, like a triangle. That still holds good when there's four, just so long as the two at the bar move apart a bit to make room for two folk facing in. But the trouble really comes, when you get five or more. That's when you need one bloke to take what I call pole position,' and he turned his ample girth through ninety degrees so that all of a sudden he was with his back to the bar, leaning against it to become effectively a fulcrum for his admiring acolytes. 'See, now another bloke can lean on that side and you can build up a second group that's still part of the big group. *And*,' he stressed with a twinkle in his eye, 'you maximise your control of the barspace (since George I have never been able to think of that as other than a single word, like airspace) so that you can always get another round in without queuing. It's your go, lad.'

Within weeks we were on the fourth-floor newsroom, shifted and shunted from here to there, amidst the endless chatter of teleprinters and typewriters. From the busy sports desk to the slow-paced features desk to London Bureau – where we actually got to go out and cover (minor) stories as part of the team that reported the UK for the rest of the world – and then, inevitably to the, for most of us dreadfully dreary but increasingly important, Econ, newly rechristend RES: Reuters Economic Services. And then, bliss oh bliss, the place we all wanted to be: the holy of holies, the grandly named World Desk, then still the hub of Reuters' global operations. It would be some years still before the telecommunications revolution would mean the 'world desk' could be moved seamlessly with the clock from London to New York to Hong Kong and back again. For the moment London was still supreme, the reins held by four senior editors known collectively as the Four Horsemen of the Apocalypse.

These were the men who monitored incoming copy, decided how urgent it was and which journalist should look it over and prepare it for publication. There was a 'top table' of the best and fastest workers. We trainees were decidedly 'downtable'. Often we were rewriting copy, turning the bare facts sent in by 'stringers' – part-time local correspondents – in places as diverse as Srinagar or Caracas into the 'inverted pyramid' form expected by mainstream English-language newspapers: most important facts at the top, second most important next, subsidiary information to follow, background and colour merged in after that. The idea was – still is – that the story could be slotted into any 'hole' on a newspaper page and literally 'cut to length': you could remove any number of sentences from the bottom and what remained above would ideally still make perfect sense. It was the mainstay of news-agency journalism.

Reuters in those final days before the whirlwind advent of electronic information and financial services that would transform it, was still a trust owned by a conglomerate of British and former imperial media interests. The business founded by Paul Julius Reuter, a German Jew, using carrier pigeons to link fledgling French and German telegraph lines had moved to London in 1851 after the laying of the Dover-Calais submarine cable, and subsequently spread a network of correspondents across the world. Reuters got a famous scoop in 1865 when a correspondent arriving on a ship from New York passed a message to a waiting boat off the coast of Ireland enabling the news of President Abraham Lincoln's assassination to be telegraphed to London and the continent nearly a full day before the mail ship docked in Southampton.

The agency had always aimed at the widest possible international coverage and a reputation for impartiality, but during the Second World War its London base and British and Imperial ownership meant it effectively became an arm of the Allied propaganda machine. By the 1970s it was once again moving towards status as an independent international operation (it would eventually be publicly floated in 1984), but there was still a fair amount of the old mindset amongst senior figures on the editorial floor.

For example when a delegation of German business people were being escorted round the office, with a view to signing them up for the still embryonic financial information services that would dominate the company's future, one of them politely asked a senior filing editor, 'Have you ever been to Germany?' He grinned back and answered, 'Yes, but only at night.' When this was met with a slightly puzzled look, he added, 'And we never got below 10,000 feet.' The message was met with a frosty smile.

When eventually – as a signal indicator of the changes to come – the News Service got its first German editor, a jovial cheery plump man called Manfred Pagel, his beaming rounds of the newsroom were often accompanied by a strange hissing sound and, when his back was turned, older staff pointing to the new air-conditioning units. There has never been any shortage of black humour on 'the Street'.

If I was surprised to find the 'Don't Mention the War' attitude still held sway, it wasn't until one evening while eating dinner in the seventh-floor staff canteen that I gained an inkling of understanding. Most of the canteen fare was unimpressive but in the quieter hours of the late-evening shift, the chef had a way with offal, serving up the most exquisite griddle-fried lamb's kidneys. I was tucking into them when I noticed the view for the first time: a clear vision of floodlit St Paul's Cathedral, barely half a mile away, and wondered how it must have looked from here during the Blitz as the firemen fought the blazes around it. And then there was St Bride's, literally just outside the window, the great soaring white wedding-cake spire of Sir Christopher Wren's other masterpiece, beautifully restored but which in December 1940 had been completely gutted by firebombs. The men who worked at Reuters then – and there were a couple still here – had been in the front line indeed.

There was also a remnant of Empire concealed in the codes which designated where in the world a particular story would be sent. Once raw copy had come in, been handled by the desk and judged of sufficient merit to be sent out to the world, it went to a 'filing' editor who decided which parts of the globe would be most interested. He accordingly scribbled on it, usually in ink, a three-letter code which would then be transferred into electronic signals by the battery of telex operators who sat behind him. Often these codes were self explanatory: UKP meant United Kingdom Press, EUS was South Europe, EUN North Europe, EUR all of Europe, SAF was South Africa, NOR North America. They mostly reminded me of the rather simplistic codes Ian Fleming had the Secret Service use in the early Bond books: Station B for Berlin, Station Z for Zürich, Station J for Jamaica. Some were more obscure: CCC meant all main regions of the world, while anything that included Asia for some reason began with a Y. My absolute favourite was YCW. Attach those three letters to the top of a story and it went, apparently quixotically, to Hong Kong, Australia, New Zealand, South Africa and the West Indies. Every part of the world that cared about cricket.

All journalists were required to have a two- or three-letter code for themselves – usually their initials – which was added to the bottom of the story, after the word REUTER, which indicated its end. This made clear who had handled it from the first reporter to the last sub-editor. It was the sports desk which first gave me the opportunity to add my own to the score of a football match in the Republic of Ireland. Hardly a major world event – and I had not altered the copy – but I still felt a brief gush of pride at affixing the letters PYM at the end. (PM and PJM were already taken, so I chose a 'Y' at random. The editor of *The Sunday Times* still occasionally refers to me as PYM, but only when he's being polite.)

The reign of the Four Horsemen, however, did not extend into the small hours of the morning. Despite the fact that the World Desk in London was the nerve centre for the whole global network there was a period, between when New York would down for the night and when Hong Kong/Tokyo woke up, of relative lull. There were still things to watch out for: the west coast of the USA in particular was still wide awake – and one day there would be that San Francisco earthquake – but by and large the world was a less busy place. From eleven p.m. therefore until officially nine a.m. the next morning (though the day shift arrived earlier) the world passed from the control of the Four Horsemen to the Princes of Darkness.

There were two of them, both called Jim. There had to be two, because each worked a seven-day shift, followed by seven days off, with an overlapping staff, each of whom also had an opposite number whom they never saw. Jim Forrester was a large, grey-bearded, bespectacled, scholarly gourmet from Edinburgh. Jim Flannery was a rangy, ginger-bearded, woolly-hat-wearing, Sinophile from Australia. Both Jims were drawn to things Asian. Scottish Jim's interest tended towards the Indian subcontinent, Ozzie Jim's towards Peking (as it still was) and Hong Kong. This was reflected in the overnight shift's culinary traditions, although in supposed deference to one another (in reality because it was a good excuse) both traditions were honoured each week: Friday night was therefore the Dark Prince's Curry Club, while Saturday night saw the Hong Kong and Oriental Dining Experience.

Some hours after the last of the hectic day shift had departed we would push together the big rectangular desks at each of which between four and six sub-editors would work during the day, extra long sheets of teleprinter paper would be pulled from spare rolls in the store cupboards and ripped to length to form, when aligned together, a makeshift tablecloth. Two of us, the most junior and one other would be sent out to a takeaway to bring back an assortment of Asian delights.

For the Indian night we varied our custom, depending on opening hours of establishments in Covent Garden or The Strand but the Chinese always came from the Lido restaurant on Soho's Gerrard Street. This was partly because this cavernous establishment on four floors served some of the most exotic and authentic Cantonese cuisine to be had in London, and at a reasonable price. But also because it stayed open until four a.m. which meant our dining was less likely to be interrupted by such inconveniences as world emergencies. At four a.m. GMT pretty much everywhere on the planet has either wound down or not yet wound up.

The trip to Lido was also something of an adventure, not least because the Soho pavement outside was by three a.m. regularly lined with Mercedes and even Bentleys, all of them zealously watched over by improbably bulky Asiatic strongmen who had watched *Goldfinger* one time too many and modelled themselves on Oddjob. Lido back then infamously also boasted on its top floor (inaccessible to us *gwailo* natives) one of Soho's most high-rolling *mah-jong* gambling dens. When the restaurant was subsequently burnt down there were never-substantiated rumours that it was not just due to a kitchen fire.

Back in the office, bottles of beer or wine would emerge from private lockers, and we would settle in for several hours of relaxed dining, drinking and telling of tall stories by the old hands. To those outsiders who knew, and who could blag entrance by means of personal acquaintance, a return from exotic parts, or a good bit of Fleet Street gossip, the late night weekend dining parties at 85 Fleet Street were the hottest tip in the town for a drink after the eleven p.m. pub closing time.

It was on a long midweek night, however, when we had no more culinary aspirations than a packed sandwich or a sausage roll from the late trolley, that I learned another essential trick of the journalistic trade. If you can't use your eyes, use your brain. And your imagination.

At around one thirty a.m. on a quiet Tuesday or a Wednesday, a brief report came up on the English language service of AFP, the French news agency. It concerned a shooting at a fiesta in a Corsican village, apparently involving suspect Corsican separatists. Two bystanders were injured. Police returned fire and gave chase, unsuccessfully, losing the men in the forest. That was it. Nothing more. Just the bare bones of a minor incident in a relatively lawless part of southern Europe. We would put it out, just like that, more or less. It might make one of the solitary paragraph snippets in the NIB (News in Brief) section that the *Daily Telegraph* ran to give the impression it had a global remit. Or might not.

Dave Goddard had other ideas. Dave was another West Countryman, with an accent that shouted his origins. Crucially he had also worked for tabloid newspapers as well as in the more cerebral – he would and occasionally did say 'sterile' – world of the wire services (us). 'Here you go, young Peter,' he said. 'See if you can turn that into something the *Daily Mail* foreign pages will snap up.' I stared at him in blank amazement.

'There's nothing there,' I said. 'Just a few lines.'

'Just a few lines now, but wait until you've worked your magic.'

'Eh?' was the best I could manage, gazing at the torn piece of printer paper in my hands and wondering where the magic wand was supposed to come from.

'Dear, oh dear, oh dear,' muttered Goddard good-humouredly, shaking his head in a 'young folk these days' sort of way. 'Use what's there, lad, build on it.'

'But there's nothing there.'

'What do you mean there's nothing there, there's masses. How many English village fetes end up with gunfights and car chases?'

'Er, not many,' I ventured.

He smiled: 'Right. So what have you got?'

I shrugged.

'A human interest story. A good one. Well, good-ish. Have a go.'

I didn't know where to start and my face said so.

'Try this,' said Dave and he grabbed a typewriter, scanned my piece of agency copy for a second and produced something like this: 'A party in a sleepy Corsican village exploded in gunfire and bloody mayhem as two revellers were caught in crossfire in a shoot-out between militant separatists and armed local police.'

I looked at it for a minute and thought, ye-ess, I see what you mean, but, 'How do you know it was a "sleepy" village.' Reuters fact-training had got to me.

He gave me a pitying glance. 'It's the Med. If they're not whoop-ing it up, they're having a kip. Ever been down the south of France.' I had to smile. I had.

'Right,' he said. 'Now let's get cracking.'

It was like pulling teeth – or maybe fitting them – but over the next hour under Dave's amused but professional and unrelenting supervision I had turned a five-line bulletin into a 'two-page' (about 450 words, Reuter pages are short) news story.

'People screamed and ran for cover ...' Dave put into my mouth. 'How do you know that?' 'There's blokes firing guns for Christ's sake!' '... as bullets ricocheted off the whitewashed walls ...' 'But it doesn't say anything about ...!!' 'Do you think they all hit their targets? No, OK so they hit something else first, that's a ricochet.' 'But what about the whitewashed ...' 'It's Corsica, everything's bloody whitewashed!'

'Ambulances rushed to the scene to tend the wounded amid scenes of chaos ...' 'Wait a minute there's nothing here about ambu-lances!' 'You think they didn't call one?' 'No, but ...' 'Tsk, tsk!' '... the gunmen fled at high speed in their getaway car pursued by the wail of police sirens ...' 'There's nothing here about, oh I see.' I was begin-ning to. 'They had a car, right? You don't suppose they drove off at a leisurely pace?' 'No. And I suppose the police would have ...' 'Used their sirens? Too bloody right they would.'

When we were finished, I was exhausted. Exhausted and incredu-lous. And exhilarated. All at once. Dave was beaming. 'Well done, lad, we'll make a decent newsman out of you yet.'

Something inside me still niggled, told me this was dishonest, but then I looked at it and read it again, and the original, and thought, no, it's not. It's a story. 'It's not just about telling people the news,'

Dave told me another night, 'it's about making the buggers read it. Making them care.' And he was right. And the story? It made the *Daily Mail*. Not big, but it made it. And the *Telegraph* too.

I had lost my virginity. I was a proper journalist at last.

The completion of my Reuters training involved a year in Brussels, an experience I have not gone into in detail here because as the office junior much of my time was spent playing pinball and drinking beer in a succession of mock Irish and English bars that adhered like plastic leeches to the periphery of the European Commission's Berlaymont building.

The highlight of the average day in the office was watching as one by one the sun-sensitive external Venetian blinds on the concave wall of the Berlaymont facing us rattled down slowly a blade at a time. Clack. Clackety. Clack. The greatest intellectual challenge was striving to figure out what a Green Pound was, and understanding the thick Irish accent in which the commission spokesman gave his daily midday briefings in obligatory French. The journalistic highlights were an endless series of commutes to the European Parliament in Strasbourg or Luxembourg to write stories nobody ever published on debates nobody cared about. Wry amusement came from studying the strange pond life symbiosis between British tabloid journalists and government ministers, such as when portly Labour Agriculture, Fisheries and Food minister John Silkin would emerge from a meeting and declare, 'Gentlemen, fish have come up but the chips are not down!' Brilliant, John, love, just brill!

On return to London, with the threat of a move to the ever more important but deadly dull economics desk looming, journalism was fast losing its lustre. On the other hand, my private life was settling down. I had just moved into a shared house with Jackie, a girlfriend I had known from university, and the 'm' word, as yet unspoken, was hovering just over the horizon.

It was at that point that somebody mentioned the 'b' word: Berlin. The idea struck me like a thunderbolt hitting a lightning conductor: a shock out of the blue and yet all of a sudden blindingly obvious. I'm not sure whose spectre haunted the city more in my mind: Liza Minnelli, Adolf Hitler, or Michael Caine. But I was sure of one thing. Berlin was exciting, and scary. All at once. And totally irresistible.

Berlin was a name that in the early eighties still worked like an incantation. Not least because there were two of them. Or maybe three. Nobody born in the second half of the twentieth century did not have a mental vision of the Berlin that had vanished: the dark, foreboding capital of the thousand-year Reich, of monumental architecture draped in swastikas, red and white and black above a sea of stiff outstretched arms. Berlin was Mordor, the lair of the Dark Lord, the Heart of Darkness, the city where Liza Minnelli in that poster above my Paris bed had given sultry embodiment to the black magic of stockings, suspenders and jackboots; pre-war Berlin was Sodom and Gomorrah and like them had sunk in dust and ashes.

In the 1970s we thought primarily of West Berlin, plucky little West Berlin, talisman of the Cold War, the brave city that had been cut off by the engulfing communist sea, that had stood besieged, isolated and alone against the Soviet juggernaut, risking starvation; the city British and American airmen had risked their lives to feed during the 1949 blockade when the Russians had tried to starve the Western part of the city into submission; the city where US President John F. Kennedy had proclaimed – in only slightly mangled German – that the proudest boast anyone could make was to be one of its citizens. A city that still sat there, ringed with a siege wall unlike any other in urban history, wealthy, glitzy, ever so slightly tacky, a capital that was no longer a capital, not even legally part of any country, a beacon of freedom. And a magnet for spies.

Then there was the other side: East Berlin, the less than half a city that was the capital of less than half a country, where jackboots still strutted dilapidated streets, where citizens spied on one another and their own soldiers shot them if they tried to leave; a city of crumbling tenement blocks, cobbles and comical cars, where the red banners of the Nazis had been replaced by the red flags of communism and secret policemen lurked in every alleyway on the lookout for secret agents.

I had read Len Deighton's *Funeral in Berlin*, seen Michael Caine play Harry Palmer on the big screen and was as willing to believe they were as likely to smuggle live men in coffins across the inner-city border as well as swapping American spy plane pilots for KGB colonels in tense exchanges on isolated bridges. There was no doubt about it, Berlin was magic. Black magic, maybe, but that only made it all the more appealing.

3

A Place of My Own

There was more: I would have an office of my own. No boss sitting over me. My own little fiefdom.

A fiefdom, of course, was precisely what it was intended to be: technically subservient to Reuters Bonn, the large office which covered the economic superpower that West Germany had become. It housed dozens of native staff who ran the German-language news and economics service. There was also an office in West Berlin, with two West German staff. But for reasons both political and historical the East Berlin office was staffed from London, by a Briton. The main reason for this was that Berlin had in theory remained under the control of the victorious World War II Allies. This meant that when Reuters, still emerging from its role in the British wartime propaganda set-up, opened a separate office in the Soviet sector in the 1950s, (in itself a controversial move as it implied recognition of the division of Germany that had already *de facto* occurred) no one ever suggested the correspondent should be anything other than one of the 'Allies'. Despite Reuters' claim that it had since become an 'international' agency, as far as the East Germans were concerned it was still British and that meant the correspondent had to be too.

Reuters were not exactly entrusting me with the front-line bureau it might have seemed. Berlin may once have been the potential flashpoint to spark a new world war, but the Wall had – as both sides tacitly acknowledged, without mentioning it overmuch to the Germans – stabilised the situation: a concrete agreement to differ. By 1981 the Berlin Wall was twenty years old and it seemed as if it would be there forever. It was easy to forget that in the first hours of its creation there had been what appeared to be a Mexican stand-off: if the armed forces of the West intervened, what would happen? We will never know. It was a deadly game to see which superpower could outstare the other. The West blinked first.

On August 13th, 1961, the authorities in the East, having seen their population gradually drain to the West through the open plughole that was West Berlin, had simply stopped the leak by doing what everyone had thought was impossible: building a wall. Not just through the heart of the city – and therefore also dividing the underground rail system and the river traffic – but all the way around West Berlin, mirroring the impassable border erected in 1952 between the two German states.

The Wall had gone up overnight. Almost. At first little more than a barbed wire fence manned by armed soldiers it quickly became concrete. Literally. Bricks were laid rapidly to a height of two metres, at least a metre back on Soviet sector soil so the workers, watched over by armed troops, could work on it from both sides without standing in the West. Then they built a second wall behind it, to leave a 'death strip' in between. Over the next twenty years the Wall evolved into its final form: a largely anonymous cinder-block wall some three metres high in the East and a vertical concrete slab construction facing the West, also three metres high but topped with a 'half-barrel' rounded top that effectively denied purchase to anyone trying to climb it. From either side.

The truth in 1981, however, was that the situation in Europe had stabilised in a balance between East and West that people weren't exactly enamoured of, but at least had come to live with. The focus of the ongoing tension between the superpowers had moved. Primarily to the east, where the 1979 Soviet invasion of Afghanistan had provided a new arena for Moscow and Washington to fight their proxy war. The Soviets had got bogged down supporting a puppet secular atheist communist government, and the Americans had retaliated by supplying arms to religious fundamentalist patriot resistance fighters. They called themselves *mujahideen*, those who were involved in *jihad*, or righteous struggle. Many of them went on to be even more famous under another name: the Taliban.

The situation in Europe however, thanks to the conciliatory 'Ostpolitik' practised by West German chancellor Willy Brandt and the 1975 Helsinki Accords on Security and Cooperation in Europe, could roughly have been described as 'all quiet on the Western front'. That is not to say there were no tensions brewing. The two sides, ever watchful of each other's supposed military superiority, were just beginning a new arms race, with the US deploying new medium-range missiles in Britain, Italy, the Netherlands and West Germany, and the Soviet Union doing the same in Czechoslovakia and East Germany. In the end, and sooner than anyone expected, that new arms race would have an effect on the Cold War, but not at all in the way either of the power blocs intended.

In the meantime, East Berlin had become a bit of a backwater in news terms. It was seen primarily as a source of features which would be translated by the Bonn office and fed out to West German newspapers to tell their readers about the lives of their less fortunate former fellow citizens. Bonn, of course, would have preferred the correspondent to be a West German, but the East German authorities, who when it suited them could choose to play the old 'four-power' game they otherwise refuted, wouldn't hear of it. There was clearly a feeling amongst the communist authorities that a Briton would stand out more, would be less likely to get under the skin of the country and thereby would cause less of a nuisance.

And they might have had a point in my case, because there was one distinct problem when it came to me accepting the job. Well, two actually, though the first seemed – to me at least – clearly the most important: I didn't speak German. Well, I did, but not properly. I had done it at A-level and got a grade A, but my steep learning curve in Paris street slang had made me realise how far even the best schoolboy command of a foreign language falls short of real working competency in the country. Since leaving school I had concentrated on my French and my Russian, working as hard as I could – given the even greater difficulty of spending long periods amongst native Russian speakers. My German, meanwhile, was limited to the sort of stuff they taught seventeen-year-olds in 'conversation classes' at school: I could order an ice cream and ask how to play *Skat* (though not understand the answer, it's a card game whose rules I've never got the hang of) or say '*Borussia Mönchengladbach* are my favourite football team', but that was it. The idea of reading newspapers, dealing with official press releases, asking questions at press conferences or talking to dissidents was terrifying to say the least.

The other problem was in its own way every bit as pressing: I couldn't drive. This would be a serious impediment in Berlin, as although I would be based in the East, I would be expected also to cover the West. I could do that by getting across on public transport, although it would mean queuing with tourists and other pedestrians at the two recognised border crossing points, but the real problem was that the office in the East relied on most of its basic supplies – printer paper, ink, telex ribbons – being brought over from the West. And lugging several dozen heavy boxes on foot wasn't going to be easy, not least because there would be customs checks every time. I had taken lessons, of course, at some stage, but I hadn't needed a car at university; there was no place for student parking, and not much for anyone else either, in the medieval, bicycle-friendly streets of Oxford. And moving to congested, crowded London with the Tube and buses hadn't made me see the need for one either.

All of a sudden things were different. My girlfriend, although apprehensive about me going abroad again – this time for an indeterminate period – and with our future not exactly decided, bravely volunteered to give me a crash course. Pun intended. This mostly involved doing lengthy three-point turns in the narrow streets of Peckham, south London, in the car she had inherited from her grandfather: a venerable Hillman Imp. With only weeks to go before I was due to leave, I fought my way through the tortuous meandering suburban route that on the whim of some bureaucrat with more inspiration than common sense is called the South Circular to a test centre in Wandsworth. I had decided it would be good for me to drive the whole way and as a result was exhausted by just the strain of getting there on time, which we nearly didn't. I took the test. And failed.

Driving was something that would have to be put on the back burner, to be sorted out in Berlin. Reuters were hesitant about this, but someone in the Bonn office suggested I could write a fun feature about taking the driving test in East Germany. And that was that. From then on it was my problem. The other one was my domestic situation: we decided to get married, but not until the summer when my wife-to-be would have completed her own professional exams even though she would not be able to practise as a patent attorney in a communist country. It was a brave step on her part which I appreciated. But the magic of 'Berlin' was potent for both of us. She would not come out to join me, however, until after the wedding which meant I would spend my first few months there alone. I suspect the Stasi were glad to hear that because waiting for me in the flat in East Berlin were two women: the fusspot and the honeypot.

I arrived in Berlin for the first time in the late spring of 1981. Summer was in the air and the laid-back youth of Europe's most student-oriented metropolis were drinking beer in leafy pavement cafes and smoking dope in the green parks and along the beaches of windsail-dotted lakes. It wasn't at all what I had been expecting. But then this was West Berlin. 'Our' side of the Wall. Like a version of London centred on Chelsea and Hammersmith and surreally severed from The City and the East End, West Berlin had turned its back on the East, forgotten where its roots lay for the sake of enjoying a glitzy affluence that its inhabitants all knew deep down was fragile.

While paying lip service to the aim of a reunification that none of them imagined they would see in their lifetimes West Berlin's politicians and business people had created a whole alternative city structure. They might not quite have forgotten that the fractured metropolis's roots lay in the East, that the original ancient city of Berlin lay wholly within the district of *Mitte* (Centre), now on the other side of the Wall, but they simply didn't bother much about it. Out of sight and out of mind. They were more concerned with the tax incentives and financial aid from Bonn that kept the semi-isolated city's commerce alive.

Shortly after I arrived – by then already installed in my more sober surroundings in the East – I was given an aerial tour of the extraordinary entity that was West Berlin, courtesy of the British Army which maintained a small fleet of helicopters on a base at Gatow in the far west of the city. They graciously picked me up from a more central, and more imposing venue: the main athletics field of Hitler's vast 1936 Olympic Stadium, which then housed the British Army's Berlin HQ. (It has since been hollowed out, refurbished and partly roofed over to serve as the scene for the 2006 World Cup Final.)

Lifting high into the sky in what was little more than a tiny glass bubble we soared towards the Kurfürstendamm and other central landmarks so I could get my bearings, then turned towards the outermost perimeter. What astonished me at first was the vast amount of greenery and lakeland – the Grunewald forest and the Tegelsee, Havel and Wannsee lakes (a house near the last was the scene of the notorious 1942 conference that decided on the Final Solution to the 'Jewish Problem'). If West Berliners were cut off from the surrounding countryside, they still retained easy access to vast swathes of leisure land that most urban dwellers would have envied.

And then came the cut-off point: the long, winding, erratically twisting double wall of concrete with white sand in between, dotted with watchtowers like malignant mushrooms on concrete stalks, patrolled by armed guards, men with jeeps, and dogs. The total circumference of the Wall which looped out into the countryside all around West Berlin was 156 kilometres. From the air it looked not so much like a ribbon running round the Western half of the city as masking tape sealing it off, a wrapping around an awkward-shaped object, that in the middle got tangled up in it, as the 'death strip' narrowed to begin its urban incursion. From the air it was more cruelly apparent than from the ground how the Wall cut streets in two and turned thoroughfares into cul-de-sacs. We did not venture across into the East, which would have been seen as a 'provocation' in Cold War language, a violation of Warsaw Pact airspace, but we could hover just to the west of the Brandenburg Gate and stare down the long majestic and all but empty avenue of Unter den Linden that lay in a straight line in front of us, leading to Alexanderplatz, and beyond it – for me at least – home.

On the way back to the base the pilot diverted out beyond the Tegelsee towards what appeared to be a strange little walled garden just beyond the so clearly marked boundary of West Berlin itself. When I asked, he explained – shouting over the roar of the rotors – that that was exactly what it was: a walled garden. I was already aware that the Berlin Wall had been the greatest – and most cruel – postcode lottery of all. When the Allies had come to divide up the city, they simply did it along the lines already drawn up by the city post office. This had led to the front doors of the houses in Bernauer Strasse being sealed up while their inhabitants were still inside them. But here it had resulted in something altogether more odd: the 'walled garden' was a set of allotments, which because they were owned and used by people with a postcode in what was now West Berlin, had been bizarrely, with a scrupulousness that verged on the stereotypical German, left alone. East Germany had not appropriated the land. In fact, the West Berliners still used them.

If I looked down, hundreds of feet below our whirling rotors, I could just make out something I would not otherwise have believed possible: a door in the Berlin Wall. And next to it, what else but a doorbell! It was permanently guarded, the pilot explained to me. If a West Berlin allotment-owner fancied spending Sunday afternoon doing a bit of weeding, he rang the bell and an East German soldier escorted him along a track lined with barbed wire fencing to another door in a concrete wall, behind which lay his vegetable plot. When he wanted to come back, he repeated the procedure. 'I wouldn't be surprised,' the pilot said as we wheeled around and headed back towards sanity, 'if every now and then they slip one of them a cabbage or two.'

As we headed back to the landing ground he showed me one more of the Berlin Wall's anomalous 'exclaves', as bizarre as the isolated allotments: the hamlet of Steinstücken. By any sensible point of view Steinstücken was part of Babelsberg, a suburb of Potsdam, the old city of royal palaces south-west of West Berlin (and therefore in East Germany). But because for more than 200 years this particular little parcel of land had been owned by farmers from the Berlin suburb of Wannsee, it was legally part of that district, and therefore belonged to West Berlin. When the Wall was built the East Germans logically tried to occupy it, but the Americans stationed a three-man guard post there, helicoptered in and out. The East Germans responded by building Steinstücken its own Wall, all the way around the hamlet with its 200 inhabitants. For the next eleven years, the regular American helicopter flight was the only source of Steinstücken's supplies. The problem was only 'solved' in 1972 when following an exchange of uninhabited territory elsewhere East Germany gave West Berlin a road link to Steinstücken, a corridor 1.2 kilometres long and twenty metres wide, lined with a high barbed wire fence, and a wall behind it.

For twenty-eight years, from August 13th, 1961 until November 9th, 1989, West Berlin was the largest, most populous walled city the world has ever seen, a wall built, like those of other walled cities of the past, to keep people out; the difference was that it was built by those who lived outside it. In 1981 it was a city of the very young and very old. Large numbers of the middle-aged middle class had grown tired with the restrictions of living in a city you had to fly or travel more than 120 miles to get out of. The enclave might have been rich enough in its leisure facilities but it was a long way from the industrial powerhouses of affluent West Germany. And that was not to mention the latent threat of the grizzly bear parked on its doorstep.

The famous old '*Rotes Rathaus*' – the 'red city hall' (a reference to its crimson bricks – lay in Mitte. It was still the seat of city government for the East, but the West had simply moved into the local government offices of one of its *Bezirke* (districts), all of which had their own imposing buildings much as Greater London's boroughs do. West Berlin was therefore run from the town hall for Schöneberg district. It was from the balcony there that JFK had delivered his famous '*Ich bin ein Berliner*' speech in June 1963, two years after the Wall was built. (The popular joke that what he actually said was 'I am a doughnut', is only partly true. When a German says he or she comes from a city, they omit the article: the proper way to say 'I am a Berliner' is simply '*Ich bin Berliner*'. Inserting the article 'ein' gives the impression one is referring to an object and in most of Germany 'ein Berliner' is the term used to refer to one of the old city's specialities: a large round jam-filled doughnut. In Berlin, however – where the doughnut is at home – the same thing is called '*ein Pfannekuchen*'. If there were wry smiles amidst the emotional tears in the eyes of most Germans who heard his words, the Berliners themselves would scarcely have noticed.)

But while Berlin and its Wall were regularly used by Western politicians to make public points about the evils of communism, the fact was that the city's divided status was actually the result of a sulky but peaceful agreement to disagree between the old allies turned Cold War enemies. Following the confrontations over the blockade and the building of the Wall itself in 1963, this had eventually been codified in 1971 in the 'Four Power Agreement', a magnificent piece of pragmatic diplomatic obfuscation. It miraculously never mentions West Berlin by name – it is referred to only as the 'relevant area'. This laid down the rules that allowed secure links between the allied districts and West Germany, while at the same time making clear that 'the relevant area' was not legally part of West Germany. In theory, as far as the four governments were concerned, Berlin was still an occupied city, even though they all now recognised East Berlin as the de facto capital of East Germany.

Despite – or perhaps because of its bizarre status – West Berlin was a city that buzzed and bustled almost for the sake of it. On its own, with a population of 2.2 million (against East Berlin's 1.4 million), it was much smaller than old Berlin had been but still larger than any other German city, East or West (Hamburg had 1.7 million inhabitants, Munich 1.3 million). There was a hedonistic 'live for today for there may be no tomorrow' atmosphere of existence in an anomalous enclave in the communist sea. West Berlin had created a new heart around what had in any case been the more affluent, consumerist area of the old metropolis, the Kurfürstendamm.

Not that it was all glitz: far from it. There were areas such as Kreuzberg, which had the largest Turkish population of any city in Europe, and in mid-summer felt and smelled like the back streets of Ankara, with doner kebabs roasting, coffee brewing and old men jangling worry beads in doorways. These were the areas closest to the old city centre, by definition now closest to the new city's Western edge, areas that West Berlin had effectively turned its back on as if coming too close to the Wall and the ravaged heart of the old pre-war city was simply too painful.

Apart from the Turkish immigrants most of the population in these districts were students, or dropped-out students, who looked at the run-down old nineteenth-century tenement blocks near the Wall being left to rot away for lack of investment in a bleak landscape with little obvious future. And occupied them. Occasionally someone would get court orders and send in the police to evict them, but by and large the squatters presented themselves as *Instandbesetzer* (repair-squatters), and boasted that they were restoring buildings their owners were neglecting in order to write them down against tax.

Although West Berlin was effectively part of West Germany, it was not legally so. Because of that, anyone registered as a student at a West Berlin university was not eligible to be drafted into the West German army, the *Bundeswehr*, for the otherwise compulsory military service. As a result the city had a huge population of young West Germans in their twenties, diverted from their studies by its glitzy nightlife and hard-line anarchist fringe. If to the rest of the world the West Germany of the *Wirtschaftswunder* had come to be embodied by the image of a rotund, affluent businessman behind the wheel of a BMW, West Berlin was a long-haired youth in skin-tight leather trousers living in a squat and smoking dope. It also had a hard-edged techno rock culture, which allied with its scarred, fractured landscape, and traumatised Nazi past meant that West Berlin in the early eighties was the closest equivalent to urban heroin chic. No surprise that David Bowie had fallen in love with the place, moved into an apartment in Schöneberg and recorded 'Heroes' as *Helden* in German, with the Wall as a leitmotif in the background.

The August after I arrived saw the twentieth anniversary of the Wall's erection, and it seemed to me that all that summer echoed the then two-year-old Pink Floyd hit: 'Another brick in the wall.' It boomed out over hot, dusty back street courtyards all through the summer months. I made it the headline to my first big feature story, a series of reflective first impressions of my new home. It made the back page of the *International Herald Tribune* and my first 'hero-gram', a telexed pat on the back from London. But that was based on my experience on either side of the wall, as stark a difference as it was humanly possible to imagine existing in what had until relatively recently been a single city.

It was hard to say then – and even harder now – whether it was a frisson of pure excitement, or a chill running down the spine that I experienced the first time I crossed the border at Checkpoint Charlie. Charlie was the sole non-rail crossing point for foreigners into East Berlin. The name, given it by the Americans in whose sector it lay, was purely alphabetical. The first road crossing point on the way from West Germany to Berlin was Checkpoint Alpha, that where it reached the Western edge of the city was Checkpoint Bravo. 'Charlie' was simply the most famous. For a good reason.

Here the apparatus of the communist state was in your face, and in the unsmiling faces of the border guards. Westerners called them *Grepos*, a slang term derived from *Grenzpolizei* (border police). They were in fact by then officially known as *Grenztruppen*, border troops, a separate regiment of the *NVA*, the National People's Army.

They examined in detail my passport, my new multiple-entry visa, stamped both and admitted me with the words 'Welcome to the capital of the German Democratic Republic.' The words 'East Berlin' were never uttered at official level. The half-city which was not surrounded by a wall – a fact many Westerners often forgot – was referred to only as Berlin, or if necessary for clarity's sake, 'the capital'. The unmentionable other bit was, if it absolutely had to be mentioned, *Westberlin*, as if Westminster were to be excised from London.

The difference was as dramatic as in any spy film. Whereas the apartment blocks of the more chic Western districts had been lavishly restored – and even those inhabited by squatters were garish with graffiti – those in the East still had the countless bullet pockmarks that bore witness to the 'euphoric welcome' afforded by the Berlin proletariat to the Soviet champions of People's Power.

These were the ranks of six-storey nineteenth-century *Mietkasernen* (rental barracks) built by Prussian industrialists to house the new German capital's burgeoning working class. My flat was on the first floor of a typical block on Schönhauser Allee, a broad thoroughfare that ran north-south, just a few hundred metres east of the Wall, and would have been described as 'leafy' were the trees not permanently caked in the dirt of diesel exhaust and the residue from the cheap, environmentally unfriendly but plentiful lignite browncoal used in the power plants that provided heating. This was the heart of Prenzlauer Berg, a gritty working-class inner-city suburb. Today it is the bustling, Bohemian heart of trendy Berlin, alive with restaurants and nightlife. Not even in my most exotic fantasies could I have imagined that just two decades ago.

On the ground floor, just below the flat there was a bar called *Wörther Eck* (Wörther Corner), because it was on the corner of Wörther Strasse. It was a grimy place with vinyl-topped tables, and a secret staircase at the back that I would only become aware of once it was no longer used. There was a shop on the corner opposite that bore the catchy label '*Obst-Gemuse*' (fruit and veg). The communist government had replaced all traditional or family names of shops with functional ones. That Germanic insistence on exactitude was however let down by reality. The fruit and veg shop never had much of either. It certainly never had anything green, although the white cabbage occasionally had a greenish tinge. The stock-in-trade was hoary carrots and bruised onions.

Across the road was the equivalent of a neighbourhood super-market. It announced this with the word *Lebensmittel* (foodstuff), which included milk that wasn't always sour, tomato juice imported from Romania as well as barely drinkable red wine, and, thank-fully, an almost unlimited supply of still surprisingly excellent beer. The beer and the tomato juice – and some remarkably foul Russian mineral water – all came in identical half-litre bottles which were either brown or green irrespective of content, so it meant it was well worth paying attention to the label, even if it was usually faded.

The flat itself had a long, high-ceilinged corridor with a door to the stairwell at either end, three doors off to the left and three to the right. Those on the right were the bathroom, kitchen and a separate toilet; those on the left, in succession, the office, the living room, and the bedroom. The rooms were big and though it was far from luxurious it was as good a first marital home as many young couples in London could afford. The downside, of course, was that it also housed the office: I would be not so much working from home as living in the office.

And the office was the realm, let there be no mistaking it, of Erdmute. This improbable first name was derived from 'Earth Mother', and sounded just as preposterous to most 1980s Germans as it did to me. The exceptions were those old enough to sympathise with children of the thirties and forties who had been given names thought appropriate to the latent paganism of National Socialist ideology. (There are still middle-aged Russians today who labour under the name Melor, derived from Marx, Engels, Lenin, October Revolution – most of whom were called Melsor until Stalin fell out of favour). Erdmute had been employed as secretary since the opening of the office in 1959. Back then she had been a 'slip of a thing', she claimed; by now she was a jovial, self-possessed woman in her forties with heavy glasses and a shock of bright red henna-dyed hair.

As the one fixed element in a relatively transient world of young men who came and went over the years, Erdmute had a naturally possessive attitude to the Reuters office. This extended to previous correspondents, even – up to a point – those who predated her. Chief among these was one old man who was one of my first visitors in the East Berlin office: a tall thin Englishman called John Peet, who had been Reuters chief correspondent in occupied Berlin in the late 1940s and also a convinced pacifist. One day in the early summer of 1950, only months after the Soviet zone had declared itself a sepa-rate state – in response to currency reform and consolidation in the Western zones – Peet failed to turn up for work. London – to their disbelieving horror – soon found out why. He had left a neat roll of telex tape with instructions for the office clerk to send it over the wire to London. It was, in Peet's usual manner, a well-crafted little news story, properly formatted in the correct Reuters house style. But it caused pandemonium in London, swiftly followed by disbe-lief. As a result Reuters were scooped on their very own story when, a week later, Peet turned up at a press conference in East Berlin accompanied by a senior member of the communist politburo to announce his defection.

Erdmute was slightly disapproving of him, whereas she abso-lutely doted on one of my predecessors whom I believe she regarded as her 'star pupil'. In 1963 the office in East Berlin had been occupied by a young Reuters man, Frederick Forsyth, who had yet to turn his hand to the thriller-writing that would make him a fortune. The famous anecdote about him on the World Desk back in London was that he had come close to sparking World War III by sending in a flash report late one October night that massed tanks were heading for the city centre (and by implication West Berlin). He was right, but only just. And his interpretation of the 'evidence' of his eyes was dodgy to say the least. They were being redeployed for the next day's 'Anniverary of the Republic' military parade. To be fair, as Erdmute insisted I should be, that had been just four months after JFK's 'Berliner' speech, and only two years since Western tanks and East

German soldiers had faced each other on the night the Wall was built. It still gets a bit of a laugh though in journalistic circles.

Erdmute also lived up to the stereotypical Prussian love of order. Every word of copy sent to London since 1959 had been kept, neatly arranged in chronological order on yellowing telex paper in box-files stacked like ministerial archives around the walls of the office. This orderly filing system had the curious result that such historical gold dust as reports of the first reactions of Berliners to the building of the Berlin Wall and the eyewitness account of the Reuters man who was the first to pass through it, were buried amongst obscure coverage of football results. One such game between Lokomotiv Leipzig and Ballymena, Northern Ireland, was the first story it was my privilege to file; a rude reminder that even in the espionage capital of the world the job wasn't all glamour.

There was also a cupboard off the hallway which contained a flush toilet and a pile of yellowing newspapers: *Neues Deutschland*, the official organ of the central committee of the Communist Party, also dating back to the opening of the office. Erdmute liked to portray this pile of decaying newsprint as a secret treasure trove, it being theoretically illegal to hoard old newspapers, for two reasons: firstly, it was considered wasteful in a society where recycling was done for economic rather than ecological reasons, but also because the communist authorities regarded archive material as something only they should control: history was also deemed to be at the service of the party.

Erdmute was not a party member. But she was an employee of the communist state. Her contract with Reuters was handled through the wonderfully named *Dienstleistungsamt für Ausländische Vertretungen*, the 'agency for provision of services to foreign representations', DLA for short. It was to the DLA that any Western body, be it embassy, company or news organisation was obliged to apply if they wanted to employ East German staff. The DLA was then paid in West German Marks, and paid its workers the same sum in East German Marks, which on the black market were worth barely a quarter.

If the British Army had shown me West Berlin from the air, Erdmute showed me East Berlin by car, a bottle-green Wartburg

– named for the castle where Martin Luther took refuge in the Reformation and a significant one up on East Germany's most common runabout, the Trabant (for a start the Wartburg's chassis was actually made of metal). 'Soviet Embassy, British Embassy, Humboldt University, Foreign Ministry, Alexanderplatz People's Police Station,' she would rattle out as we whizzed along the broad, empty thoroughfares. 'Marx-Engels Square, Council of State building, Palace of the Republic'. The last of these was a giant showpiece conference/concert hall cum cultural exhibition centre, built on the site of the old Hohenzollern Kaisers' palace, bomb-damaged but torn down by the communists in 1950 as a political statement. The asbestos-ridden Palace of the Republic has since been demolished and a replica of the Hohenzollern palace is being re-erected, including the only bit that survived, having been preserved by Erich Honecker, the de facto dictator, as a balcony for his Council of State building.

She would test me on what I had learned that day back in the office over coffee and biscuits provided by Helga. If Erdmute was the fusspot, Helga was the honeypot: the 'cleaner'. Helga was a dark-haired, dark-eyed, slender beauty of maybe thirty – a couple of years older than I was – divorced with two young children. She, like Erdmute, was officially employed by the DLA state organisation, in the role of cleaner and general housemaid. But the role she had played throughout most of the tenure of my predecessor had been that of mistress.

'Wir lebten zusammen, wie Mann und Frau,' (We lived together like man and wife), she told me one day, at the door to the bedroom, her big brown eyes staring pointedly into mine.

Helga had for the previous few weeks become something of a pal. It was hardly a bad thing to have an attractive woman, the nearest person to my own age I had come across, to show me what there was to a fun side of East Berlin. We went for a drink in a couple of bars together, we even went to a disco of sorts once where youngish East Berliners drank heavily – the East Germans thought booze rather than religion an allowable opium for the masses – and indulged in fairly dirty dancing – think John Travolta without the white suit – to domestically produced pop music or, more rarely, an officially sanctioned Western hit. And Helga could writhe with the best of them.

We even went swimming together once, along with her children, at one of the many lakes of the Brandenburg countryside to which East Berliners, unlike the hemmed-in West Berliners, had unrestricted access. But all along, I was wondering just what game Helga was playing. For she was undoubtedly playing a game, as became clear when she spilled the beans about her sexual relationship with my predecessor in a way that clearly suggested that if I was interested, the privilege went with the job.

The man I had taken the place of in the office, if not the bedroom, had little in common with me physically – apart from a relatively diminutive stature – and even less in personality, being a ruthlessly ambitious career journalist with his eyes already set on a high executive position he eventually achieved. It seemed unlikely to me, therefore, that Helga found us both equally attractive. That left only two other possible solutions, both of which were equally credible, and may even have intermingled: first, that she was merely a young divorcee looking for a man who had easier access to the finer (i.e. Western) things in life than most of her compatriots, or, secondly, that she was an employee of the *Staatssicherheitsdienst*, the state security service, the infamous Stasi.

The likelihood that both these possibilities co-existed is the one that I found most plausible at the time, and continue to do so today. The greatest – and in the end most frightening – element of the Stasi's control of the East German population was not through direct monitoring (though there was enough of that, as I was to find out) but through a vast network of IMs, an acronym that stood for *Inoffizielle Mitarbeiter*, 'informal collaborators'. These were people recruited either because they volunteered, occasionally for ideological reasons but more usually for personal advancement, or who had themselves been compromised, or had simply been told that the job they were in required such 'active collaboration'. There were tens of thousands of them in a population of just seventeen million, and IM 'skeletons' keep turning up in the cupboards of prominent people, including politicians and show business figures, even today in a Germany reunited for nearly twenty years. Everyone knew of the

45

existence of the IM network, but nobody admitted being one. But as I was to find out, the result was that everyone watched what they said in the company of strangers. And often even friends.

So was Helga Stasi? Or at least an IM? I don't know for sure, but from records I have seen since, I suspect the answer is as complicated as the question. It was impossible that anyone working for the DLA, given that they were employed exclusively in the service of foreign organisations, was not at the very least required to answer any questions that may be put to them as to their immediate employers' activities. It was also absolutely certain that among her friends would be at least several IMs. The same thing obviously applied to Erdmute, but if the Reuters correspondent was actually sleeping with the maid, it would be the easiest thing in the world to keep tabs on almost every other aspect of his life, both private as well as professional.

I have to say here, however, that it was not on account of such professional scruples that I declined the apparently obvious invitation. Nor was it that I didn't find Helga attractive: she was gorgeous, intelligent and apparently – insofar as appearance meant anything – honest. It was just that I was already spoken for. I was happily engaged and planning – albeit at a distance – my wedding to the woman I was intending to spend the rest of my life with. If Helga was bait, tasty bait she might be, but the fish wasn't biting. A few months after my wife arrived, Helga was transferred elsewhere – she wouldn't say where, and I have never seen her since. Her successor was a hatchet-faced little woman in her sixties.

That we were spied on was a given. The extent of it was something I would discover only later. We simply assumed there were microphones in the walls. Everywhere. Even in the bedroom. If it felt uncomfortable at first, it surprisingly quickly became just something you lived with. It could be tempting to fall into what John Le Carré would call 'tradecraft': turning on the radio or the water taps and whispering if we had something to say we preferred not to share with the secret policemen. But at least in the early days when our circle of acquaintances among the native population was extremely limited, there was less of that than you might imagine. We weren't spies. And although the regime was repressive, we weren't its citizens. East Germans under a similar level of surveillance might, we assumed, have felt obliged to watch every utterance. But I didn't have to worry about what I said. My antipathy to the 'workers' and peasants' state' was something the minders took for granted. I represented, after all, 'the class enemy'. I was a 'tool of the imperialist powers'. If I felt like shouting 'Erich Honecker is a wanker' aloud in my own flat, I could. Although I would have been advised not to shout it out the window.

I did undertake one minor act of sedition: on the occasion of the wedding between Prince Charles and Lady Diana Spencer, a month before my own, I inflated and released a dozen 'Charles and Di' balloons from the window of the flat. Not because I was or am a committed monarchist, but just because they were there. My Reuters bosses would no doubt have sternly disapproved. There was a presumption of a sort of *Star Trek* 'first directive' on Reuters correspondents not to do anything to influence local conditions. My dozen balloons in any case hardly created a diplomatic incident; I noticed a couple lying burst in the gutter a few hours later. I would have liked to think a small child somewhere found one and was allowed to keep it. But I doubt it.

In any case I had more important things on my plate: I still needed to learn to drive. I had bought myself an East German bicycle. In a country dedicated to sport as a means to cement its international reputation – and with ten-year waiting lists for cars – a bicycle was one of the few consumer commodities that was relatively easy to come by. The problem was that even though cars could be taken through Checkpoint Charlie, for some mysterious reason, bicycles could not. To cross to West Berlin, therefore, I was reduced to cycling to Checkpoint Charlie or to Friedrichstrasse station and then proceeding on foot. Friedrichstrasse station was where the overground S-Bahn railway network in East Berlin came to a brutal end. The same line, of course, ran on through West Berlin, but the trains no longer did. The station was divided into two. Anyone getting off the S-Bahn in the East would have thought this the end of the line. And for most of them it was. But Friedrichstrasse, once the busiest station in Berlin, was still most famous to ordinary East Berliners. It was the only spot where those entitled to go to the West – mostly pensioners considered no longer of economic purpose to the state – could cross.

Long lines of them could be seen in the downstairs underpass where they queued for access to the closed-off half of the station, waiting to pass one by one through the steel border control gates where their documents were inspected. To cross here I had to join them. The platform itself looked like a scene from some Hollywood vision of a World War II movie, with the silhouette of a jodhpur-clad guard with automatic weapon slung over his shoulder marching along the gantry against the glass wall below the arch of the station roof. From here increasingly dilapidated trains ran their Cold War shuttle service to the West. The tracks and trains themselves were one more of the surreal anomalies of divided Berlin. With partition in 1947, the railway lines in Western Germany belonging to the old *Deutsche Reichsbahn* had been renamed the *Deutsche Bundesbahn* (federal railways). The lines in the communist East, however, had – despite its imperial and Nazi connotations – retained the old name. And because Berlin's S-Bahn overground urban rail service had always been operated by the Reichsbahn, it still was: the trains that ran through West Berlin were owned by East Berlin, and still ran the same old run-down rolling stock. A bizarre counterpoint to this was that several of the old U-Bahn (underground) lines started and finished in West Berlin but passed under East Berlin, where the stations, however, had been closed and the entrances bricked up. But these trains, owned and operated by West Berlin public transport still passed through extra slowly in case someone tried to jump aboard.

Despite being employed by East Berlin public transport, the staff of the S-Bahn in West Berlin of course had to be West Berliners (otherwise there would have been queues of East Berliners trying to join), but their uniforms were supplied by the East and they were paid by the East (in Western D-Marks). For a time after the Wall went up West Berliners had boycotted the S-Bahn as a token protest, refusing to give money to the regime that had built it. They gradually drifted back, but in the meantime service and timings had deteriorated to almost Eastern standards.

To take the train from Friedrichstrasse west therefore was to take a little bit of the East with you in your soul, at least until you got off at West Berlin's Bahnhof Zoo. As its name suggests this had until 1945 been merely a large station convenient for the Zoologischer Garten, but with many central stations destroyed, it had by default and partly because of its situation near the 'new', Western-shifted 'city centre' around the Kurfürstendamm, become the long distance transport hub for West Berlin. It was hardly an advert for the city, however. That year, 1981, West Germany as a whole was still in a state of moral shock caused by the new film *Wir Kinder vom Bahnof Zoo* (We Kids of Zoo Station), with its David Bowie soundtrack and its disarmingly depressing tale of underage prostitution and drug abuse in the shadow of the station. Here more than anywhere else it was clear that West Berlin, for all its superficial glitz and glamour, was a city of the *déracinés*. Here people I got to know in the West, from West German journalists, local politicians and British military types still based in Hitler's Olympic stadium, all thought they lived in the real Berlin, and marvelled when I disappeared East 'like Harry Lime going down some manhole', as one diplomatic wife put it in a slightly mismatched analogy. But for all its privations, I slowly began to feel more at home in the East, a city that was somehow quieter, less frenetic, and, I was gradually coming to understand, for all the resentment of its population against their government, more sure of what it was, and where it was: a city with – significantly there is no better word than the German one – a *Hinterland*.

Bizarrely it was thanks to my limited means of transportation that I was discovering that '*Hinterland*' at close quarters. The bike also had the advantage of allowing me to get definitively out of the eye of whoever might be watching me. The Stasi didn't ride bikes. On several occasions in what was a glorious warm spring, I had cycled out of the city altogether, something no West Berliner could do. Cycling along dirt tracks through fields of waving golden corn and then stopping for a beer at a little village bar unchanged since the 1920s was a surreal experience that contrasted radically with my everyday life in the office with Erdmute and Helga or the hectic traffic-clogged bustle of West Berlin.

But I was determined to pass the driving test before my wife arrived, so as not to be dependent on her to ferry me across the frontier. And as I was living in East Berlin it seemed only sensible to take their driving test. It would, after all, make a nice feature for the German service in Bonn, for whom the lives of their compatriots on the other side of the Iron Curtain was a matter of endless fascination, fuelled by not a little *Schadenfreude*.

The only thing was that I could not exactly take the test precisely as an ordinary East German might, even if I had wanted to. The regulations declared that as a foreigner I had to go through that wonderful organisation, the *Dienstleistungsamt für Ausländische Vertretungen*, the DLA, partly because they wanted me to pay the money for lessons and the test itself in hard currency: D-Marks. I duly signed up and went along for my first lesson, an introduction to the theory test which was in itself rather intimidating, not least because it would obviously be conducted in German, but also because at that stage the concept of a theory test didn't exist in Britain.

I met up with my instructor in the offices of the state motoring school. He was a genial grey-haired man who clearly thought the whole business of teaching a Westerner somewhat amusing and could indeed see the problem of me learning some of the more obscure auto mechanic terms in German. This sent a further shudder of panic through me. I had no idea that the 'theory test' also included elementary mechanics (it has only in the past few years become part of the British test) even though it should have been fairly obvious, particularly in a country where repair garages were few and far between, and spare parts were notoriously hard to come by.

He gave me a curious smile, however, and said he was sure we could find a way around it. After all, I would be driving a Western car, wouldn't I, and they were famously reliable. We then had a brief discussion of European road signs which reassured the two of us that the standardisation across the continent did indeed apply to both sides of the Iron Curtain (not a phrase we actually used as such of course). There turned out to be just three significant differences: the universal East German upper speed limit of 100 kph (just over 60 mph), compared to the West which famously had none at all; the fact that if there was a painted sign with a right-facing arrow next to a traffic light, it meant it was legal to turn right on red, provided it was safe to do so; and that the 'little green man' on pedestrian lights wore a hat. (This last turned out to have been a specifically Berlin thing, which was discarded in West Berlin after 1945 but engagingly one of the few East Berlin features to cross over when the Wall finally came down.)

Somewhat to my surprise, rather than spending any length of time on the technicalities of the driving test we drifted into a genial conversation about life in the 'Capital of the GDR'. He hoped I enjoyed the rich variety of goods that the Socialist economy produced for its citizens, and mentioned – simply in passing – that he did remember tasting French brandy once and thinking it was very good.

I got the message. For our next appointment, I arrived a few minutes early with – on Erdmute's advice – a little present: a bottle of Courvoisier, purchased in West Berlin, purely he should understand as a thank you for fitting my lessons into his busy schedule. He smiled in supremely professional feigned astonishment, locked it away in his cupboard, and we sat down to study the road signs again. After about half an hour, he said he thought I was up to taking the theory test straightaway. But rather than produce a formal paper, he took me through about a dozen of the road signs we had just been discussing – all of them essentially the same as in Britain – and then with a flourish produced a form from his desk, signed it and handed it to me. 'Congratulations,' he said. 'You've passed.'

That only left the practical examination. I was actually hoping the lessons here might be a bit more rigorous. I genuinely had things to learn. For a start I was driving on the right rather than the left as in Britain. This is much less difficult than people who have never switched from one to the other imagine, particularly if one is in a car with the steering wheel on the proper side. And this one definitely did: it was a Lada, bright orange, both a car and a colour that most East Germans considered highly desirable. It belonged, of course, to the State School of Motoring. My instructor, however, was not the genial fifty-something of the theory department, but a bright-eyed short-haired young man about my own age who had that sort of 'when I grow up I want to be a policeman' look about him. And maybe he was. I decided in this case not to mix drinking and driving.

There were other hazards that I hadn't anticipated to driving in East Berlin, including at least one that we really should have covered in greater detail in the theory part: the tram. Trams ran down the middle of most main streets and had absolute priority as did the pedestrians who jumped off them whenever they stopped, which meant you had to be pretty damn careful to make sure you did too. And that meant knowing and understanding the very different traffic lights for trams, which were always white but vertical for go and horizontal for stop. The tram also posed another danger: because it ran on rails deeply embedded in the rutted cobbled streets, cars with thin tyres, such as a Lada, could get stuck in them. Cars shared the same lanes as the trams but were supposed to get out of the way fast by pulling in to the right if they noticed one approaching behind them, which was hard to avoid as the conductor unfailingly announced his presence by ringing a piercingly loud bell. Unfortunately if you were literally 'in a rut', sometimes getting out of the way wasn't as easy as it seemed, which meant you could continue for several yards driving as if stuck in the groove on a Scalextric track with an impatient deafening bell from behind clattering in your ears.

My test, for which I was judged ready gratifyingly quickly, was something of an experience in itself. It was to be taken, as I had expected, in one of the State School of Motoring's Ladas. What I hadn't expected was that there would be four of us in it. The system routinely tested two candidates at once, swapping over as driver halfway through – accompanied by the instructor as well as the examiner. It felt a little crowded therefore as I piled into the back seat alongside my instructor, while the front seat next to the examiner was taken by a jolly but clearly nervous woman from the Ghanaian Embassy, who, she revealed, was taking the East German driving test for the sixth time.

It soon became obvious why. She almost immediately fell into the tram track trap – happily without a tram just behind her – meaning she was nearly unable to follow the examiner's instructions to turn right into a side street. When she eventually did manage to do so, she accelerated with relief, unfortunately just at the point where two children aged about nine or ten decided to skip out onto the cobbles after a bouncing ball. The examiner averted disaster only by jerking the wheel to the left. We careened to a sudden stop. By this stage the optimistic smile on the face of the young woman behind the wheel had been replaced by a rictus of resignation. He told her to drive to the end of the street and pull in.

It was my turn. And I have to admit I am forever grateful to that young Ghanaian woman. I didn't get stuck in the tram tracks and I didn't nearly kill any young comrades. After half an hour of blissfully uneventful pootering along the cobbles of Prenzlauer Berg, I pulled up back in front of the School of Motoring building and was told I had passed. The Ghanaian girl shrugged and went off to prepare for a brave seventh attempt. I sometimes wonder if she ever made it. My prize was a little grey plastic-coated booklet embossed with the 'hammer and compasses' coat of arms of the German Democratic Republic and the word *Führerschein* on the front. This, to my amazement, caused some hilarity amongst my West Berlin colleagues, whose driving licences said *Fahrerlaubnis* (driving permit). One of them joked that it had to be a communist country that would still issue anyone with a licence to be 'Führer'.

At a stroke, however, my life was transformed. At last I could take possession of the two-year-old VW Golf in British racing green which had been sitting immobile on the pavement outside the flat since I arrived. It had a distinctive blue licence plate, as did those of all non-diplomatic foreigners, and the registration QA (signifying foreign press) 41 (the United Kingdom was the forty-first country to recognise the GDR as a sovereign state) – 04 (it was the fourth ever registered). In short I was going around in a car that shouted my identity aloud to anyone who cared to know. But what did I care? I had wheels. Even the famously frosty border guards at Checkpoint Charlie were impressed. Their icy demeanour had with time begun slowly to thaw, thanks to their amusement at seeing me padlock my bicycle to the railings next to the border post entrance. One of them was a big burly bloke with curly hair who smiled occasionally, which was a lot more frequently than most. I had already mentally nicknamed him the Bear, although I would only know his first name on the day he became unemployed. He looked at the car, looked at me, smiled and said: '*Gratuliere*' (congratulations). I smiled back.

I was due to go back to England in a few weeks' time for a holiday, the focal point of which would be our wedding. But when my wife finally arrived in Berlin, at least I would be able to pick her up in style.

4

Going Underground

'Newsman and Bride to Make Home in East Berlin,' read the head-line above our photograph in the weddings section of the *Scunthorpe Evening Telegraph*. I suppose it was more exotic than Grimsby. East Berlin made even Scunthorpe seem smart.

Our honeymoon was spent modestly, driving up to Edinburgh for a few days and back via the island of Lindisfarne. It was the first time that I had driven legally on the left-hand side of the road. Concentrating on it wasn't made any easier by the fact that my new brother-in-law had thought he would make our first few married nights that little bit 'hotter' by applying an invisible layer of Deep Heat to the steering wheel.

There was one other aggravation. We had only five days together before, at Reuters' unsentimental insistence, I was due back in Berlin. The event dragging me back was not exactly earth-shattering: the annual Leipzig Trade Fair. But this was one of those occasions when a rare glimpse of the East German leader Erich Honecker in person could be guaranteed and, as always with reclusive Soviet bloc leaders, there were rumours about his health.

Honecker, as it turned out, was in fine fettle, as I discovered by accidentally getting into the close entourage strictly reserved for the obedient East German press. It was only when I tried to do the unthinkable – ask the man a question – that my presence was imme-diately noticed and I was politely, if extremely firmly, escorted back to the holding pen where the foreigners were kept.

It was a week later when I finally picked up Jackie at West Ber-lin's Tegel Airport, and took her on an introductory sightseeing tour. As would be our custom with all future house guests, last stop was the viewing platform on the Western side of the Brandenburg Gate, where US presidents and other dignitaries visiting West Berlin were taken to view the concrete evidence of communism's 'inhumanity'.

Next to us, dark and looming, sat the great grey stone bulk of the Reichstag, just in the West but still bearing black scorch marks from the 1933 fire and patched bullet holes from the 1945 Soviet conquest. In front of us, as we climbed the wooden steps of the platform, was a piece of pure theatre: the great neo-classical triumphal arch starkly floodlit with the communist 'hammer and compasses' version of the German flag flying over it in the dark night sky. Save for two goose-stepping guards shouldering Kalashnikov rifles, beyond there was no sign of human life, just the distant glistening orb of the East German television tower, a mile away. Immediately below us the Wall stretched out in an obscene bulge, designed to keep viewers on the Western platform all but invisible from the East. Set back from it, close to the Reichstag wall, was a line of white crosses, each bearing the name of a Berliner shot dead trying to flee to the West. And in front of the Wall itself the ubiquitous placard which by now to me had already become so familiar, the warning spelled out in black letters on white: '*Achtung! Sie verlassen jetzt West Berlin.*' Warning! You are now leaving West Berlin. Not that you could do so very easily with a ten-foot high wall in the way.

'Where are we going now?' asked Jackie.

I pointed into the glare of the floodlights and said, 'Over there.'

Unsurprisingly it took her a little while to settle in. But we were young, adaptable, and both taken with the exotic romance of living in East Berlin. It was undoubtedly a bit monochrome, but then so was *The Maltese Falcon.*

The language, of course, would prove an initial problem for Jackie, although at least she was not required to work in it. She had done German at school but only to O-level and now gamely signed up to take lessons provided by the ubiquitous DLA, which meant her class included the wife of the Yemeni ambassador, several North Koreans and a smattering of Hungarians, Poles and Yugoslavs.

It was only after a couple of weeks that we realised she was learning German with a difference. Some of the variances between her textbook, 'German for Foreigners 1a', and those we had known back at school in England were immediate: 'Here is a 100 Mark note. The 100 Mark note has a picture of Karl Marx.'

A few took a moment to sink in. Like most in the genre, the book followed a typical family as a means of learning everyday vocabulary. Here is an example from the chapter entitled: 'A Typical Day at Work': 'Herr Sander is a fitter in the People's Own Enterprise "Red Star". His shift begins at six a.m. At five thirty a.m., Herr Sander arrives at the factory, and by six a.m. on the dot he is standing by his machine in Hall 2. Before breakfast the party secretary comes into the department. He asks about the export contract for Cuba and discusses the five-year plan with the workers.'

Little things like that reinforced the fact that we were living in a wholly alternative version of Germany. A further complication was that they didn't actually use the full expression 'People's Own Enterprise' but an acronym of the German *Volkseigener Betrieb*: *VEB* (pronounced Fow-Eh-Beh). As virtually everything in East Germany was owned and operated by the state, this was an important word in its own right. East Germans used these acronyms all the time, often because, as in the case of the infamous DLA, they were a lot easier to pronounce than the full-out version. Another in everyday use was LPG, which was the East German version of the Soviet collective farm, or *Landwerkschaftsproduktionsgenossenschaft*, an 'agricultural comradeship'. To call a spade a spade.

One of the results was that when Jackie would practise some of her newly-learned German on West Berliners, she would tend to use VEB or LPG instead of 'firm' or 'farm'. It was what she was being taught every week by native speakers for heaven's sake, but it still caused the future 'Wessies' to collapse into laughter. Not at her accent, but at this unknown vocabulary. Even so, hardly encouraging if you're struggling with a new language.

Happily, back on what was now definitely 'our' side of the wall, she faced no such patronising sarcasm. All these terms, including FDJ – for the *Freie Deutsche Jugend* (Free German Youth), the communist youth organisation Herr Sander's daughter, like every other DDR child, belonged to – have vanished, an alternative language faded into history. It should be remembered (particularly by former West Germans) that there is a whole generation of African, Middle Eastern and South American industrialists and agriculturalists out there who used those same textbooks. And even if some of them may also have forgotten the socialism, their command of German still owes its allegiance to *VEB Roter Stern*.

But language wasn't the only difficulty. There was the fact that we were not so much living above the shop as in it. With two other women. Getting up in the morning to have breakfast wasn't quite what it should have been for a young couple when the breakfast table in our kitchen was already occupied by Erdmute and Helga, both chain smoking, and gossiping in a language that strained my still growing command of colloquial Berlin dialect and was certainly beyond Jackie. Nor was it helped by Erdmute with her sweetest smile volunteering to put the coffee on again for us. It felt like being houseguests in what was supposed to be our own home.

Helga was another matter. I think for a while she genuinely wondered if she and Jackie could become friends. But men in other places had other ideas: barely a few months after Jackie arrived, Helga was transferred. We never saw her again. Her place as cleaner was taken by Frau Neumann, an elderly harridan who fussed and bustled around the place, generally annoying all three of us (Erdmute included). Perhaps the most signal sign of her real obligations to her employers was the time we had a late party with a gathering of East German friends, a babble of voices that the microphones in the walls obviously couldn't distinguish. Frau Neumann turned up in the early hours of the morning, claiming she had decided to come over and do our ironing because she 'couldn't sleep'. The secret state never does.

In the meantime we were getting on with what we could under the circumstances to make our 'own mark' on our first marital home. I had persuaded Reuters in London that they really had to spend money on refurnishing the flat, something that under a succession of bachelor correspondents had not been done for years. They agreed, but only if I kept costs to a minimum. The other complication, of course, was that there was simply no furnishing worth having to be bought in East Berlin. The average standard of goods in shops – when there were any – was of a quality to make Ikea's bargain basement products look like Chippendale. We did, therefore, the only thing any man with a young wife and an albeit limited expense account for furniture would do: we went shopping in the West. And before long had found ourselves a nice, relatively modestly priced brown leather sofa. There was a problem, however: nobody would deliver to East Berlin, at least not without prohibitive charges that included protracted dealings with customs officials – which I suspected involved substantial backhanders all round – and visa formalities for the delivery men.

So we opted for the only logical alternative, as it turned out totally illogical in our circumstances, but we didn't know that at the time: we hired a self-drive van. This was a bit of a challenge in itself for a relatively novice driver, but we loaded up the sofa and set off for Checkpoint Charlie. Everyone, from the West Berlin office staff to the man at the sofa shop, said we were mad: they would never let us through. It simply hadn't occurred to us. I had, after all, a customs exemption certificate for East Germany; I hadn't considered that it might not be valid for the import of larger household goods. And sometimes, as all journalists will tell you, it's just best not to ask that extra question. When we turned up at Checkpoint Charlie they opened the barrier as usual but waved us to one side into a loading bay while a relatively junior border guard dashed into the prefab huts that made up the border post to fetch his superiors. The senior officer who emerged frowned at first when he saw my customs declaration form, then turned to ask something of another who turned out to be the burly, curly-haired one – Yogi Bear – who had congratulated me on passing my driving test. He smiled again. I liked it when he did that. Then he went to fetch one of his colleagues who was even more unusual: she both smiled and was female. She had a nickname too. We called her 'Lovely Rita', not because she was called Rita – we never knew her name – or was particularly stunning, though with long dark hair and an easy smile she was pleasant enough looking, but because of the Beatles song: 'Lovely Rita, meter maid,' which included the line, 'and the bag across her shoulder made her look a little like a military man.'

She wasn't actually military but customs, but she was definitely a woman and when she looked inside the van she had only one comment on our unusual and possibly illicit cargo: 'Hmm, nice sofa! Real leather!' And that was it. She stamped the forms and off we drove. Several hours later I drove back to West Berlin to return the empty hire van – to the amazement of my Western colleagues and the man from the furniture store who had been expecting his goods returned. On the way out, the Checkpoint Charlie guards all turned out to watch, and 'Rita' came over to ask if we'd got the sofa into the flat all right. Not one of them looked in the back. For all the tortuous schemes that would-be escapers from East Germany devised, from hollowed-out petrol tanks to secret compartments under the floors of freight lorries, on that occasion I could have had a dozen escapers in the back and nobody would have noticed.

Ever afterwards, if it happened to be 'Rita' on duty when we crossed through Checkpoint Charlie she would make a point of asking, 'How's the sofa doing?' I never had the courage to admit that a week after we bought it I had fallen asleep on it with a felt-tip pen in my rear pocket and put a series of indelible scrawl marks all over it. Come to think of it, I didn't tell Reuters either. It was hard enough telling the wife.

If we shopped when necessary in West Berlin, I was determined that it would only be when necessary, and we would not live our social lives over there. Jackie probably wondered about the wisdom of this as we wandered up Schönhauser Allee past shops that were a million miles from the glitzy establishments just the other side of the Wall: a flower shop that bore the name *Blumen* (Flowers), but didn't actually have any most of the time. Then there was *Uhren Schmuck* (literally: Watches, Jewellery), the name for all of what passed for jewellers' shops in the communist paradise, most of which contained no more than a few, usually second-hand watches, old brooches and – just occasionally – cheap pieces of amber from the coast of neighbouring Poland. By the time we reached Dimitroffstrasse, once Danziger Strasse but since Danzig had become Polish Gdansk, renamed in favour of a Bulgarian communist (it has since reverted), we were in need of a little light relief.

Around the corner were two old-fashioned bars, though just how old-fashioned we were still to find out. They faced each other on opposing corners across the broad main street. One was called *Schusterjunge* (Cobbler's Boy), the other *Hackepeter* (Chopped Peter). In reality these referred to two traditional, complementary Berlin culinary specialities: the former was a small brown rye bread roll usually served with the latter: a dish of spicily seasoned raw minced pork. It was a neat conceit therefore for them to be the names of two facing pubs. The opposition had been rather more pointed in the early 1930s, before Hitler's rise to power, when one had been a drinking den for Nazis and the other for communists, and they had traded insults and hurled cobblestones at each other. We had no idea which was which. It didn't take long to form an opinion.

Hackepeter was like something transplanted straight from the set of Cabaret, without the singing girls: brown-painted walls, dark, smoky, lit by low-wattage bulbs in low-hanging yellow shades. On a small raised stage a two-piece ensemble of keyboard player and drummer who used mostly cymbals trotted out tunes from the fifties. There were two waiters, one rotund, balding and middle-aged, the other scrawny and ancient, both in stained white jackets, carrying trays of quarter-litres of state-brewed Berliner Pilsener beer. Sitting over a couple – regular service ensured by the astute tip of a single Western D-Mark – felt like being in a surreal time warp. Over the bar hung a faded photograph of a woodland scene, a young boy and girl holding hands in a forest glade in the Harz Mountains. It looked sentimental and bucolic. Until I squinted to read the caption: *Buchen Wald im Harz*. Had it always been there, I wondered, from the time before Buchenwald became a synonym for evil, or for the time when it became one? But then the occasional sinister frisson was part of the essential Berlin experience. In the West money and conscience had sanitised all traces of the past. There was less of each in the East.

Ironically it was in the West that the real remnant of Nazism remained, alive if not quite kicking. In 1981 Rudolf Hess, Hitler's right-hand man arrested in Scotland on a controversial mission (the subject of countless conspiracy theories) to make peace with Britain prior to the Nazi invasion of the Soviet Union, had for many years been the solitary inmate of the vast redbrick Spandau Prison. By then eighty-seven, Hess was on what newsmen consider a perennial death watch, and Reuters news desk asked me to 'redo' his obituary. The message from London added the rider – in the even then outdated telexese from the days when costs were calculated per word – 'though realise he ungotaboutalot recently'. Hess might have 'ungotaboutalot', but the fears of his imminent demise were serious enough to have his son Wolf-Rüdiger come to visit him. I met him outside. Having been just three years old when his father made his ill-fated mission, and having not seen him again until he was in his thirties (Hess was allowed only one thirty-minute visit per month), he could tell me little. As I shook his hand in farewell, it occurred to me that I was now just 'two handshakes' away from Adolf Hitler. A chilling thought.

Back in East Berlin I had happily found another local pub to call my own, one where the past also lingered, but without the same taint. It had been a balmy evening in early summer when I first discovered Metzer Eck, while returning from a day 'on the other side'. I was also responsible for providing reports in English for Reuters from West Berlin, which made life occasionally schizophrenic. This had been one of those days covering the hijack of an airliner by Poles claiming political asylum in West Berlin, followed by a minor riot between squatters and police near a bar named after Bobby Sands, the IRA hunger-striker. So it was with all that Western confusion rattling around in my head that I ventured up a side street and stumbled into the secret heart of East Berlin.

As I got out of the U-Bahn at Senefelder Platz, I had decided to explore a little. Instead of my usual plod up Schönhauser Allee, past the great bulk of the Volkspolizei station and the wall of the old Jewish cemetery, where the arrangement of the brickwork still displayed Stars of David, I took the back streets, past where an architecturally interesting old nineteenth-century water tower stood. But before I reached the water tower a welcoming glow from a corner bar beckoned. The sign above the door read Metzer Eck. As I creaked open the door and glanced into the warm smoky atmosphere, the bar appeared as welcoming as any I had yet encountered in East Berlin: not very. There was the immediate sharp sense of mistrust, the unspoken question: 'Who is it? What does he want here?' In the Western half of the same city the answers would have been simple and obvious: 'A passing stranger, in search of a quick beer.' In the East there were always second thoughts. It is always disconcerting to walk into a bar for the first time in a part of the world you do not yet

know very well. All the more so when it is a part of the world controlled by a paranoid totalitarian state, where you still have a foreign
accent and society is riddled with informers.

I was therefore not totally at ease as I took up a standing position
by the bar and ordered a small Pils. It is one of the English-speaking
world's more common myths about Germany that the natives drink
lager beer in huge litre jugs called *Steins*; they do occasionally in
Bavaria, particularly at Oktoberfest time, and the great jug is actually called a *Krug* (*Stein* is a German-American term). In Berlin,
they almost invariably drink Pils, much drier and hoppier, and
mostly from a tiny twenty-five-millilitre glass with a delicate stem,
and usually with a little doily arranged around the base to catch
any drips. Anyhow that – minus the doily, which the East had run
out of – was what I was holding in my hand, trying to sip noncha-
lantly, when the man with the beard and thick black-framed glasses
approached me.

Even though I had indeed gone into the bar, not just for a beer but
in the hope of striking up a conversation, I was still more than a little
unnerved by his approach. It was not just the fact that the beard and
glasses, coupled with a black polo neck and battered leather jacket
made him look a bit like a comic book caricature of a spy, nor even
the – substantially disconcerting in itself – fact that he appeared
to be wearing a human molar tooth on a chain around his neck,
but that his first words, albeit heavily accented, were undeniably in
English. Spooky. How did he know? Was I exuding some subliminal
Anglophone aura? And then I realised: tucked under my arm was a
copy of *The Times*. What the bloke with the beard was asking was if
he could have a look at it.

This immediately placed me in a quandary. Could he? Well, of
course. But should I? Was this a test? Was he a Stasi plant who had
been tailing me, pre-empted my subconscious and realising I was
bound to gravitate towards the pub, had gone on ahead to lie in
wait for me, so he could catch me out disseminating hostile propaganda to solid socialist citizens of the workers' and peasants' state?
On balance, I decided probably not. And on second thoughts, did
I really care? The 'Star Trek directive' only went so far, and if he
actually asked to see the paper, then who was I to deny him. It was

surprising enough to come across anyone in East Berlin who could actually read it. It is another one of those myths about Germans that they all speak perfect English. Very few do, other than businessmen, bankers and car salesmen. And certainly in those days, on the eastern side of the Wall, next to nobody did. They didn't even learn it in school; the only compulsory language on the curriculum was Russian. And if they went abroad at all it was usually only to Poland or Czechoslovakia, where the inhabitants mostly had some German, if only because the Germans had a not wholly appreciated habit of popping in over the years, usually in large numbers.

While I was reflecting on all this, of course, the bloke with the beard was staring at me in a strange way, probably because I hadn't answered him yet. He repeated the question in German. I answered in German and his wary attitude returned – after all what sort of East German had access to foreign newspapers? Only the sort you didn't want to ask too many questions of, if you were an ordinary citizen, not that for a moment I suspected he was. I handed over the paper, and he perused it for a bit, glancing mainly at the headlines. I had no idea how much he was taking in. Then he turned back to me and made a few comments in English. And I slowly realised he was testing whether my command of the language matched his. I could see him grudgingly, wonderingly, admitting that I might be the genuine article, an adventurous tourist perhaps strayed way off-course. His name was Jochen, he volunteered. I told him my name and he bought me a beer. I bought him one back and for the next hour or so we stood there next to the bar, on either side of the shoulder-high tiled oven that was the most traditional form of Berlin central heating, and talked quite a lot about very little. It was a form of verbal fencing, that I was to discover was the prelude to any friendship, even the most casual in a society founded on mutual mistrust.

After a few beers we agreed to meet again a few days later, and yet again stood on either side of the *Kachelofen*, resting our beers on it. He insisted on talking English – he was desperate to practise his – which I found mildly irritating – I was keen to improve my Berlin German. There was also the fact that it made me feel conspicuous. Jochen, I was to find out, liked being conspicuous, particularly if it meant demonstrating his learning. He was a stage designer, which went some way towards explaining his penchant for the dramatic in his clothing, not just the tooth – which I never quite managed to ask about and he never explained – and the leather jacket, but a wide-brimmed fedora hat which accompanied them. His sexual preferences were, I quickly decided, ambiguous, though he never demonstrated them.

He doted on his mother. She was a specialist in Latin America and travelled to Cuba; the two of them were working together, he told me, on a book about the history of the Sandinista movement in Nicaragua. It was Jochen's one overt gripe against the party that they never allowed him to travel with her. He never told me if she was a member of the Communist Party, though I would have occasion to come to believe it. He was not, he insisted, probably because he didn't relish the thought of too much inspection of his private life. But he was, he proclaimed, a convinced socialist, mostly it turned out for private reasons. His father had been a soldier in the war and had abandoned his wife shortly after Jochen's birth in the early 1950s to move to the West. She was one of the few who deliberately chose the communist East. It soon became clear that Jochen's personal and political life, had become fused, his hatred for capitalism developed out of scorn for the father who abandoned him for it. His devotion to his mother led to devotion to her ideology. He was a textbook case of Freudian Cold War psychology.

Jochen became my first East German friend, although it was a slightly odd relationship with, for me, too many aspects that were to say the least ambivalent, although my wife's arrival cleared up at least one of them. Jochen had a Bohemian lifestyle at a 'garret artist' level as a semi-freelance in a profession subsidised by the state, which approved of the arts as long as they kept in their political place. He had little money and did little work, living on beer and basics. His living conditions made our spartan apartment seem luxurious: a tiny studio flat with shared toilet facilities on the landing. I went round for dinner one night and he introduced me to home-made Prussian potato soup, a Berlin speciality ever since Frederick the Great introduced the humble spud in the eighteenth century. It was surprisingly good and I told him so. And he puffed with pride and said that was proof all the West's money didn't make for a better lifestyle. He wasn't wholly right, but he wasn't wholly wrong either. No East German ever made soup by opening a tin or a packet. For one very good reason: they didn't have either.

My conversations with Jochen at the bar had the advantage of making me an accepted fixture in Metzer Eck, if still for the moment considered an outsider. Standing at the bar meant, inevitably in the course of ordering and paying for beer, that I also got into conversation with the man behind it. He would turn out to be more influential on my attitudes to East Germany that anyone else I would ever meet. Alex Margan was a wry, witty, thoughtful man by then in his mid-forties, and he had one of those things that in East Germany was not best publicised: a naturally inquiring mind. For that reason alone he was fascinated by having a genuine 'foreigner' in his pub. He had listened to me speaking English but had not been entirely convinced at first, he told me. He had come across people who pretended to be foreign, to seem more interesting. Then when that suspicion faded, he wondered if we could have a conversation as he had no English. It was only when I was in there a few evenings on my own and we got talking in German that he really began to open up.

He would later reveal that I had accidentally aroused a certain level of suspicion simply from my association with Jochen, who was known to openly express support for the government, which most of his regulars – I was to learn – considered downright weird. Jochen was a tolerated regular in the pub but behind his back they called him 'Tarn', a nickname that suggested he was there 'in disguise'. I had, of course, had my own doubts too. Our suspicions, in the end, were mostly – if not totally – unfair, but that was something I would find out only years later when their world had been swept away and I finally opened my Stasi files.

Either way, Jochen was not invited to the *Stammtisch*, that table closest to the bar where our hosts themselves would sit down when they had a moment free and mix with their most valued customers, those they considered friends. The *Stammtisch* is an institution in every German bar but at the time I was only vaguely aware of the honour when one evening, Jochen not being present in his usual position near the *Kachelofen*, Alex motioned to a place on the

bench next to him and told me to sit down. He introduced me to
the others: an immensely fat man in his thirties called Manne who
had damp palms, spoke with a lisp, and sat in the corner nursing his
hundred grams of schnapps; a big bearded bloke with an iron handshake and a loud laugh whom Alex introduced only by his surname,
Busch; a musician from the East Berlin philharmonic called Bernd,
and Uschi, his loud bottle-blonde wife who spoke in a thick accent
with long vowels that I later learned was the hallmark of Saxony, and
Dresden in particular. There was also Axel, who produced docu-
mentaries for state television; Udo the overweight clarinettist; Ulla,
the gap-toothed waitress from the bar down the road; Günter, an
actor with the Volksbühne company who was allowed to pour the
beer for the after-hours crowd and would deliver bursts of opera as
he did so; Erwin the bus driver; Lothar the stocky landlord of the
pub across the road who came in on his nights off, and the lads from
the bakery down the road who came in to fetch draught beer in
buckets for the night shift. Like the best of well-run pubs (an institution that the Germans treasure and modern Britain neglects to its
peril), it was a vibrant microcosm of the district's society. Indeed,
particularly under the circumstances, it kept that society sane.

It was our landlord Alex's own story, gleaned over the weeks
and months that followed as I gradually became integrated into
the *Stammtisch* crowd, that seized my imagination first among the
many extraordinary tales of these 'ordinary' locals. Alex had become
something of a professional Berliner; he made a point of cultivating
the city's old traditions in the bar, including a collection of draw-
ings by Heinrich Zille, a famous nineteenth-century caricaturist
of Berlin street scenes. He maintained a vintage street market cart
which on special occasions he would bedeck with a panoply of hard-
to-come-by treats, sausages, salami and cheese, usually acquired on
the black market. Once a month, providing Alex could rustle up
the wherewithal from his remarkable network of contacts, most of
whom were grateful to be accorded the status of occasional *Stammtisch* guest in Metzer Eck, he would serve up *Berliner Eisbein*, boiled
pork knuckle accompanied by potatoes and mushy peas.

For all that, Alex was not a Berliner by birth. He had been born in
Danzig, a city whose vanished name was to me already as redolent

with historical connotation as Babylon or Nineveh and in the years
to come would, as Gdansk, accrue as much again when it became
the birthplace of the Polish free trade union Solidarity. Later I travelled there to meet Lech Walesa, the shipyard worker turned political firebrand who would kindle the first smoke amid the dry timber
of the Soviet Empire. Alex had been on the threshold of his teens
as the Second World War lurched towards its end, and towards
his home. Like all young boys he had been compulsorily enrolled
in the *Pimpfen*, a politically-directed organisation for children,
whose members were supposed to graduate to the Hitler Youth. He
remembered being inordinately proud of the small silver trumpet he
learned to play and being desperately upset when his mother took
it and hid it as the Soviet troops neared the outskirts of the city. The
runic, lightning flash letters on the little banner that hung from it
meant nothing to him; his mother suspected the Russians would not
look on the SS with such indifference.

She was right too, his partner Bärbel chipped in over the *Stammtisch*, a cigarette as usual wobbling on her lower lip. She contrib-
uted the story of how her brother Horst, who had been a few years
older and already enlisted by the Hitler Youth had been arrested by
the Soviets several months after the conquest of Berlin. 'It meant
nothing to him, no more than being in the Boy Scouts. Besides he
didn't have a choice. Nobody did.' That didn't matter to the Russians.
They came one morning at dawn – the secret policeman's favourite
calling time and took him away. They never saw him again. Bärbel's father, a lifelong socialist who had rejoined the party and supported its forced merger with the communists, had been outraged.
He wrote a succession of letters demanding his son's release or at
least visiting rights. In the end his campaign apparently succeeded
when they got formal notification that Horst would be set free. It
was followed, just a few days later, by notification that he had died
of tuberculosis in Sachsenhausen, the former concentration camp
north of Berlin which they had taken over and continued to run,
only with different inmates. He was just seventeen. Bärbel did not
have much time for the communists. Or the Russians.

Her son, from an earlier, failed marriage, was – inevitably – called
Horst after his unfortunate uncle. And as his uncle had been forcibly

conscripted into the political youth movement of his day, so young Horst had been made painfully aware that to continue his studies beyond elementary level he would have to don the blue shirt of the young communists, the Free German Youth. 'For one generation it was brown shirts, for the next it's blue shirts,' Bärbel would mutter cynically taking a long draw on her cigarette and a snifter of schnapps. It was a reminder to me that hers was a generation of Germans for whom freedom of expression was a luxury to be enjoyed only in private. That was why membership of the *Stammtisch* inner circle was such a privilege.

She and Alex had got together almost by accident. His family had come to Berlin as refugees when Danzig was given to Poland and the German population expelled. His parents found a billet amidst the ruins of the Prenzlauer Berg district for themselves, Alex and his sister Renate. Young Alex, in search of a way to contribute to the stretched family budget, signed up on a course to learn hairdressing. As an older teenager he went to see his older brother Norbert who on his return from the war had settled in one of the Western provinces. He did so without even thinking about the fact that Germany was already divided, and got stopped at the recently erected border with the West. He spent the night in a cell and was told to go back to Berlin. Instead he found a forest track that led through the still permeable frontier and spent several weeks hitchhiking, even into Austria – though crossing that frontier too was illegal – which had so recently been just another part of the now vanished Reich.

But at the end of it he came home, qualified as a hairdresser, met a pretty young woman, married her and settled down to life back in Berlin, a city with two currencies and two social systems but still one city for all that. Alex's wife, however, was a devout communist – her father worked for the Stasi and when Stalin's death was announced she burst into tears. Alex was not. She tried to convert him to the cause, get him to join one of the other small political parties that were allowed to exist under the umbrella of communist supremacy. It didn't work. The building of the Wall in 1961, which left Alex separated from his sister Renate who had been working in the West when they closed the frontier, had stunned him. The political climate had soured Alex's relationship with his wife and in

1967 they divorced. Her reward for political correctness was custody of their two children; Alex's was redundancy from his hairdressing job. He took part-time work in bars, working as a waiter in the few that remained in private ownership, one of the few branches of the economy to escape total nationalisation, unlike all the breweries and distilleries. Bärbel was glad to hire him. The little girl who had seen her brother plucked from the family home never to return had grown into a handsome woman richly endowed with street-wise common sense and a love of old Berlin. Her two children, Horst, and a striking dark-haired girl called Kerstin, made up to some extent for the two sons Alex had lost. He moved in and it was not long before they had a child of their own: pretty little Alexandra.

But everyone in Metzer Eck had stories to tell, and before long – over enough late evenings downing cold Berliner Pilsener and the occasional *Korn*, a traditional Berliner vodka-like schnapps – I had heard most of them. More than once I was made to see things from a perspective I had hardly considered. As when somebody on one rare occasion did mention the war and I said my father had been in the Royal Air Force. At this, Kurtl, the little frog-like accordion player went misty eyed. 'Ah yes,' he said, 'I remember we would hear on the radio: raiders approaching, direction Wolfsburg, Magdeburg. That meant it was our turn again. My mother would hurry me down to the shelter as we heard the bombs falling. It was when we came up from one of those, and climbed through the rubble to get back to our flat that we found the telegram to say my father had been killed at Stalingrad'. All of a sudden, I was seeing the old Reuters filing editor's joke about only visiting Berlin at night from the other side.

There were also times when they failed to understand things too. As when I tried to defend Britain going to war with Argentina over the Falkland Islands and one of the regulars, a mother of two boys serving their time in the National People's Army, said: 'Think of all those innocent young lads called up and sent to their deaths.' I tried to tell her nobody in Britain had been called up, that we didn't have military service any more and that all the troops sent to the Falklands were reasonably well-paid, volunteer professionals. She wasn't having any of it.

Amongst the most poignant, and in its way tragi-comic, stories was that of the fat man I met on my first evening at the *Stammtisch*. Manne (short for Manfred) Schulz was the grandson of a shoe-maker who had seen the company he worked for nationalised, and both quality and wages collapse. In the fluid, complex world that was Berlin in the 1950s he found a better job in a company in the Western sector and took his son, Manne's father, with him. With the city still half in ruins, everyone found accommodation where they could. Manne's mother remained with the children in Pren-zaluer Berg, near her parents, until her husband found something other than working men's hostels. By the time he did, Manne was so settled at school they decided he could continue to live with his granny and grandpa.

On the night of August 12th, 1961 they had all been over to his mum and dad's new place near Tempelhof Airport. The grown-ups had a few too many and came home by U-Bahn bleary-eyed in the small hours of the morning, not noticing anything untoward at the 'sector boundary'. They still had hangovers when a neighbour woke them at seven a.m. to tell them the world they knew had come to an end. Manne still remembered bouncing out of bed and running to nearby Oderberger Strasse, where armed guards were supervis-ing the construction of a concrete block structure behind barbed wire. He did what only an excitable ten-year-old could: he found a hole in the barbed wire and squeezed through, running off to his parents' house to tell them what was happening. They, of course, already knew. They were just relieved to see him on the right side and were wondering how they could let his grandparents back in the East know he was all right, when he slipped away again: to go back and tell them himself. It was another two years before his mother next saw him: at Christmas 1963, the first occasion after the build-ing of the Wall on which West Berliners were permitted to travel east. By then he was twelve and although he was delighted to see his mother again, he was not upset that he could not go back with her.

He took me to see his grandmother, now in her eighties, and she just smiled when they recalled the story and said: 'Yes, I just had a feeling I'd be stuck with him.' Ironically, by the time I got to know him, his grandmother could come and go across the Wall whenever she felt like it and life was about to change radically for Manne too.

The East German regime had no qualms about letting its old-age pensioners travel west; they were no longer productive workers and if they chose to stay on the other side then it was simply one less drain on the 'workers' and peasants' state'.

Manne, though only in his mid-thirties, was about to fall into the same category. The sprightly lad who had clambered around the rubble in the Berlin of the 1950s had grown into an immensely over-weight adult. He had worked as a shelf-stacker, then an asphalt-mixer preparing tar to pour over the cobbles on the streets of Prenzlauer Berg. He had become one of the regulars at Metzer Eck, famous for knocking back *Korn*. He would drink it in hundred-gram measures, jovially referred to as '*sto gram*', the only bit of Russian most East Germans could remember from their compulsory lessons at school. But the year before we arrived in Berlin, he had suffered a perforated appendix. Because of his obesity what should have been an urgent but simple operation became a major surgical task. No sooner was the appendix removed and the wound sewn up than the stitching failed. Then he suffered a rupture. In the end he needed a total of seven operations and was ill for seventy-eight weeks, long enough for his sickness pay to expire. He was scarcely fit to return to mixing asphalt, but he had only two choices: to return to work of some sort or run the gauntlet of red tape to be declared an invalidity pensioner. To take a pension was to take a colossal cut in wages, but it meant freedom from the one right guaranteed citizens of the German Democratic Republic, the right to work, and its corollary: that not to work was a crime against society punishable by imprisonment.

But the pension also carried one inestimable perk: the right to go west. After visits to three doctors, thorough examinations, endless trips to police stations and government offices, he finally received the certificates that entitled him to a passport, with a valid visa for exit up to thirty days in a calendar year. If the state expected him not to come back, it was sorely disappointed. Invalidity was what Manne had been waiting for all his life: from just a fat bloke in the pub he became the centre of society. The first time I met him was just a few weeks before he received his passport: the transformation was incredible. On his return from his first visit west, he kept the *Stammtisch* spellbound with his stories of the luxuries on sale along the Kurfürstendamm, about the opulence of KaDeWe (the Harrods of West Berlin) and – more down to earth – the endless supplies of fresh fruit and vegetables on sale from stalls in the street. The regulars sat there in awe. They knew of course that I could – and did – go to West Berlin whenever I wanted. But this was one of their own. He told them about the stereo systems, the flash cars, the endless variety of pop music. Bärbel's impressionable fifteen-year-old daughter, Kerstin, sat hanging on to his every word, stars in her eyes.

Manne's disability certificate had overnight made him a centre of attention, but it was also a career move: he became a full-time smuggler. The first few times he crossed the Wall to visit his parents or siblings, he would return home with the little gifts they had given him and some Western currency. There were a few other things too that his brothers slipped him: well-thumbed hardcore pornographic magazines wrapped in plastic bags which he smuggled through with ease by slipping them down his trousers, secured with the bandages that supported his swollen stomach. It was a still a wound that would put off investigation by all but the bravest of customs officials.

He developed another trick. The East German state operated hard currency stores for its own citizens – a means to remove from them any D-Marks sent by relatives in the West – in which it sold, amongst other things, Western brand cigarettes at what amounted to duty-free prices, some twenty-five per cent cheaper than in the West. More importantly for Manne's new trade, one of the most popular brands, Marlboro, could also be had for East German Marks. Albeit Marlboro made in Moldova (then the Soviet Republic of Moldavia). At over seven Marks a packet, these cost almost double the best East German brands. But Manne did his sums. He worked out that a carton of 200 would cost him about seventy-five East Marks, which at the black market exchange rate was the equivalent of only fifteen D-Marks, whereas he could easily sell them to his brothers in the West for twenty D-Marks. That gave them a fifteen D-Mark discount on the West Berlin shop price for 200 Marlboro, and him a profit of ten D-Marks, which was equal to fifty East Marks, or half a week's wages for a waiter. The profit on two cartons gave him the equivalent of a week's wages.

'I can remember the first time I tried it,' he told me one evening at the *Stammtisch*. 'In theory you're only allowed to take out one carton of cigarettes, but in practice they don't care about us taking out anything that isn't in short supply over here. So I took three cartons of cigarettes in my dufflebag. By the time I got over, I was still sweating just a little, so I stopped at a bar on the way for a West-beer. And when it came to pay for it, I sold two of the cartons to customers in the bar.'

He did not, however, run the risk of converting D-Marks into East Marks at five to one in West Berlin and bringing them back with him (that was currency smuggling and a major crime). Instead he found something even more lucrative: he bought up cassettes of Western pop albums, brought them home, re-recorded them and sold each copy for twenty East Marks. He bought a tape-to-tape copying machine to make the business easier and had top quality speakers built to order in the East, paid for in D-Marks, a turntable and amplifier, and set up his own disco for hire at private parties. The fat roadworker had become a celebrity DJ. He even found a girlfriend. For Manne Schulz the Wall had become not so much a barrier as a door to a new life. Although he would never have said so publicly, the last thing he wanted was for it to be opened to everyone. But then nobody imagined it ever would be.

Of all the others who gathered round the *Stammtisch* several nights a week, the only one who had regularly visited the West, and not just West Germany, was Bernd. As a musician with the Berlin Symphonic Orchestra, he regularly travelled on trips that were designed to show that the communist state had every bit as great a command of the cultural arts as it had of sport. And that at least would not turn out to have been the result of performance-enhancing drugs. Bernd had been to Belgium and the Netherlands and he was very excited because now, for the first time, he was going to Britain. 'You'll love London,' I told him. 'Ahh, we're not going there,' he replied. 'Oh,' I said. 'We're going to Wales,' he said. It appeared the level of cultural reciprocity East Germany aspired to hadn't quite been achieved. The Berlin Philharmonic (West) played at the Albert Hall and the Queen Elizabeth Hall on London's South Bank; the Berlin Symphonic (East) were playing in Cardiff and Llandudno.

That didn't stop Bernd being excited though. Not particularly because he was going to Britain, but because he was going to the West and that, as always, was a shopping opportunity. Particularly when he had a wife as demanding as Uschi. (Wives of course were not permitted to accompany their spouses on foreign trips, to diminish the chances of defection, although for obvious reasons even that occasionally didn't work.) For the next two weeks, however, I had only one task every evening Bernd was present in the pub: to school him in the correct pronunciation of the one English phrase he desperately needed to know if his home life was to be worth living over the coming year: 'Please can you sell me a pair of orange leather ladies' trousers?' I tried in vain to explain to him that no matter how well he pronounced it, he was going to get odd looks in Llandudno's Marks and Spencer. But he wasn't having it; according to Uschi they were all the rage in West Berlin. And the West was the West, wasn't it? He came back several weeks later, sadly empty-handed and completely bemused by the 'very rude' reception his request had received.

There was one other regular who had been in the West, but not for a long time. Hans Busch was the exception at Alex and Bärbel's *Stammtisch*: he was a communist, an actual card-carrying member of the Socialist Unity Party of Germany, the 'leading force in the state', created by an enforced merger of the Socialists into the Communist Party when both became legal again in 1945. Ironically, Busch was the grandson of a wayward Polish nobleman who had lost his fortune gambling in the heady days of the Weimar Republic, survived by selling off his title and settled with a German wife in a little town near the Dutch border. Hans's mother Liselotte became a committed communist, a political affiliation she concealed during the Nazi era by marrying a staid conservative businessman and producing babies. Hans was born near the end of the war and in 1956 his mother finally followed her convictions and decided she and her children would up sticks to experience the new 'socialist state on German soil' for themselves. Hans was therefore a chosen son of the GDR who, when challenged that East Germany was only communist because it was the ideology of the occupying power, replied: 'You could make the same conclusion about capitalism in West Germany.'

Busch's youthful enthusiasm for his mother's ideology had taken a few knocks over the years however. Initially he had the convert's zealousness mixed with the quirk that being a declared revolutionary was accepted by the establishment. He delighted in the vocational training in forestry he received through the state-sponsored apprenticeship scheme, and at eighteen even volunteered for the *Bereitschaftspolizei* (the public order police). Unlike most East Germans who regarded the compulsory school subject as a chore, Busch had been as eager to learn Russian as a Muslim might be to learn Arabic: because it was the language of his religion. Alex, a lapsed Catholic, teased him that the party's prescribed 'self-criticism' sessions were akin to confession. 'Maybe it's because it's a form of lapsed Christianity that I believe in it,' Busch retorted.

In truth his faith had lapsed too. As a good-looking young man he had had a string of girlfriends in a state where sex was positively encouraged as a distraction for the young, not least because of a falling birth rate due to cramped living conditions. But when he lost his job because of an affair with a visiting West German girl who was deemed a 'security risk', he began to wonder about the party's insistence on dominating every aspect of his life.

When the party refused him permission to attend his father's funeral in West Germany, an even deeper disillusion set in. In the end Busch had devoted himself to the apprentice scheme he so firmly believed in, and was now warden of a residential home around the corner from the pub, which provided temporary lodging during the week for youngsters from the provinces come to learn about the print industry. He would still go through the motions of defending socialism – despite Alex's jibes about 'our friend Lenin here' – but privately he would admit the truth of the old maxim about life under communism: 'They pretend to pay us, and we pretend to work'.

But it was Dieter and Hannelore, the husband and wife team who when I first discovered Metzer Eck worked there as waiters, who had the most heart-rending tale of the inhumanity of the Wall. It took me a while to understand it, not least because 'Hanni' had the most impenetrable Berlin accent I had yet encountered. But also because it followed an inhuman logic all of its own.

It concerned her uncle Eberhard, whom the family nicknamed 'Pieps'. Pieps had lived in Teltow which all his life he, and the rest of the family, had considered an outer suburb of Berlin (like someone in Orpington or Harrow might be considered to live in the outer suburbs of London). But Teltow had a Brandenburg rather than a Berlin postcode, so in August 1963 it suddenly found itself on the other side of the Wall. To the inhabitants of such fringe suburbs the sudden severing of their lifelines to the city they thought they belonged to was unbelievable. Teltow was little more than a straggle of streets where the Greater Berlin that had grown up in the nineteenth century sprawled out into the countryside. On its own it was nothing, yet now, literally overnight, this little overflow of urban sprawl had been designated a rural village. It was an anomaly on a par with the 'walled garden' allotments I had seen from my helicopter tour when I first arrived. It was true that Pieps and his neighbours could still drive into 'Berlin' – at least the eastern half of it – but now it was a journey of some forty kilometres just to reach the edge of the city and when they did it was a part they were completely unfamiliar with.

But far more importantly, they were severed from much of their lives. Many of them had worked in nearby parts of the city. Now their jobs – earning valued D-Marks – were forever inaccessible. For Pieps and a couple of his mates, there was one thing that was even worse: they had been permanently cut off from their local pub. One night late in that fateful summer of 1961 – a quiet night, as all nights had now become since their road ended in a barbed wire fence illuminated by searchlights – Pieps and two of his friends were drinking in the bar they had perforce used since they could no longer get to Franz's, only half a dozen streets away. At last one of them stood up and said, 'I've had it with this. I'm going for a drink at Franz's.'

Bleary with beer, the three of them staggered into the night. The one who had made the suggestion strode forward with deliberation in his step, the other close behind, while Pieps who had had a bit more to drink, staggered confusedly after them. It was only when he saw the lights and the barbed wire that he half-sobered up and realised what they were facing. He ran after them. But his two drinking buddies had been prepared. They simply hadn't told Pieps all of it. As they came close to the fence they dived for a hole in the ground, an area where they had previously scooped out earth and surreptitiously snipped through the barbed wire. Now they pushed their way through and ran for the second fence as if the hounds of hell were on their heels, as they soon would be. Only poor old Pieps, not quite in on the plan, ended up struggling with the wire, trying to follow them but caught hopelessly, and was unable to find the gap his two friends had squeezed through. As it seemed he might have found a hole big enough, two crashing rifle shots rent the air, and splintered the bone in his leg. The people in the pub they had just left watched silently as the guards took him away.

He was taken to Rummelsburg, the strict security detention centre in the south-east of Berlin, where a quarter century later I would – thankfully only briefly – also find myself. Pieps was sentenced to a year's imprisonment; but when he emerged it was not only as a political misfit with a mark on his identity card that doomed him to menial work, but as a cripple, one leg an inch shorter than the other. He died not long after. Hannelore's father was in the National People's Army and considered his brother-in-law an unwelcome embarrassment. But she remembered him. Alex opened a bottle of his best Nordhauser Korn, and we all honoured poor old Pieps the way he would have wanted: with a round of schnapps.

It was for both Jackie and me an initiation into another world a Germany nobody had taught us about at school, and at the same time an invitation into the large extended family of friendship in a totalitarian society. We were becoming at home in a world that most correspondents at best only visited. At Christmas that year we held a party in our flat and served English roast turkey to a group of twenty that included Alex, Bärbel, Udo, Manne, Hannelore, Dieter, Günter. Even Jochen too. Alex brought bottles of best Berliner Pilsner. And we turned up the music for the benefit of the microphones in the walls. And drank and talked and told jokes.

But it was Dieter's recasting of the legend of the Pied Piper of Hamelin that got the loudest laugh: 'There was this plague of rats down at the offices of the party,' he started, already getting chuckles from his audience. 'Along comes this little girl and she says she can get rid of the rats if they promise to give her whatever she wants afterwards. After a lot of umming and ahhing, they agree. So the little girl puts her hand in her pocket and brings out a clockwork mouse on a string. She leads it out of the building and as she does all the rats come running after her. When she reaches the River Spree, she kicks the clockwork mouse in. All the rats jump in after it and drown. The comrades are delighted, and say, "That was marvellous, little girl. Now we will keep our promise: what should we give you?" And the little girl smiles her sweetest smile and says, "A clockwork Russian soldier.'"

I almost hoped the men with the microphones could have heard it. After all, it was only a fairy tale. Wasn't it?

5

Swords to Ploughshares

'I don't know what he wants,' said Jackie, her face reflecting something between panic, despair and disgust, as she pushed the rear door of the flat to, and summoned me to deal with the caller. I walked down the corridor and opened it again. And understood in a flash. It was Müllerchen. And all three of Jackie's emotions were perfectly understandable.

For a start Müllerchen looked like something no self-respecting cat would drag in. To say he was rat-faced was to do a grave disservice to most rats. He was a small man, about whom the word 'mousey' springs to mind, except that people keep mice as pets which give altogether the wrong impression. He had lank, greasy dark hair and a moustache that suggested he had himself tried to pick up some rodent with his teeth and half of it had remained stuck there. His name was Muller, the universally used diminutive Müllerchen being a reference to his size and general weediness rather than, as it might have been, an endearment. He lived with his wife and an unconscionable number of children in the ground floor flat where he fulfilled a modicum of the duties of a concierge.

His official title was 'KVW-leiter' which stood for *Kommunalwohnungsverwaltungsleiter*, or communal accommodation supervisor. But everyone called him the *Hausmeister* (housemaster), a title he not only hated but which was hugely politically incorrect because it had been the word used under the Nazis when whoever filled the role was supposed to report to the Gestapo any suggestion of 'treacherous' talk about the party. There was, of course, little reason to suggest that that element of the job had changed, although Müllerchen was far too dim, and almost invariably far too drunk to take in, let alone report any whisperings of discontent against the SED.

To make things worse, he spoke German as if it were a cross

between Mongolian and Dutch – with apologies to both – a hissing, sibilant, nasal version of the language with a backstreet Berlin accent that confused consonants and had only the remotest idea of what grammar might be. Imagine a German with a sound but basic command of the Queen's English being faced by a Glaswegian-born Cockney with a lisp.

Even so, Jackie had managed to grasp the essence of what he wanted: 'I think he wants our newspapers.' This was said with some trepidation. And rightly so. Because what Müllerchen wanted was not our copies of *Neues Deutschland* or any of the other esteemed, two-a-penny publications of the official East German government-backed media, but the West German newspapers we also had delivered daily. These were, of course, taboo. Despite the fact that most East Germans could watch West Berlin television and listen to West Berlin radio, the idea of them actually getting their hands on words in print that had not been passed by Communist Party censors was anathema to their masters.

Our newspapers were delivered specially, not by a newsagent, but by a hand-picked courier in the pay of the East German postal service, and undoubtedly vetted for party loyalty by the Stasi. They were not pushed through our letter box but had to be handed over in person to one of us, or to Erdmute in her role as office secretary. Reading the Western press was for Erdmute one of the big perks of her job, and no doubt explained why the Reuters subscription also included several of the more popular West German glossy magazines which she and Helga could be found perusing over coffee in our kitchen during their mid-morning fag break.

None of these publications were supposed to leave the office. Even when read, they were supposed to be disposed of in a special waste bin earmarked for incineration, though every now and then I did notice one of the glossies stage a successful escape bid via Erdmute's handbag. Müllerchen, however, was another thing altogether. Jackie's caution was admirable. For a start, if he really was conscientiously performing the duties of a *Hausmeister*, which I seriously doubted on grounds of his general incapacity, might this not well be a trick? A trap to compromise my standing as a correspondent on the grounds that I was 'disseminating' anti-GDR propaganda, such as the price of a discount three-piece suite, the ready availability of imported Greek asparagus, or adverts for holidays in Majorca?

Certainly the idea of Müllerchen poring over the lengthy intellectual political leaders in the columns of Die Zeit, or perusing the foreign pages for 'anti-socialist' dispatches about the latest Soviet reverses in Afghanistan, seemed improbable to say the least. I decided initially to play the straight bat: I told him that unfortunately I needed the newspapers for my work and that even when finished with them, his government forbade me to let them leave the flat. I have rarely seen anyone look quite so crestfallen. If this was some sort of Stasi entrapment game, Müllerchen was playing a blinder. 'Für die Kinder,' he bleated. For the kids. 'Just one page.' I was puzzled. None of the broadsheet heavyweight newspapers we took regularly were famed for their funny pages. And I didn't have the Muller family down as great sports fans. Which page could he mean? And then he told me, and I realised I should have known all along. 'Die Fernsehprogramme.' The television schedules. Of course!

The East German government had long since given up the nigh impossible task of jamming the strong signals which not so much leaked over the Wall as were poured across it. After all an endless diet of soap opera from the dubbed import Dallas to West Germany's home-grown Black Forest Clinic was just as effective an opiate for the masses in the East, as in the West. Better that they should escape into a television fantasy world rather than escape across the barbed wire fences that confined them in the real world. But in those days, long before on-screen electronic programme guides, nobody had any idea what was on and when. No publication available anywhere in East Germany published a schedule for almost anything anybody ever watched. Yet here was Müllerchen with the answer just upstairs. He gave me his most ingratiating smile. How could I say no? It was easy. I wrapped myself in his government's flag and told him I couldn't possibly go against my host country's regulations. Call it hard-hearted if you like but the idea of having a mendicant Müllerchen rapping on the back door on a regular basis just didn't bear thinking about.

But the inhabitants of our flat block weren't all quite as antipathetic as Müllerchen or the unseen secret policeman in the flat next door. At quite the other extreme to both of them was Volker. If Müllerchen looked like a half-drowned rat, Volker looked like Bjorn from Abba. He had long blond hair which fell to his shoulders and a little wispy blond beard clearly cultivated from adolescent bum fluff to make him look older than he was. He was a would-be hippy who worked – given that not having a job in the workers' paradise was illegal – as a gravedigger.

Volker lived in the *Hinterhof*. The word translates literally as 'back yard', which is far from inaccurate but doesn't quite do the concept justice. The big Berliner 'rental barracks' of the nineteenth century were built to a remarkable uniformity: all six stories high, but each roughly square in shape with the centre hollowed out to form a quadrangle open to the sky, the idea being that it allowed light and air to circulate to the living accommodation around it which was invariably cheaper than the 'prestige' apartments which faced onto the main road. It worked well in theory but even from its inception only to a limited extent in practice. For obvious reasons the sun only shone down into it when it was directly overhead, so for most of the day, and all of the winter, the *Hinterhöfe* and those who lived in them inhabited a world of deep shadow. Ours, however, was better than many, largely thanks to the Royal Air Force who had done the poor people of Berlin the favour of removing the apartment block immediately behind it. Instead of being enclosed on all four sides, therefore, our *Hinterhof* had three six storey sides and one bounded by a ten-foot wall and a patch of wasteland.

Historically, because the *Hinterhöfe* accommodation was cheaper it had been lived in by the poor which meant the rich folk living in the apartments that faced the main road treated it like dirt, which invariably was what it was full of. Everybody kept their bins there for a start, even if it was the only playing space for most of the apartment block's children. Under communism of course, there was supposed to be no such thing as rich and poor, but it was still remarkable how it tended to be people like Volker who ended up living in the basement. He had a one-room flat that opened onto the bin storage area, but because of the missing apartment block on one side he occasionally got a few rays of sunlight. Not that Volker noticed them.

Like most would-be hippies – or maybe just a lot of kids his age with too much time on their hands – he spent a lot of time in bed. This might, of course, also have been because he had a very attractive girlfriend called Kathrin, a leggy blonde who spent a lot of time wandering around in one of Volker's shirts and not much else. She was younger than him and possibly too young to be spending as much time in his flat as she did, but that was none of my business and in any case we were pretty certain her father knew about it. He was, Volker confided behind a hand – as if the man himself might be watching – a 'sort of policeman'. We could all imagine what sort. On the other hand our confidence in her father's omniscience might have been misplaced – how many fathers dote on their teenage daughters to the extent of wilful blindness? The alternative – which I very much doubted – was that her dad was using her to keep tabs on Volker and his mates, who liked to think of themselves in a small way as 'dissidents'.

They were not of course 'dissidents' in the sense of those cultural and intellectual figures who particularly in the Soviet Union made a point of taking a public stand against totalitarianism. They were primarily disaffected, with a similar attitude that many Western kids have towards their parents' society: not so much active rebellion as passive resistance. If in the West this often manifested itself as left-wing engagement, in a supposedly communist society it took the form of anti-establishment libertarianism. Rather than organise themselves, they resisted organisation, preferring to hang about in small groups grumbling about things. Maybe not that different after all. Their biggest statement, if their parents let them get away with it, knowing what it would mean for their career prospects, was refusing to join the FDJ. But then the concept of 'career' meant relatively little in East Germany: unless you were eminent in science, sport or classical music, or were a dedicated party apparatchik, there wasn't much you could do to raise your living standards far above the average.

Most young people did join the FDJ, not out of ideological conviction but because it was the line of least resistance, plus they organised regular camping trips and had a fairly liberal attitude towards sex. In some ways this was a direct continuation of a similarly relaxed attitude in their immediate predecessor Nazi organisations which glorified the body (and approved of large numbers of pregnancies to boost the workforce). But there was also the general official view that as an activity it was 'mostly harmless'. Refusing to join was, therefore, not just a statement but almost an act of self-denial. However, it obviously hadn't hindered Volker's success with the opposite sex.

Dissident youth didn't actually do much most of the time, except get together late at night, drink beer and occasionally smoke dope if someone had got his hands on some – there were more than a few interesting window boxes in the *Hinterhöfe* despite the relative lack of sunlight. One of his mates, however, did a bit more: Martin wrote and sang songs. He was about ten years older, in his early thirties, but also had shoulder-length hair and a beard, though he looked more like an overweight Jimmy Page than either Bjorn or Benny. His songs, however, sung to the accompaniment of raucously strummed acoustic guitar were in an altogether different tradition, that of caustic irony. His idols were the American Tom Lehrer, the great Russian dissident singer-songwriter Vladimir Vissotsky and of course, East Germany's own Wolf Biermann.

Biermann was the son of a communist murdered by the Nazis who in 1953 at the tender age of seventeen had moved from West Germany to the East to work for the communist dream. He had his eyes rudely opened by the building of the Wall and the discovery of just how repressive his supposedly ideal regime could be. The communists who had at first adored this talented young actor, singer and songwriter turned on him with a vengeance when he began singing songs with a sting in the tail. He was refused membership of the party, then declared a 'class traitor' and banned from publishing his music or performing in public. But his fame as a countercultural icon was assured. In 1976 he was surprisingly allowed to go on a concert tour in West Germany which turned out to be a pretext for getting rid of him altogether, by revoking his citizenship and refusing to let him back into the country.

He was Martin's hero and he would perform Biermann songs to admiring audiences of kids like Volker at late night spontaneous 'gigs' in people's flats or in summer at impromptu lakeside picnics. He also wrote his own. One of my favourites was a catchy, gently satirical take on the government's tendency to treat Westerners – or anyone in possession of hard currency – better than their own people, stuck with no more than the money the government itself issued. The prefix 'Inter' – supposedly as in 'International' – was a clear indication to most East Germans that whatever it was attached to was not for most of them. 'Intershops' sold imported Western goods – from hi-fi equipment to good quality coffee – as long you paid for them with Western currency. These were usually situated in the lobbies of Interhotels, which were for Western guests only and again accepted only hard currency. 'Intertank' filling stations on the autobahn between Berlin and the West German border had better quality petrol, never ran out and accepted only West German D-Marks. They were officially only to be used by Westerners travelling between West Germany and West Berlin, and were occasionally used for clandestine meetings by family members separated by the border, and for smuggling (the strict border checks at either end were primarily looking for people). The East German airline was called 'Interflug' and although it was theoretically possible to buy tickets for East German Marks, this was academic as most East Germans did not possess passports.

Martin took the system to its logical if somewhat exaggerated conclusion suggesting that the autobahn filling stations also had 'Interloos': 'Not for the likes of you and me: we're not good enough to have an Interpee.' And that Interhotels also operated Interbrothels, 'If you have D-Marks you're in luck, you can get a first class Interfuck.' Every time he sang it he was risking a jail term.

Conversation at these late night 'speakeasy' gatherings never ever turned to how to change the East German system, however. That, it was assumed, was impossible. There was always one huge, insurmountable obstacle to even the slightest protest or campaign for reform: the Red Army. Some 380,000 Soviet soldiers (twice the size of East Germany's own conscripted National People's Army) and 6,000 tanks were based permanently in East Germany. In theory they were the front line protecting good socialist citizens against a Nato invasion. In reality they were the army of occupation that had rolled in in 1945 and apart from the now much regretted withdrawal from the Western sectors of Berlin, had simply never gone home. They had, of course, occasionally gone on excursions – into Hungary in 1956 and into Czechoslovakia in 1968. On both occasions, the forces stationed in East Germany had, as the most convenient, been in the forefront of the invasions. And they had, of course, taken their East German colleagues with them.

It was with little short of wonder, therefore, that Volker and his mates all sat around and watched on West German television as lots of denim-clad, bearded, long-haired students and dropouts – people who looked almost identical to them except in scruffier jeans because they didn't have to worry about when they might get a new pair – marched through the streets of Frankfurt, Bonn and Düsseldorf complaining about the stationing of new American short- and medium-range Cruise and Pershing missiles on German soil. They had not the slightest doubt that if they made the same sort of protest about the Soviet SS-20 missiles that they knew – only from Western television – were currently being based all over their own country, they would end up behind bars. Sharpish.

The official East German line – when it was forced to refer to the topic at all, which was only in reply to questions from Western journalists like me at rare press conferences – was that only Western missiles were evil. Soviet missiles by contrast were friendly missiles, based on East German soil simply to deter attack by the nasty Western missiles. The state was happy enough to organise the occasional peace protest, usually for the benefit of West German camera crews, it was always directed at the West: their placards in fact were identical to those carried by the West German protesters.

The wild card suddenly dropped in the midst of this game of double entendre hypocrisy turned out to come, of all places, from the unlikely quarter of the Protestant Lutheran and Evangelical Church. Quietly, unassumingly, they had come up with not so much a slogan as a biblical quote which they would argue was in no way out of line with the government's theoretical enthusiasm for disarmament. It was a line from the book of Isaiah, chapter 2, verse 4, referring to 'God's universal reign' due to follow the Day of Judgement. In full it read: 'They shall beat their swords into ploughshares and their spears into pruning hooks. Nation will not lift up sword against nation. And never again will they learn war.'

The full quote was on posters put up on the walls of churches, to accompany sermons on the need for global peace. But the stroke of brilliance came when it was turned into a visual symbol, a badge that people could wear; more specifically an embroidered badge that East Germany's unrecognised 'army' of disaffected youth – Volker and his mates – could sew on their jeans. The symbol chosen was a stroke of pure genius: an image of a man bending a sword with a hammer. But what made it genius was the fact that the original image was a statue which stood in the garden of the United Nations building in New York: not only a work in the tradition of Socialist Realism, but a gift from the Soviet Union. The result was a symbol – effectively of passive opposition – which could not be banned, because it was, after all, an image 'borrowed from Big Brother'.

Just how far the churches in the GDR were actively agitating against the communist government was – and is – a moot point. There were some pastors who had all along been happy to cohabit with the regime in a climate of mutual tolerance. Their wages were paid by the church itself which remained in full communion with – and financially supported by – the churches in the West. But the collaboration – a word it is still hard to use without the suggestion of a taint – had allowed certain important works to restore church buildings which had lain damaged or even in ruins since the end of the war in 1945. Notable amongst them were the (botched) restoration of the bomb-damaged Berlin Cathedral on the Spree island in the city centre, and of the gutted medieval Nikolaikirche. Church and state in the latter case worked together on a mammoth task which included building a new tall double spire which was lifted by giant cranes onto the restored towers like popping two upturned ice cream cones on a child's sand castle. Around it a new development of housing and even shops and restaurants were thrown up, admittedly of less than top quality construction, all as part of the forthcoming 750th anniversary of Berlin which was itself intended to celebrate the 'normalisation' of the GDR as an established, 'proper' country in its own right.

On the other hand, for every pastor who was content in his or her accommodation with the communist regime, there were others who secretly rejected it, despising the regime's repression of free expression and its hypocrisy on matters of conscience, not least concerning arms control. These included a vivacious bearded balding cleric called Rainer Eppelmann who was frequently in trouble with the authorities for his outspoken sermons, and was happy to let himself and his large rambling house on the outskirts of the city become a focus for disenchanted youth. Headquarters of the Swords to Ploughshares movement – though the word is too strong for what was at most a nexus of like-minded individuals – was a little information office operated by the churches in common located on Oranienburger Strasse, just a few yards from the shell of the great Berlin synagogue, which had been targeted and largely destroyed in the November 1938 *Kristallnacht* pogrom. From there a dumpy little blonde-haired woman who was effectively the PR person for the Protestant churches in East Germany disseminated information about 'church activities'. She tried hard to imply their main focus was 'pastoral work', but showed little surprise when most of the enquiries directed to her had an ill-concealed political angle.

I am sure that she and others in the church believed that Swords to Ploughshares was at least in part a way to bring young people to God, even if it had other aspects. In much the same way English churches will run youth clubs, even if they know that the young people who attend often drink a bottle of cider first. It certainly had the effect of moving the perception of the church amongst youth from the marginal and irrelevant to a central element of society, and caused churches themselves to be seen almost as they were in the Middle Ages, as potential places of asylum. That would become particularly the case eight years later as events accelerated – in a development not remotely foreseen by anyone back in 1981 – towards the socio-political revolution which brought the Wall down.

In the meantime, however, it looked as if the real country in which the church was on a collision course with the communist state was further east: Poland. The overwhelmingly dominant church in Poland was the Catholic church and it too for years had lived in a state of uneasy cohabitation with an officially atheist government. There was an old joke I heard in late 1981 on my first visit there about the average Polish worker going to church every Sunday because it annoyed the Communist Party leader, and to strip clubs every

Saturday night because it annoyed the bishop. The Poles, having been invaded by the Germans and then the Russians in quick succession in 1939, had subsequently seen their entire country forcibly move 100 miles westwards and then had a communist government imposed on them by their so-called 'liberators', could be forgiven for having a deliberately cynical and obstreperous cast of mind. But in 1979 an event had happened that had picked Poland up by its bootstraps and set the whole country on perceived higher moral ground and with a huge, self-confident smile on its face: the election of the first non-Italian pope in centuries: a Pole.

Karol Wojtyla of Krakow, wartime resistance fighter, rugged outdoorsman, and inspired multilingual orator, was no sooner installed as Pope John Paul II than he did something else no one expected: he embarked on a series of global pilgrimages, starting with his homeland. Overnight Stalin's old jape about 'how many divisions does the Pope have?' took on another dimension as millions of Poles turned out to welcome a local hero of global status who would not have attracted more devotees if he had been the messiah himself.

The pope did not actively spark revolt or opposition to the status quo in any way, but the mere fact of his existence and the massive crowd-pulling power of his presence, gave an entire nation a boost to its sense of identity and its belief that with faith and a bit of effort nothing was impossible. In the wake of his visit strikes at the big shipyard in Gdansk (which under its old German name Danzig, had seen the first shots of the Second World War) gave birth to the communist world's first trades union not controlled by the Communist Party. It was called Solidarity and in the best tradition of trades unions anywhere it had brought the hard-currency-earning shipbuilding business to its knees with the result that the government reluctantly, and with one eye over its shoulder at what it knew would be disapproval in Moscow, had recognised it. Chief among its spokesmen was a chippy little electrician called Lech Walesa, a devout Catholic who always wore on his lapel a badge of the 'Black Madonna of Czestochowa', an icon which had allegedly saved the city of Czestochowa from Tatar invasion. It was also one of the new pope's designated holiest sites.

In the autumn of 1981, then, with Jackie having just about found her feet in East Berlin, I was obliged to abandon her there for several weeks at a time on two occasions as I was drafted in to the one-man Warsaw office to help correspondent Brian Mooney cope with an ever increasing news flood. Solidarity was expanding, spreading like wildfire across the country, far beyond its original base in the shipbuilding industry at Gdansk. By midsummer there was hardly a factory or office in Poland that wasn't setting up its own branch of the free trades union. And in the same way as the trade union movement in Britain had given birth to the Labour Party, so Solidarity's local and national leaders were beginning to make demands that went far beyond conditions in the workplace. It wasn't long before it would quite clearly be a fully-fledged opposition party, something which no state in the Soviet bloc had ever tolerated. And most of us were certain that none ever would. We had Budapest and Prague to remind us.

The Polish story in the autumn of 1981 was an experience both frustrating and exhilarating. Working with someone else from a cramped office in a backstreet of central Warsaw was not easy, or convivial, but being out on the streets among people who were increasingly not scared to say aloud and in public what they thought of the government, in a state where you could still disappear into a cell for an indefinite time at the whim of some party official, was both exciting and moving. Nightly vigils had begun outside a church in central Warsaw in memory of a priest who had died under dubious circumstances in police custody. People held candles aloft in the cold night air and faced down hostile police surrounding them to sing the national anthem as an act of defiance in a way you can only do when you live in a country that has frequently been wiped off the map of Europe by its neighbours and your national anthem includes the line: 'Poland isn't lost yet'. This use of songs officially approved but sung with different intent was something else I would experience again – and join in with – in East Berlin in 1989. But right now I was too stunned especially as the Poles went one step further with a song designed deliberately to taunt the leader of the Communist Party – and therefore their president – the Soviet-trained General Wojciech Jaruzelski. 'There will be a Poland, there will be a Poland,' they belted out over the heads of the watching police, 'without a

Russian general.' I had a passing grasp of Polish from my knowledge of Russian, but I had to doublecheck with Wiktor, our office translator, to be sure I was hearing right.

It was during my second two-week spell in Warsaw that I made my own single biggest contribution to the Polish economy. It was early December, 1981, and by now the crisis in the Polish economy was coming to a peak with the result that petrol supplies were severely limited. An empty tank meant a wait of several hours in a queue that could stretch for over a kilometre to get to the pumps. People took it in turns to stay by the car, usually having to push it along a few yards at a time: fuel was too precious to waste starting and stopping the engine in the queue. Petrol could be paid for in zlotys, but the national currency was plummeting so fast with rampant inflation that almost everything worth having that wasn't an absolute necessity had to be paid for in hard currency. While in East Germany this meant D-Marks, in Poland it meant US dollars, not least because whereas most East Germans had relatives who sent them money from West Germany, most Poles' relations abroad lived in the United States, mostly in Chicago.

The government, willing to do anything that encouraged the influx of hard currency into the economy, allowed Poles to keep US dollar bank accounts. The Reuters office ran almost entirely on dollars, drawing notes in large and small denominations weekly from the bank. The customary thing at a petrol station was to slip the attendant a one-dollar bill to make sure he filled your tank right to the top. When eventually my turn came and I pushed the East Berlin office VW Golf up to the pump – I was leaving for home in a couple of days' time and did not want to run out en route as, especially in the provinces, it could take a couple of days to fill up again – I gratefully pushed a note into his hand and drove off. It was only some hours later, back at the office, when I was settling how much money I had to leave in Poland and how much I had drawn on my own account, that I realised I was $100 short. Well, $99 to be precise. With my only trip to the US having been as a child many years previously I had failed to reckon with the only world currency which had all its notes the same shape and colour. Instead of $1 I had slipped the petrol station attendant $100. There was no point in going back. To a Pole at that time $100 was practically a life-changing sum of money. The Warsaw man laughed and said it was a lesson well learned, if a trifle expensively. I took the hit. And rejigged my expenses claim for the trip.

The drive back to Berlin was a nightmare: eight hours on bad roads through a building blizzard. As night fell and I approached the East German border, with still an hour to go before I got back to Berlin I was staring through the windscreen at what looked like the scene from the bridge of the USS Enterprise when Captain Kirk engaged warp drive. I had no choice but to carry on; I was already cutting it fine for the next day was the date set for the biggest set-piece story of my whole time in East Germany. For the first time, a West German chancellor – Helmut Schmidt – was paying an official visit to East Germany. After all the years when Bonn had refused to recognise the East German state's legitimacy, the bridge-building begun by Willy Brandt was finally reaching the apparently logical conclusion. Realpolitik would win out over sentiment. The Federal Republic of Germany would from now on treat the German Democratic Republic, in theory at least, in the same way as any other country. It was a legitimisation that Erich Honecker, the diminutive East German dictator, himself a West German by birth, had long hoped for. For Schmidt – if not for all his fellow countrymen – it was an overdue piece of gesture politics that would improve Bonn's relations with Moscow and the Soviet bloc as a whole. East Berlin, normally little regarded by the world press, had become a media circus for the event. I certainly was counting for the first time in ages on a front-page story. In the event, it barely made it into most papers.

I awoke the next morning with the television in the office already blaring as Erdmute sipped her coffee watching the build-up to the official handshake. But it was the reams of paper spewing out of the teleprinter that grabbed my attention, and the regular rows of bells. I gave her a questioning look. 'Oh,' she said, 'something's happened in Poland.' I ripped the copy from the teleprinter. Something had happened. Overnight, probably only hours after I had crossed the Polish-East German border, General Jaruzelski had decided enough was enough, that if he didn't act, then the Russians would and, as so long dreaded yet anticipated, Warsaw would be added to the list after

Budapest and Prague of brutally crushed experiments in reforming the communist system. He had declared martial law. Solidarity was banned. Overnight Walesa and its other leaders had been dragged from their beds and imprisoned. The borders had been sealed, mail suspended and telephone wires cut. The reports on the teleprinter were being written in London head office from official statements released by the Polish government. There was no way of establishing independent contact with Warsaw. If I had stayed, I would have been stuck there, albeit on top of one of the major news stories in the world. But with no way to get reports out of the country.

My own reporting on the big Berlin 'summit' was perfunctory and completely overshadowed by the news – or lack of it – from Poland, all of which was dominated by official pronouncements on radio and television. The only thing I could do, after long conversations with London, was to drive back the way I had just come, to Frankfurt-an-der-Oder, the little town which effectively straddled the border. It straddled it because, prior to 1945, the Polish-German border hadn't been there; it had been some hundred miles further east. Since Poland's forcible movement west, the bit of Frankfurt that lay on the east bank of the Oder River had been renamed Slubice. But it was still scarcely possible to pretend it was really a town, being as it had always been little more than the overflow suburbs – rather like the bits of old Berlin where Hannelore's uncle Pieps had lived, cut off from the rest of the city by the Wall. As a result the border regulations were relaxed for locals on either side. As there was virtually no industry in Slubice, most of the inhabitants crossed the little pedestrian bridge over the river daily to work in Frankfurt.

With few other possibilities of getting live, independent news out of Poland itself, my idea was over the next few days to drive out there on a regular basis and simply hang around the Western end of the bridge waiting for Polish workers to cross to ask them for information about what life was like under the martial regime. It was a good idea in theory and yielded news that schools and universities had been suspended, and that the curfew imposed from dusk to dawn was being strictly enforced by armed soldiers on every street. But there was a limit to what my Polish could manage, no East Germans were being allowed to cross the other way, and the number of workers actually crossing had reduced to a mere trickle. So after a few days spent standing around in snow and sleet at one end of a bridge in a bleak, barren and mostly empty landscape, I decided it was no longer productive.

Just when it seemed that the Poles had locked down news out of their militarised state for the foreseeable future I got a sudden telephone call that changed everything. It came from West Berlin and was from Gail Mooney, the wife of the Reuters Warsaw correspondent, who had been given permission to leave the country with their young child. She had taken the overnight train and was in a hotel near the Kurfürstendamm and was keen to see me: she had, she said guardedly, both of us conscious that we were not the only parties to our conversation, 'lots to tell me'.

She had, too. Not only could she fill me in on masses of detail about the huge stricture imposed on everyday life in the short period since martial law had been declared, she had hidden in her underwear a tiny notebook filled with scribble in minuscule writing from her husband, giving news about the political situation, about which Solidarity leaders had been arrested – which until then nobody had known – as well as quotes from a few brave dissident figures who so far remained at large and were fully aware that making a statement that would be reported in the West might well spell an end to their freedom. It was great stuff and we sat together for several hours as I debriefed her on everything I could imagine was pertinent to the story. I then retreated to the West Berlin office and began turning Gail's words and Brian's notes into a coherent story, with his name of course and a Warsaw 'dateline'. It was the first piece of direct reporting to emerge from Poland since the clampdown and made headlines around the world. Reuters were delighted just as the Polish authorities were enraged and I had no doubt living conditions in the Warsaw office would deteriorate accordingly.

The martial law declaration in Poland was seen elsewhere however as a clear indication that the doom-merchants had been correct, that only so much red rag could be waved at the Kremlin bull. It was widely speculated that Jaruzelski had been given an ultimatum from Moscow, although he would eventually claim that the reality was quite different, that he had made the difficult decision himself in order to pre-empt an invasion which he was convinced would otherwise have been inevitable. To this day Poles argue about whether or not he was right. Either way, the flame of resistance in the Soviet empire had been snuffed out. The Swords to Ploughshares movement in East Germany did not exactly die out but tough talk in what might loosely have been called 'oppositional circles' went suddenly quiet for a while. That was why I was initially quite surprised with the news that Volker came to me with early in the second week of February 1982.

Volker told me he had heard from 'some of his friends' that there was going to be a 'sort of demonstration' in Dresden on February 13th, the eve of St Valentine's Day and the anniversary of the wartime bombing of the city. He didn't know what exactly – he was never a very precise sort of bloke at the best of times – but he thought it would be a sort of get-together around the rubble of the Frauenkirche: 'Just to say no to all bombs and stuff.' It wasn't quite as mundane as he made it sound. There was no question that the Frauenkirche would be an emotionally powerful focal point. Dresden's Church of Our Lady had seemed miraculously to survive the horrendous firestorm unleashed by the US and British air forces above a city that at that stage of the war was primarily a clearing point for refugees and prisoners-of-war.

The morning after the 650,000 incendiary bombs had consumed the 'Florence of the Elbe', reducing some of Europe's most beautiful baroque buildings to ashes and leaving tens of thousands of blackened corpses on the still smouldering streets, the great soaring dome still stood intact, even glowing amidst the swirling dust and soot. But it was glowing for a reason: temperatures inside at the height of the firestorm had reached 1,000 degrees Centigrade. Nobody – of the few who were left alive and not caring for the badly burned or burying the dead – dared even approach because of the radiated heat. It took another twenty-four hours for what was effectively a ticking time bomb to go off. At ten a.m. on February 15th the superheated stonework of the pillars that supported the great dome literally exploded, sending some 6,000 tonnes of stone crashing to the earth, plunging even into the crypt below.

But it was remarkable enough that a few of the young hippies whom Volker hung around with were planning to ever make any sort of public statement. To do so surely risked at the very least temporary arrest by the police, and possibly interrogation by the Stasi.

'Do you know how many?' I asked, in the tone of a mate, which is what I was, rather than a reporter.

'Uh, no, not really,' replied Volker with a broad smile, in that spellbindingly absent way he had of answering anything even vaguely approximating a question.

'Are you going?' I asked.

'Uh yeah, well yeah. Maybe. Don't know about transport though.' He couldn't drive, obviously. A train to Dresden wasn't hard – or expensive – but it would have required effort and imagination. And he wasn't good on either. Then the obvious occurred to me: 'I could give you a lift.'

It was more than obvious really. I had already decided that this had to be a story of some kind: the first protest of any sort by East German young people, even if it wasn't really anti-government in any way, or anti-Soviet, at least overtly. It wasn't government-sanctioned or approved. And that in those days was newsworthy enough. I knocked out a few basic paragraphs on the lines of: 'Young East Germans affiliated to the Swords to Ploughshares peace movement are planning to stage a demonstration against the spread of medium-range nuclear missiles in Europe at the Frauenkirche next Saturday night, sources close to the movement said.'

Not altogether to my surprise, it made a brief item on the next night's evening news on ARD, the first West German television channel, although it added that the network's own correspondent had been unable to unearth any more details. I knew that. He had rung me up. Without putting Volker in the frame, I told him what I knew, which wasn't much. He put the phone down rather exasperatedly. Like many of the other West German correspondents covering East German affairs, he lived in West Berlin. His 'dissident sources' were semi-professional; mine were the neighbours.

Just how reliable they would turn out to be was another matter. Two days later, on the Saturday afternoon, we piled into the car, me and Jackie plus Volker and a mate of his, and drove the three hours down to Dresden. I had been to the city before, marvelled at the scant remains of its baroque glories nestled along the banks of the curving River Elbe – the seventeenth-century Zwinger palace, designed to be the Versailles of Saxony, was still undergoing a forty-year restoration – and been horrified at the bland, faceless flat-blocks and empty pedestrian zones imposed by the diktat architecture of Socialist Realism in the 1960s (though much of it no worse than what British planners did to Coventry). But the great rubble heap of the Frauenkirche still dominated the town centre, in its own way a more poignant monument to war's brutal destructiveness than anything conceived as such (its post-1990 rebuilding is a masterpiece of restoration but it has eliminated another memory of horror).

We parked the car in a side street and walked towards the great mound of charred stone, now liberally dusted with the fine snow that had been falling for several hours. That there was something going on was unmistakeable. Here and there a candle flickered in a glass jar amid the ruins. As we got closer we could make out at least several dozen people milling around, with more slowly gathering. And beyond them, a watching line of several dozen policemen, not interfering but watching both the gathering crowd and each other, as though waiting for a signal. I told Volker to go and join his pals, expecting there to be a gaggle of them at least that he would know. It seemed there wasn't. At least not at first. Then he spotted a girl and went off to talk to her, although whether it was because he knew her or just fancied her, I was less than certain. I took out my notebook. Immediately two of the policemen took an interest in me.

One of them came up to me and told me to put it away, there was nothing going on. I looked at him as if he was from Mars, though I knew the truth was that in his eyes I was the Martian: East German press did what they were told. And provincial policemen never encountered any others. I then did something even more unexpected in his eyes: I walked away, mingling with the crowd, now several hundred in number, milling around and over the snowy rubble. Most had the familiar Swords to Ploughshares patch sewn on their jeans or jackets. There were several dozen candles in jam jars placed in sheltered spots amid the heaped ruins. I started asking people why they were there and got the answers I expected, in accents that suggested most of them had travelled to get here: 'We're against the missiles.' 'No more wars'. It was the sort of thing even the party's faithful FDJ could be relied upon to trot out, as long as they made clear it was only American missiles in West Germany they wanted no more of. 'All missiles?' I asked a couple of people. 'Including Soviet ones in the GDR?' I got a cautious nod from one, then a loud enthusiastic, 'Of course,' from the girl beside him, pulling her scarf up over her face as she spoke. 'Absolutely,' said another, looking over her shoulder. The police had doubled in number and were beginning to form lines that looked like they might at any minute advance.

I began asking how people had spread the word about gathering here tonight like this. It was only when I noted a remarkable coincidence of answers that the terrible truth began to dawn on me. 'I heard about it on the television,' was the almost unanimous response. Like a cold shiver creeping up my back, I realised what I had done. I had broken the Prime Directive: the old Reuters rule of thumb that we correspondents liked to pretend was taken straight from *Star Trek*, when we were told 'to boldly go' on our five-year missions: no interference with the internal affairs of other civilisations. We were supposed to be reporters, not movers or shakers. We wrote about what went on; we didn't influence it. And yet that was precisely what I had done. Nearly every one of the young people at this small but still unprecedented 'spontaneous' demonstration was here because they had heard West German television say there was going to be an unprecedented spontaneous demonstration. It also explained why there were relatively few local accents in the crowd. Dresden was widely joked about in the rest of East Germany as '*Tal der Ahnungslosen*', or the Valley of the Clueless, because its geographical situation (in a valley) and distance from the West Berlin transmitters meant it was the only major populated area in East Germany that couldn't receive West German television.

Would there have been a demonstration at all if I hadn't reported it in advance? Probably? Possibly? I asked Volker in the car on the way back how widespread the talk in Berlin had been amongst the Swords to Ploughshares crowd. 'Oh, I dunno,' he replied. 'I think it was just something somebody said would be a good idea.' I almost crashed the car. 'What?' 'Yeah, but it was good, wasn't it? I mean they organised it well. Lots of people turned up, and stuff.' If I hadn't been driving I would have closed my eyes. In the end the 'demonstration' had passed off peacefully. The police – cowed to some extent by the presence of several West German television camera teams – contented themselves with looking menacing. The demonstrators did nothing more than sing a few songs and hold hands rather longer than the police would have liked them to. And a few of them had their photographs taken. Not by the press.

The same 'amateur photographers' also took pictures of me. Their colleagues of course had been doing that for some time, occasionally with more interesting cameras than I had imagined. But then just how much attention the men and women who made up the 'Sword and Shield of the party' had been paying to me, I would only find out some years later, when the sword had been blunted and the shield discarded.

6

Spooks

It is one thing to assume you are being spied on round the clock, that there are microphones in the walls of your flat and men in plain clothes tailing you. It is another thing again to know it for sure. And something else altogether to see the proof of it, in black and white, words on paper and photographs taken by hidden cameras.

The whole time we lived in East Germany – and even more so when we moved to Moscow – we took the secret state for granted. For a while it was tempting to try to spot any signs of surveillance. To do things like suddenly turn around on the street and walk back in the direction we had just come from, to go down into a U-Bahn station and come out the other side, without actually catching a train. But after a while it gets boring, especially if you never spot a tail. Even then you know that doesn't mean they aren't there, just that they are professionals and you are a rank amateur. Which is just as well, because if you are a professional, they will spot that too. And draw the appropriate conclusions.

The result is that like everyone else living in such a society, after a while the fact of being spied upon – however frightening and intrusive it may seem to someone who has never experienced it – becomes something you simply live with, like an unpleasant pattern on the wallpaper in a rented flat.

It was only afterwards, when it was all over, when the Wall had come down and the Stasi were no more, that I – like tens of thousands of ordinary East Germans, got concrete proof of the extent to which the everyday facts of my life had absorbed the attention of an industry which itself employed tens of thousands. Although in the last frantic days of communist rule the Stasi had gone into overdrive, shredding the evidence of their existence. In vain. There had been too many of them, for too long, and they had generated a mountain of paperwork that would have challenged even the bureaucrats of any British government department. Small wonder, when there was a file larger by far than any medical records, on virtually every single man, woman and child in the country.

The building complex in East Berlin's Normannenstrasse, not far from what had once been Stalinallee, served the Stasi as not just headquarters but a city within a city, home to 33,000 people, complete with well-furnished apartments and shops stocked with Western consumer goods. There was, therefore, a particular irony when after the Wall came down – and the flats were redistributed to ordinary citizens – that their headquarters were chosen as a museum to their abuse of power. The Stasi's files were given into the custody of a government-financed independent body under the control of an East German Lutheran pastor, to whom anyone who suspected they might have a file (which was nearly the entire East German population) might freely apply for access, in a reading room in the old Stasi headquarters. It was there that I turned up on a sunny summer's day in the mid 1990s, more than a decade after the Stasi first opened their file on me, to look inside it. All 286 pages of it, marked *MfS Hauptabteilung II – gesperrte Ablage*. (Ministry for State Security, Chief Directorate II – Counterespionage – restricted access), archive number: 14904/83.

My codename was *Strömer* – Streamer – don't ask me why. I had started out as *Insel*, Island. Because I was young and alone? Then quickly metamorphosed into Streamer. Because they didn't know which way I would flow? Because they found it hard to keep track of me? Maybe. Maybe not. Somebody somewhere for some reason decided I needed a watery theme. My wife Jackie became Sea. Karin, one of our East German friends with a brother jailed for trying to escape to the West, was Jellyfish. Because of her 'unkempt' hair, as noted in her description in my files? The men from the Ministry of State Security obviously liked neat haircuts. It was hard to put reasons to it all. Other acquaintances and friends became 'River', 'Brook', 'Trout'. An old university friend, by then the wife of a Bristol greengrocer, came to visit for a long weekend and received the codename 'Mussel'.

My case-officer was a Colonel Lehmann. He collated, typed up and ordered all the information, summaries not transcripts of telephone calls, of 'private' conversations picked up by the microphones in the wall. Twenty-nine of them, Reuters estimated when they finally took the walls apart to find them after the Stasi had ceased to be. The flat next door, allegedly inhabited by a 'policeman', but which I had long suspected was the home for their battery of tape recorders, had indeed been just that. It was no surprise, however, that we never saw anyone entering or leaving. There was a secret staircase from the back of the bar downstairs which gave direct access. The men who took turns working their shift monitoring our lives would pass through the bar each day on their way to and from 'work'. Their overseer was a Lieutenant Weichelt. Perhaps he stopped at the bar for a quick one. I was glad I had made somewhere else my 'local'.

Weichelt thought there was a strong possibility I was aware my flat was bugged. Bright bloke. I had honestly never considered any other possibility. But then I had seen those Michael Caine movies and he hadn't. If I had referred repeatedly to 'Harry Palmer', he would probably have listed him as an 'important contact'. He noted that I appeared to employ, 'a few standard methods' of making his life difficult. In fact the tone of his report is one of sustained resentment, as if by turning on the taps in the kitchen or the radio in the living room I was somehow not playing by the rules: 'He uses sonic disturbance, e.g. loud music, to create difficulties for the work of ministry operatives.' Bless. Actually, lieutenant, you were right, but sometimes I just turned it up loud because Robert Plant sounds better like that.

Anyone who is granted access to their Stasi files may see certain names and/or addresses 'redacted' in the modern jargon, in other words blocked out so that they cannot be read. This is not censorship on behalf of the modern German government, but done because one of the guiding rules laid down by the Lutheran pastor who first took over the onerous custody of the files was that 'nobody should discover from sight of their own files that their neighbour was committing adultery'. In other words the 'product' of the communist state's snooping should not become a snoopers' charter for latter-day busybodies. Nonetheless I did discover pertinent things about some of the people I knew and why the Stasi were particularly obsessed by my contact with them.

A keen example was the only one of my predecessor's 'contacts' I had kept in touch with, simply because we got on well together and I spoke his language: Nikolai (Kolya) Makarov, was – is – a Russian artist of considerable merit, whose sombre but technically impressive paintings today hang in leading Western galleries. Back then he was not long married to an East German woman and just beginning to make a name for himself. I knew his father was 'something important', relatively hush-hush back home in Moscow, but Kolya didn't talk about it. I vaguely suspected he might be related to the Nikolai Makarov who had designed the Makarov pistol, which was to handguns what the Kalashnikov was to machine guns. But I never actually asked. It would have seemed an abuse of our friendship. Kolya never liked to talk much about his parents or Moscow, so it would have been rude to push.

But my own Stasi file told all: 'Makarov is the son of a former liaison officer between the KGB and (Stasi) Chief Directorate I (which dealt with the Minister for State Security himself, the obnoxious Erich Mielke)… During his student days, Makarov belonged to the dissident movement in Moscow. For this reason his father was obliged to leave the KGB. It is not known to what extent Millar uses Makarov as a source of information. But we must also consider the possibility that Makarov is using Millar for subversive goals.' There is nobody who creates spy conspiracy theories better than the spies themselves. Kolya didn't have any information, except about where to get decent oil paints. And he certainly had no intention of 'using' me for subversive goals. All he wanted was to make a living out of his inspired, eccentric, ever so slightly depressive art. And sell it for D-Marks. Happily history was on his side.

But then Col Lehmann was building up a bigger picture here: 'Operative control measures on Streamer give growing evidence of deliberate contacts with persons from the circle of relatives of members of the Ministry for State Security or the National People's Army … Millar's activity is the expression of an increasingly intensive, direct and clearly secret-service-controlled attack by enemy forces against the socialist security organs.' You have to love it: the Stasi saw themselves as victims. But then Lehmann had his 'evidence': he knew who I knew. The difference was that he assumed

I knew as much as he did about them. The chief corroboration for his theory that I was some sort of MI6 plant focusing on relatives of the guardians of communism, was not just Kolya, but Volker the gravedigger's sixteen-year-old girlfriend, Kathrin. We had always assumed, from her exasperated unspecific references to 'my bloody dad' that he was something in the police or more likely the Stasi. Here was proof: according to my file her father was not any old common or garden domestic informer or dissident interrogator, but the nearest thing East Germany had to James Bond. He had been seconded to the East German Embassy in Zanzibar under diplomatic cover and had spearheaded a successful covert mission to entrap a CIA officer. Bloody hell! Kathrin just moaned about him being an old fuddy-duddy.

Col Lehmann's need to prove I was something more than I seemed pointedly noted 'similarities but also differences' between my predecessor's more orthodox attitude to journalism (one that has served him well in his subsequent career) and my own, and were suspicious of them. 'In contrast to his predecessor who looked for information from so-called prominent dissidents, Millar looks for information from people who are neither well known in the GDR or internationally, including those in church circles. His frivolous appearance which would make it difficult for him to make contacts amongst official circles, by contrast makes it easier for him to make illegal contact with young people and those connected with the church.' (An example of how already for the Stasi the church was linked to the seeds of opposition.)

'Millar's contacts seem to be primarily people he meets in pubs round about, people who represent a sort of Berlin backstreet community' (how the communists scorned the working class!) 'and who have a hostile attitude towards the GDR' (as they would have had towards almost any government). 'He seems primarily interested in getting to know people of his own age or younger (students and young adults).' Hey, I was one too! But there were gratifying words as well: 'It would appear that Millar is successful at making honest relationships with GDR citizens of the above mentioned social sphere.'

But they attributed somewhat greater ambition to me than I ever actually harboured: 'The particularities of Millar's circle of contacts suggest that he is involved in attempting to create a political underground in the GDR. It is not currently possible to ascertain if these efforts are something of his own making or if he is acting in accordance with a set of orders.' They saw snakes in my background: 'There is a political-operational relevance in the "break" between Millar's field of study at university and his choice of career; this suggests the intentional intervention of third-party individuals or institutions.' It was hardly stupid to assume that MI6 went headhunting at Oxford, particularly amongst linguists, to steer them into the service, although you might have thought if they'd wanted to infiltrate East Germany they wouldn't have gone for a French and Russian graduate. And then the Stasi never for one moment were capable of putting themselves in the place of a young British graduate in the recession-hit seventies desperate to find work as anything other than the 'advertising account executive' which was all the university careers officer could suggest.

'It is therefore important to put more effort into identifying and analysing Millar's contacts. To this end, we recommend stepping up the activities of Chief Directorate VIII' (charged with surveillance of persons believed to pose potential risk to the state), 'including increasing the efforts put into voice identification by Department 26' (the microphone men). Department 26's report of 26.1.1982 indicates Millar is in possession of the addresses and telephone numbers of contacts we have not as yet identified.' Ha! Ha! They never got their hands on the little address book I never let out of my sight. And what did I have in it? The addresses and telephone numbers of people who in their world scarcely existed: friends!

At some stage it was decided to put Lehmann's conviction that I was a spook to the test. Up until now, the file revealed, I had indeed been subject to surveillance on the streets, even though, gratifyingly, considering I was not employing any 'counter-surveillance' methods by that stage, they occasionally lost me. Just after midday on June 22nd, 1981, for example, only a few months after I had arrived, a certain Major Bonitz followed me from the flat – on foot at that stage as I had still to pass my driving test – to the Eisenberg furniture shop on Senefelder Platz. I see from his notes I spent only two minutes there – I have no recollection of the event other than vaguely recalling trekking round East Berlin a couple of times seeing if I could order some new furniture for the flat from local sources rather than West Berlin.

Major Bonitz – or his team – followed me to Warenhaus-Centrum, the city's rather sad excuse for a socialist department store, on Alexanderplatz. No luck there either; it was closed. After that I tried the 'Intershop' hard currency outlet in the Stadt Berlin Hotel, where I apparently filled out an order form for some item of furniture. I no longer recall what it was, and the Stasi failed to take a note. In fact they were slipping up in a big way here. Within twenty minutes of me entering the Intershop they were forced to note: '13.12 Contact with subject lost.' I can only suspect Major Bonitz got distracted by all those Western goodies on display. Bizarrely the case log continues blank until '16.30 Operational surveillance terminated,' apparently without them ever having caught sight of me again.

Up until now, however, incidents of such detailed 'tailing' had been sporadic, the files revealed. Even so it produced details which to a British mind might suggest they were trying a little too hard, but I fear to a German mind (East or West) implied potentially seditious intentions: 'He has crossed the road illegally while the pedestrian light was red.'

Now, however, they turned the searchlight on, big time. For up to ten days at a time, teams of watchers would follow us from before dawn to long after dusk. They would begin their day seated in a car parked somewhere outside our flat on Schönhauser Allee, wait for us to emerge and then stick on our tail, to produce at the end of each day a minute-by-minute account.

Their diary for August 4th, 1982, in the middle of one such ten-day surveillance routine, read as follows:

07.30 *Operative surveillance of Streamer at his apartment block continued.*
VW Golf car parked in front of block.

They had a long and fruitless wait. It had been a late night in Metzer Eck the night before and the weather was warm and listless, one of those Berlin summer days when the hot cobbles repel and the deep green of the Brandenburg countryside dotted with little lakes beckoned. When we finally crawled out of bed, we decided to go on a picnic. The Stasi came too.

13.05   *Streamer and Sea leave Apartment Block Schönhauser Allee 27 via stairwell 2 and get into the above-mentioned vehicle. Streamer is driving. They follow the route: Schönhauser Allee, Berliner Strasse, Granitzstrasse, and eventually join the slip road to the autobahn at the Pankoz-Heinersdorf junction.*

13.15   *They join the autobahn, heading north towards Rostock.*

13.28   *They leave the autobahn at the Birkenwerder junction then rejoin it heading back towards Berlin.*

Clever counter-espionage measures? Not quite; my wife was map-reading.

13.35   *They leave the autobahn at the Mühlenbeck junction and head towards Summt.*

13.38   *They park the car in Summt at the North Bank car park for Lake Summt, and walk to a stretch of beach next to the Lake. Streamer is carrying a basket.*

13.42   *They find a place to lie down on the beach, and strip down to their bathing costumes. They then lie down to sunbathe and look through newspapers and magazines.*

15.00   *They get up and go for a swim in the lake. After about five minutes they leave the lake again,* (it was cold, and I'm not German!) *and go back to sunbathing.*

15.25   *Sea changes back into her clothes, while Streamer just pulls on a pair of shorts over his wet swimming trunks* (I admit it, I'm a slob). *They then pack up their things and at …*

15.31   *… set off towards the car. Streamer is carrying the basket.*

15.41   *They both get into the parked car. Streamer puts the basket on the rear seat and drives the vehicle off …*

15.42   *… towards the motorway back to Berlin and the apartment block.*

16.02   *They stop in front of the apartment block, get out of the car and at …*

16.03   *… enter the apartment block. Streamer is carrying the basket.*

16.25   *Streamer and Sea again leave the apartment block, get into the car and drive along Sredskistrasse, Knaackstrasse, Prenzlauer Allee,*

> *Liebknechstrasse, Unter den Linden and stop at the Ministry of Foreign Affairs. Streamer is driving.*

16.35   *Streamer parks in front of the Ministry and gets out. Sea stays in the car.*

16.36   *Streamer enters the Ministry of Foreign Affairs.* (I was picking up a repeat multiple-visa application.)

16.42   *Streamer leaves the MFA, gets back into the car and drives via Werderstrasse, Französische Strasse, Friedrichstrasse, and Clara-Zetkin-Strasse to Otto Grotewohl Strasse where at ...*

16.48   *They get out of the car* (the timings show how little traffic East Berlin's streets had) *and at...*

16.49   *They enter the VERSINA shop.* (A shop only open to foreigners where, behind closed curtains, they sold a basic supply of Western quality foodstuffs for D-Marks.)

17.00   *They leave the above-named establishment.* (The timing reflects how little there was to buy.) *Sea is carrying a cardboard box, dimensions approx. 40cm × 40cm × 30cm, which Streamer then takes and puts in the boot. They get into the car and take the most direct route home.*

17.09   *Streamer parks the car outside the apartment block, takes the cardboard box from the boot and both individuals enter the building at ...*

17.10

20.00   *The operational surveillance is brought to an end.*

In other words, they sat out there while we had dinner and left before we went to the pub, thereby missing a whole world of insight into who our real 'contacts' were in East Germany, that segment of society they least wished us to get to know well: ordinary people.

But Col Lehmann still found a way to do me damage. In my file he affixed a photograph of the two of us leaving the VERSINA shop. He was probably very proud of it: it had been taken by one of those little bits of kit that the James Bonds of this world are so very fond of: a concealed camera. Concealed in the tail-light of a little Trabant parked outside the shop. It was marked, 'secret'. But it was the note he appended next to it that caused the most damage to my way of life: 'On such expeditions, it would appear Streamer makes his

109

wife carry the heavy objects.' She has never let me forget it. Thanks, colonel; I really owe you for that one.

At the end of this concentrated period of surveillance, however, the man who was in charge of what in the world of John le Carré were called 'lamplighters', sitting on my tail day and night, was forced to conclude: 'During the period of intensive operational surveillance on Streamer from August 2nd, 1982 through August 20th, 1982, we could not identify any active counter-surveillance techniques.' (I'd long since assumed that if they wanted to follow me they would.) 'His driving by and large obeyed the rules of the road although he has been observed driving after consuming alcohol.' (I was young, and occasionally a bit silly. I admit it. Maybe you should have stopped me.) 'When driving, he usually chatted to whoever else was in the car, and almost invariably took the most direct route.' (Yes, I wasn't trying to shake you off because I didn't really know you were there. If we took wrong turns, it was usually because we'd got lost.)

My file also contained a list of the codenames of the IMs (*Informelle Mitarbeiter* – part-time collaborators), the everyday leeches who spied on their acquaintances or friends for the state. 'Constructive analysis of the possibilities of using the Reuters office cleaner as an IM.' Damnation of Helga? Maybe. Of Frau Neumann? Definitely. There was also a list of 'contacts' I had inherited from my predecessor: 'Armin,' 'Tobias,' 'Walter,' and 'Walter Fichte.' There was not enough evidence for me to pin down specifically which was which, but I had a clear vision in my head of the 'friends' of the colleague who had occupied the post before me, who would turn up uninvited, to 'keep up the relationship,' to invite me out for a meal or a drink, to offer me titbits of meaningless gossip that suggested insider knowledge but in fact revealed next to nothing. They would 'leak stories' that were about to appear in the next day's official press. Armin tried to feed me a story about an upcoming minor regional party conference. It was hard to tell him I couldn't care less. He reported to his superiors that I had left lying about 'as if by chance' a copy of the West German news magazine *Spiegel* – was I trying to entrap him? He admitted to them he had found it 'interesting'.

I had little to do with any of them: I simply wasn't interested enough in them or their supposed, so clearly calculated, 'insight'. If

East Germany had a story, it wasn't to be had from these people. The Stasi obviously recognised that their old strategy wasn't working. Amongst the tasks 'in hand' listed was: search for and identify an IM among Streamer's GDR acquaintances. They would succeed but not as much as they had hoped.

'Tobias,' reported that, 'because of his appearance and attitude, Millar really wasn't on the same wavelength. But he would do his best all the same.' I clearly wasn't fastidious enough. His physical description went down in my file: 'Approx. 25 years of age, short with long, curly unkempt hair, uncared-for clothes: frayed jeans, tatty shoes, loose shirts, unmanicured fingernails.' I admit it all. I haven't changed that much even now.

Contrary to what I – and certainly Alex or Bärbel or many other of my East German friends might have suspected, I was pleased and gratified to find no clear sign of Jochen amongst those who informed on me. For all that they called him 'two-face', he did not feature on the list of the Stasi's IMs. In fact the only reference to him specifically exonerated him: Col Lehmann noted: 'We have no hopes for using him directly.' The operative word, however, was 'directly'. Their key informer was the mother he doted on. In November 1982, Jochen had invited Jackie and me to come and see a play for which he had designed the stage sets. It was the first evidence of any real work he had done in all the time we had known him. I was delighted to accept, not least because the play was being performed in the delightful little medieval town of Quedlinburg in the Harz Mountains. Jochen was delighted we accepted, not least because it appeared he had been counting on us to give him a lift. Him and his mother.

She was a plump, giggly and self-consciously learned academic woman in her fifties, with dyed jet-black hair and saw herself as a self-proclaimed intellectual advocate of the 'developed socialist society'. She was also a Stasi collaborator, codenamed 'Pauline'. Her report on the trip was detailed, beginning with the fact – probably to her and her controllers my most shameful failing – that I turned up to collect her from her flat thirty minutes late. En route to Quedlinburg she reported that I 'did not stick to the speed limits'. I was driving a zippy little VW Golf in a country full of fibreglass Trabants; the motorway speed limit – as opposed to in West Germany where there was none – was 100 kph (62 mph). I was however chuffed to note that she had added: 'He did however show himself to be a safe and experienced driver.' Thanks, Pauline.

She noted that our conversation over dinner following the performance concentrated on the play, then about foreign languages and different cultures, adding: 'It has to be said that at no point did the conversation touch on politics.' Why would it have done? I knew she was an old commie, but she was also the mother of my friend. I neither wanted to convert her (to what? I was hardly a neo-conservative), nor to offend her. The conversation was joined by an elderly actor who had a daughter who was also a journalist, on the official Communist Party paper, and we sat up chatting and drinking until three a.m. I am thankful to the Stasi for noting what time we got to bed. I certainly have no recollection.

Pauline sat up even later making notes of her initial impressions:

- *M appears to have studied at Oxford, probably languages.*
- *He speaks perfect German with little accent* (thanks Pauline), *and knows Russian and Polish* (bit of an exaggeration on that last one).
- *While at Oxford he took part in amateur dramatics.*
- *He is Irish, his wife English.*
- *During his childhood he must have lived in Boston, USA* (where did that come from?) *and France* (I must have mentioned my year in Paris).
- *He is a keen beer drinker and collects beer labels* (what can I say?).
- *'He only got married after being posted to the GDR.*
- *M is intelligent, witty and comes across as youthful while polite and amusing in conversation* (by this point I'm beginning to dote on her myself).
- *Despite several naive attitudes shown in his conversation he is certainly not naive in general.*

The next day she reported the details of our walk around Quedlinburg old town, that I paid for lunch for everyone (I put it on my expenses – it was fairly legitimate), and that afterwards I insisted we drove back via Magdeburg to take a look at the cathedral.

While we were there, however, she noted that 'M disappeared for about ten minutes. No explanation for this was given.' Col Lehmann has put a large felt-tip double exclamation mark next to this. And he would be right. I had indeed been 'up to no good': my detour via Magdeburg was not just to see the cathedral, but because I had been told there was an active branch of the Swords to Ploughshares movement in town, centred on the priest's house a few hundred metres away. I had snuck off to take a look and chat with a couple of kids who told me I would be best going to a different church. They told me the address and tried to draw a rough map.

Back in the car 'Pauline' noted a crude sketch on a piece of paper and reported that I asked her if she knew a 'Heimholzer Strasse' in Magdeburg where there was supposed to be an 'interesting old church'. She told me no, but then adds, 'It came up that there was a Helmholz Strasse'. Her switch to the anonymous third party is unsurprising: it was her son Jochen who told me. We drove there and located the building the lads outside the priest's house had directed me to, the St Michael Community Centre. 'Pauline' reported: 'M parked about fifty metres away and went off with his wife, leaving us in the car for about half an hour. Then he returned and we continued the journey to Berlin without further interruption.' All true. I had for the first time made contact with a Swords to Ploughshare 'chapter', if such a word could be used for such a diffuse agglomeration of individuals, outside Berlin. No doubt 'Pauline' and the Stasi would have considered it 'hostile' behaviour, possibly worse, but to me it was just journalism. If ever a serious opposition movement was to develop in East Germany I wanted to be in touch from the ground floor, and similarly if ever the 'organs of the state' decided to clamp down on these disaffected young people by imposing jail sentences on them, I wanted to be sure their friends had ways of getting that information into the Western press. My only regret in hindsight, is that perhaps I should have anticipated that Jochen's mum wasn't just the nice old lady she seemed to be.

Col Lehmann was impressed. He noted tersely on the bottom of her report: 'This source is reliable. Any verification of the information contained in this report must protect the identity of the source.'

She obviously had a long chat with Jochen about me afterwards.

Two weeks later, for the first time – a signal mark of the general incompetence of attempts at total surveillance – there is a detailed report on Metzer Eck: 'We have been informed unofficially that M is often to be seen in the pub Metzer Eck. He is considered a regular and always given a seat on the *Stammtisch*. He pays close attention to everything that is said and therefore must be considered extremely up to date on popular attitudes and opinions on political matters.' Lehmann's deputy Col Franz adds the note: 'Any verification of this information must protect the identity of the source'.

Right to the very end of my time as resident correspondent they used every means possible to observe every meaningless detail. As we were having our belongings packed up for transport to Moscow a customs official was required to visit the flat to check we were not taking away valuable historical relics. Afterwards he was required to submit a report to the Stasi. He had noticed a West German maga-zine lying on the table in the office, he told them, obviously shocked. 'During our presence in the flat, the teleprinter was running,' he noted further, adding just that extra little professional detail: 'It was a Kamp brand.' That good old Prussian thoroughness again. Well and truly wasted.

But by then they were already writing me off, for the time being at least: 'The transfer of the files to the Soviet fraternal service has been carried out'. There were no prizes for guessing who Big Brother was. Like Kolya said: I was entering the lion's den.

7

Roads to Moscow

They gave a farewell party for us in Metzer Eck. We were sad to go; they were sad to see us go. This was not a world in which people popped back and forth across borders readily. None of us was really sure when we would meet again. Or if. East Germans were required to go through the same lengthy visa application procedure as Westerners if they wanted to visit the Soviet Union. 'Big Brother' liked to limit the number of houseguests

Alex, invariably, managed to make a joke out of it all. 'How about that,' he quipped, 'they could go anywhere in the world and where do they choose? Next door to Siberia'. And then he brought out the *pièce de résistance* for the long evening of drinking ahead: a vodka bottle frozen in ice, from which he poured viscous shots into small glasses which we knocked back with mock Russian shouts of '*Na zdorovye*' – one Russian phrase every East German knew – and chased with cold Berlin Pilsener. Alex stood up and gave his mock 'loyal toast': '*Wer denkt das Saufen so viel Freude macht, als wir, die lieben die Sowjetmacht!*', which translates roughly as: 'Who is more loyal to the Supreme Soviet – than those of us who keep our lips wet?' And we hooted with laughter. And he poured another round. By which time we had got round to the usual lavatory humour from Dieter: 'Why does a Russian take three pieces of wood when he goes for a shit? One to balance on, one to lean on, and one to keep the wolves away.' Everybody cracked up, just as they always did when he told that one. It was a reflex action: even those Germans who lived under the Soviet jackboot couldn't help thinking that somehow the world had been turned upside down.

Britons on our little offshore island so often think of continental politics – when we think of them at all – either as the 'meddling bureaucrats' of Brussels or as the historical ogres who were held off by our most powerful defence: a twenty-one-mile stretch of water. It has often occurred to me that Britain's relationship with the rest of our continent would be more sane – and less marked by delusions of effortless superiority – if *la Manche, der Ärmelkannel* (only we call it the *English* Channel) had dried up. Certainly in Berlin, a city that more than many others has felt the tide of European history lap over it, there was no one without at least a modest understanding of geopolitics. When I told Reinhard, one of the two German correspondents who worked in Reuters' West Berlin office that I was planning to drive to Moscow in January, he looked at me as if I was stark staring mad: 'Remember what happened to Napoleon. And Hitler didn't even get there. What makes you think you will? In a Volvo 340!?'

He had a point. We nearly didn't. There was thick snow falling already as we drove east on the long straight *autobahn* through the pine forests that led to the drab little industrial town of Frankfurt-an-der-Oder, where I had tried to get comments about life under martial law from the few Poles who crossed over to work. Now we were about to find out for ourselves; we had a seventy-two-hour transit visa.

The first night was spent in Poznan, until 1945 the German city of Posen and one of the Führer's supposed fortress cities. It was bleak, the snowy streets empty. The car cassette player blared a track from an album by Canadian punk group Rational Youth entitled *Cold War Nightlife*. It had been sent to me by a friend in England with a wry sense of humour. The band were belting out, 'Saturdays in Silesia, holidays are for heroes.' Another track on the same album was fancifully entitled 'Dancing on the Berlin Wall.' I often wonder if they knew something the rest of us didn't.

We spent the night in a dingy hotel where the menu featured little more than *barscz*, Poland's typical beetroot soup, a thin red peppery bouillon with only a cheese straw to stir in it. We had a beer and went to bed hungry. The next day it was on to Warsaw, where I renewed acquaintance with a couple of British and American correspondents at a restaurant that served roast duck and red cabbage, if little else. The Solidarity story, they told us, had died on its feet. The spark had been extinguished. Those leaders who weren't incarcerated knew that if they did not keep quiet they soon would be.

French sector (abandoned piece of wall), 1981

View from the West near our flat, 1981

Der Führer(schein) – passing my driving test, 1981

Portrait of the artist as a young hack

Helga the honeypot

Erdmute the fusspot

Crosses (in West) commemorating those killed crossing the Wall at this spot

The Wall with contemporary English graffiti – not exactly political (Hitler's bunker underneath the no-man's-land)

Manne Schulz on his first trip West looks back towards home

Not quite the best hotel in town, 1981

Our back yard
(entry to Volker's
flat), 1981

Dresden Frauenkirche ruins – scene of demo, February 1982

Swords to Ploughshares symbol of protest movement, 1982

'You too could win this luxury car!' Berlin, 1982

Getting the coal delivered
Berlin, 1982

East German guards in the 'death
strip' (taken from the West), 1981

Keeping an eye out for his fellow citizens (death strip), 1981

Mayday 1984 in Red Square

MAYDAY MAYDAY
MAYDAY Big Brother
is watching you!
Moscow, 1984

Changing the Guard, 1987

Manne and Hannelore at Fasching (carnival) party in Metzer Eck

Tired and emotional on 'lovely Rita's' leather sofa. Sign says: out of order

Metzer Eck: Alex at the bar, your correspondent on the wrong side of it

With the Bear (Uwe)
German Unification
Day, October 3rd, 1990

Knocking down the walls (Jackie, with Oscar, 2, and Patrick, 5, one week after the Fall of the Wall, 1989)

I spy with my little eye. The next generation finds the cracks in communism

1989 Leipzig protesters on steps of Stasi offices!

Protesters march in Leipzig, September 1989

'Free Elections – Unified Germany' Berlin, 1990: The move towards unity!

On the frontier (far West Berlin), 1981

Abandoned watchtower, 1990

Wall, what wall? On the outskirts of West Berlin, 1990

There were soldiers everywhere on the streets, but at least they were Polish, not Russian. For the moment.

Day three, we drove east from Warsaw under blue skies but on sheet ice that on one occasion saw me swerve so radically that we spun off the road into a rubbish collection yard. The border post at Brest-Litovsk looked like the bridge of an ocean liner trapped in Arctic ice. The Polish guards didn't emerge, just waved me in from behind their plate-glass windows. I got out and went into the building to show them our documents. They were sitting around in shirt sleeves over cups of coffee. They didn't look like they got a lot of business, smiled sceptically and shrugged as if it was not their business to stop fools rushing in where angels would have put their feet up, had a beer and given it a second thought. Then they raised a red-and-white barrier thick with snow that looked as if it hadn't lifted in weeks and let us out. To be eaten by bears.

The Soviet frontier post was a hundred yards or so away. In the distance stretched a line of flat-blocks that marked the outskirts of Brest, a long low line of concrete between blue skies and white snow. Ahead was a barrier similar to that we had just come through, guarded by two soldiers in greatcoats and fur hats with a red star badge and Kalashnikovs held at attention. They moved forward, inspected my papers unsmilingly, gave a signal to some unseen superior and the barrier rose. Apprehensively I edged the car forward onto Soviet soil, only to see a line of black-clad, fur-hatted men emerge from the building ahead of us. I had no idea what we were letting ourselves in for.

The Russians greeted us with open arms. We were obviously the best thing that had happened in a year to a group of bored customs officials whose routine job was stamping the papers of lorry drivers carrying concrete in both directions. They pulled the car apart, of course. That was the best bit. For them. They checked out all the tapes for the cassette player, playing a few snatches here and there, not to check for seditious sermons – God knows what they might have made of *Cold War Nightlife* if they had understood the words – but to hear new songs. They inspected our clothing, our socks, our underwear as if eager to find out whether Westerners had the same anatomy. They pored over our photograph albums. For hours.

Honest. Not looking for evidence of anti-communist propaganda but out of genuine, ridiculously enthusiastic, almost childish human interest: 'So that's your nan, is it? How old is she then? And is that where you live in England? Does everybody have a house like that? What sort of car is that then? How much does that cost? How fast does it go?' It was astounding, endearing, amusing, infuriating, downright bloody maddening after five hours of it, before eventually they realised it could not go on for ever and somebody – claiming at last to have had the proper clearance from 'above' – finally let us pack up again (no offers to help there) and said, with obviously great reluctance, that we could go.

'Where are you heading for tonight, then?' one of them finally asked.

'Minsk,' I said. We had no choice: we had been obliged not only to book our accommodation in advance but also to give details of our route, and estimated times of arrival. The estimates were now shot to hell, to say the least.

'How long will it take to get there?' I asked.

He shrugged, thought a minute and said, 'How fast does your car go?'

An East German would have told me precisely how long it would have taken, driving at the legal speed limit of 100 kph. Russia, I was already learning, worked on a whole different set of rules. I put my foot down. It was late, already turning dark – despite the fact we had set out from Warsaw early and reached the border well before noon – but we made good progress at first. We were, after all, on the smart new motorway that the five-year plan decreed be finished for the 1980 Moscow Olympics, nearly eighteen months ago. It had two lanes – occasionally three – in each direction. And next to no traffic.

In fact, there was less and less traffic the further we went on. And gradually – ever so gradually – I began to realise why. It was a bit odd, after all, to see chunks of debris on the hard shoulder. And then there was the occasional obstacle on the carriageway itself: a pile of sacks of cement or something similar where the central reservation ought to be. It had been a while since we had seen traffic of any sort coming in the other direction. And then the obstacles started to become more frequent: pallets of concrete cladding in the slow lane; heaps of stone that now were clearly not just random debris but piles of aggregate. It's at times like that that the human brain does its utmost to shut out realisation of the blindingly obvious. At least until you run into it, head on. Which is what we now did, in the shape of at first one huge pothole, then another and then, definitively, inescapably, incontrovertibly – no matter how the mind tried pathetically not to recognise it – the physical end of the motorway. Not in a diversion sign, or a turn-off, or a line of brightly-coloured warning tape stretched across the carriageway, but in the sudden, immediate absence of paved surface, concrete pavement replaced by frozen mud. The car bucked, slid and juddered, as I braked hard and we swerved, bounced and rattled decisively to a halt. Possibly forever.

Ahead of us, about a hundred yards away, was what would have been a motorway bridge, had the motorway got far enough to go under it. It hadn't. The Olympic motorway not only hadn't made it to Moscow in time for the games, it hadn't even made it to Minsk, still over 100 kilometres away. And Moscow was a full day's drive beyond that. I was fast beginning to know how Napoleon – and even Hitler – had felt.

For one thing, we couldn't move. Not an inch. We had bumped our way to a standstill in a rut that was not just bigger and deeper than our car tyre – the bumper was resting on the earth in front of it – but also frozen solid. We would have to get out and push to get any chance of purchase at all. Thank God, I thought, as I lugged the heavy things out from under our hastily repacked luggage, at least we had brought snow chains. What we hadn't done, of course, was ever practise putting them on. Not even under perfect easy circumstances, like on the street outside the office, let alone at ten o'clock at night stuck in a frozen muddy rut in pitch blackness with the temperature pushing minus ten degrees Centigrade.

It wasn't easy. In fact, it was virtually impossible. With our fingers freezing we battled with fiddly catches, cold metal, hard rubber and frozen mud. 'Push this way,' shouted Jackie. 'No, pull this way. It needs to fasten here,' I replied. 'No it doesn't, I've got the clip here.' 'Well, it's supposed to be here!' These are the sort of little occasions that have been known to cause just the mildest marital strain.

Where the hell were the KGB? That was what I wanted to know. Where were the omnipotent, omniscient masters of secret surveillance who were supposed to be watching our every move? Were they lurking, sniggering to themselves, just out of sight a few hundred yards behind us, in a comfy Volga saloon, with the heating turned up, sharing a flask of vodka-reinforced coffee. Maybe, but I doubted it. They were back home in bed, tucked up and warming their feet against the backs of their well-upholstered wives. There was only so much a man would do in the service of socialism. And keeping an eye on two ill-informed, off-course Westerners who were obviously no danger to anyone but themselves was quite literally above and beyond the call of duty. And as far as I was concerned, it just wasn't good enough.

It wasn't just the whereabouts of the KGB that was on my mind. It was the whereabouts of the wolves. This might be a motorway building site in what is today Western Belarus, rather than the depths of Siberia. But at the time it didn't feel to me as if there was much difference. And I'm still not sure there is. At least not in the depths of winter. I didn't know the exact numbers (between 1,500 and 2,000 at the latest estimate) but I knew there were wolves out there. And every time I heard a howl – which was not infrequently – it might have been a mangy dog in some forsaken farmyard, but as far as I was concerned it was a prowling monster with ice-blue eyes and snow-grey fur circling in the dark, already licking its lips and summoning the rest of the pack at the thought of a tasty little Irishman and his bride for a midnight snack.

The trouble was: there didn't seem any way out of it. None at all. Even with the snow chains half-fastened – which was the best we had the remotest chance of hoping for – the wheels spun and spun. On either frozen mud or empty air. We weren't going anywhere fast. In fact, we weren't going anywhere at all. I was beginning to wonder about a Volvo 340's life-support systems. Would it be best to keep the engine running all night to keep us warm, even at the risk of the tank being empty by morning. And was there any guarantee anyone would come by in the morning? I had no idea where we were – other than halfway to Minsk – or how far it might be to the nearest human settlement. There were certainly no lights – friendly or otherwise

– to be seen in a landscape of unremitting darkness and unreflecting snow. What we needed was a miracle.

And then the miracle arrived. Out of nowhere. At least so it seemed. With no glare of headlights to announce it, just a dull gleam from dirty sidelights in the dark, puffing, grunting and farting loudly, a dilapidated, noxious gas-emitting parody of an open-backed beaten–up truck. I would later learn this was the ubiquitous workhorse of the Soviet economy, and in pretty routine condition. Then, all of a sudden the headlights came on and we stood in them illuminated like timorous frozen bunnies.

It would be another year before my Russian was up to understanding the full idiomatic and syntactic richness of the obscenities that spilled forth from the little fat man with arms like tree trunks who barrelled out of the driver's cab. (Nearly all Russian swear words, I would later learn, are, thanks to Genghis Khan and his hordes, derived from the Mongolian words for the body's private parts.) I gathered he was not pleased. Not pleased to find us parked 'in the middle of the road' where he might have ploughed straight into us had he not thought to do something as rash and energy-wasteful as turn on his headlights. Not pleased either to find the reason we were there was because we – and he – had literally come to the end of the road.

He ummed and ahhed a bit, spat on the ground a few times, uttered the names of a few more Mongolian body parts, and then shrugged and made to get back in his cab. If he was a top-level KGB agent trained to tail Westerners in deep cover, then he deserved an Oscar for his method-acting portrayal of an ignorant, half-drunk, foul-mouthed member of the lumpen proletariat who didn't give a bent kopeck for two namby-pamby Westerners and their fancy little car stuck in the mud.

'We can't move,' I bleated. 'We need to get to Minsk.' At this stage even a lift in the back of his stinking lorry seemed an attractive option.

'It's that way,' he shrugged, indicating the inaccessible bridge ahead as he climbed back into his cab and started up his grumbling engine. 'Just follow me,' he grunted, leaning out of the cab as he pulled level with us.

I was about to point out that this was not exactly the easiest thing in the world as we were stuck fast and there was no road, when I turned and saw in the glare of his headlights, a good metre higher than ours as he passed, that there was in between the lumps of snow-covered concrete what appeared to be a track. And as mercy would have it – or maybe because the weight of the truck had changed the frozen contours of the mud – I rammed home second gear and the snow chains caught. And we pulled, lurchingly, bumpily, with sounds that suggested God only knew what damage to suspension and chassis, out of the rut, following in the illuminated path taken by our unlovely lorry driver as he heedlessly rattled, occasionally at alarmingly improbable angles up what would perhaps one day be a motorway slip road but right now resembled a frozen obstacle course around the tank traps of El Alamein. And then the lights went out.

Somewhere just before reaching the brow of the incline, he turned his headlights off and fell back on the use of mud and slush-covered sidelights that offered no more forward illumination than a single candle in a hurricane lantern. In all my subsequent three years in the Soviet Union I never saw an industrial, public transport or even private vehicle that ever used its headlights properly. I don't mean full beam, but even just dipped. Whether the average Soviet citizen simply didn't believe that by the mere act of driving, he was charging his battery – who knows, maybe on some vehicles it didn't! – or whether it was somehow believed that they were saving fuel, or whether headlights were deemed a privilege only for the party elite, who flashed them relentlessly when roaring at high-speed along the priority lanes reserved for their Zil limousines, I never really knew. It was just a fact. Something you came to expect and not argue with. Like so much in the Soviet Union. Dimly lit streets required dimly lit cars. It was part of the atmosphere. As if they were following Hollywood stage directions.

We got to Moscow. In the end. Arriving at Minsk in the small hours of the morning, then on the next day via Smolensk and mind-numbingly beautiful vistas of broad snowfields littered with giant black crows, silver forests of birch trees, sparkling golden cupolas of onion-domed churches, and huge foul-smelling black cloud-belching industrial plants. When we finally pulled into the courtyard of the little block of flats that would be our new home – official address: Sadovaya-Samotechnaya 12/24, but known universally to its mainly Anglo-Saxon inhabitants as 'Sad Sam' – the Reuters bureau chief looked up almost dismissively and said, 'Oh well, better late than never I suppose.'

Over the nearly three years we spent in Moscow the Cold War reached a new icy nadir. Relations between the Kremlin and the West plummeted to a low unknown since the Berlin and Cuba crises. Leonid Brezhnev's successor, Yuri Andropov, had been ambassador to Hungary in 1956 and played a crucial role in coordinating the Soviet invasion. He returned home to become head of the KGB and had been a leading light in advocating the brutal suppression of the 1968 Prague Spring. His promotion to the top job was greeted with despair in a Poland still labouring under martial law. Washington saw him as a fittingly sinister head for what President Ronald Reagan now termed the 'evil empire'.

A few months later, in September 1983, we reached one of those bleak moments when the awful reality of the superpower standoff came home. Soviet fighter pilots shot down a South Korean airliner which had – allegedly because of a navigational error – strayed into prohibited airspace over the Kamchatka peninsula, home to some of Moscow's missiles sites. All 269 passengers and crew were lost. The 'evil empire', it seemed, was living up to its reputation. Soviet spokesmen were unrepentant, blaming the US for using civilians as 'shields' for its espionage activities. Conspiracy theories abounded, not least among journalists, given as a breed to black humour who noted the aircraft's James Bond designation: KAL 007. In the meantime, our feeling of isolation, as 'enemies in a strange land' was intensified when the Soviet state airline Aeroflot was banned from landing in almost all Western countries who at the same time ordered their national airlines to suspend flights to the Soviet Union. Although there was still the option of the long drive or overnight train journey to Helsinki, there was a feeling among the foreign community of being trapped in the lion's den.

During this period I took some memorable journeys to the outer reaches of that den, notably – in a not wholly vain search for some 'light relief' news features – to the coldest inhabited place on earth, a remote Siberian settlement called Oymyakon. It took the best part of two days to fly there, a journey of some 5,000 miles via Omsk, Tomsk and Yakutsk, a metropolis of 250,000 people literally in the middle of frozen nowhere. We landed out of an azure sky looking down at oceans of pine forest that stood up like iron filings manipulated from below by a magnet, into the grey blue fug of frozen exhaust fumes that marked the city. There were still two more flights, first to the regional centre of Ust-Ilimsk, then on in an antiquated turbo-prop Yak-16 where we sat in bucket seats facing each other along the fuselage, heated by something resembling a giant hair dryer. Most of the other passengers were dressed in sealskins. The pilot and co-pilot looked like something out of 'Biggles goes to Alaska', big men with thigh-high fur-lined boots and fur hats with the flaps flapping. I asked one why we had to sit around for two hours before we took off. 'Temperature,' he replied in the monosyllabic way men of action have – especially Russian men of action – 'we wait until it is warmer.' 'How warm?' 'Above minus 50C.' 'Oh, why.' 'Earlier – the wings crack.' It was good enough reason for me.

My photographer on the trip was a Russian called Lev – Reuters occasionally 'borrowed' local staff for non-controversial stories. He took some memorable snaps of me 'cuddling' dead rabbits that local Yakuti tribesmen had trapped and left sitting, apparently as pert and ready to bound off across the snow, outside their yurts to be skinned and eaten whenever they chose to bring them 'in, out of the freezer'. Lev had previously been foreign minister Andrei Gromyko's personal snapper, he boasted. Which made me realise I was now also just 'two handshakes' away from Josef Stalin. As links to twentieth-century tyrants went, I had done the double!

Back on the Cold War front, a memorable *Time* magazine cover named Reagan and Andropov jointly 'Men of the Year', showing them standing back to back, like adversaries about to take part in a deadly duel. The American television correspondents meanwhile were engaged in a battle of their own: trying to get their domestic anchors to pronounce the new Soviet leader's relatively simple name properly. Almost unanimously US newsreaders had taken to calling him *And*ropov, putting the stress – vitally important in Russian – wrongly on the first syllable. One of them, a Canadian working for CBS, devised what he thought was an ingenious – and for the state of superpower relations terrifyingly apt – mnemonic: 'You go to the edge of the cliff ... And-DROP-off.' Needless to say, it didn't work. It was a problem that was to recur.

Even after flights abroad were restored, the sense of oppression remained. The entire top floor of the Sad Sam building was under lock and key, and known to be reserved for KGB monitoring equipment. Phone calls to the West had to be booked hours in advance. Although under the Helsinki Accords, that back in 1973 had seemed to usher in a new era of détente but were now de facto defunct, television companies had unfettered rights to broadcast news material, in practice it didn't happen. The BBC, CBS, NBC, ITV, ARD – almost all the Western television news channels – had Moscow correspondents, but to send their material in those pre-portable satellite days they were obliged to use the facilities of the Soviet state television transmitter at Ostankino in northern Moscow. If their film contained matter that the Soviet authorities didn't like – interviews with the famed dissident Andrei Sakharov were a classic example – when it came to transmission time, the satellite link inexplicably collapsed, or some other 'unavoidable' technical failure occurred.

The result was an unexpected 'perk' for the spouses of other accredited correspondents: the birth of the 'hand-carry'. Because they too were in possession of that – for most Russians – unimaginable luxury, an unlimited multiple entry and exit visa, they could, literally, leave the country in a hurry. So whenever a TV company had a hot scoop that they reasonably feared might not make it out over the Soviet-controlled airwaves, they simply bought an instant business-class ticket and handed it, along with the tape and a 'thank you' of $100 cash to whichever spouse was head of the queue and had the time and inclination for a hand-luggage-only excursion to London. They were met at the other end by a TV company chauffeur who took the tape to the studio before depositing them at a West End hotel. Next day they were picked up again and taken back to the airport, though not before most had spent their $100, usually in Harrods food hall, though on one occasion the British wife of

an American correspondent memorably brought back a vast takeaway curry. Who had thought heaven was chicken tikka and bhindi
bhaji?

These trips were frequent enough that before we finally left, my
infant son, born a little over a year after our arrival, had accumu-
lated more then 25,000 miles of British Airways flying time. Before
his second birthday. But if our private lives had been marked by
the happy event of a birth, work was an unremitting death watch.
Andropov had not been a well man when he took over. Instead of
a dynamic change from the slurred speech and stumbling gait of
the senile Leonid Brezhnev, the new man in the Kremlin was more
often on a dialysis machine in the Central Committee's private hospital. Andropov had suffered from kidney problems for years but
they were now acute.

Within months of taking the top job he almost totally disappeared
from view, leaving keynote speeches to be given by other politburo
members, eagerly watched by those of us who styled ourselves – like
Connie in John LeCarré's *Tinker, Tailor, Soldier, Spy* trilogy – Krem-
linologists. We would hatch theories as to what speech on which
occasion, which nuance and what announcement of policy gave
hints as to who might be next in line of succession to the all-impor-
tant role of general secretary of the Communist Party.

The American correspondents had barely managed to get their
New York anchors to pronounce the Soviet leader's name properly, with the stress on the second rather than first syllable when
Andropov finally dropped off. His body was laid in state according
to tradition for Soviet leaders since the death of Lenin in 1924 in
the Hall of Columns in the Trades Union House, once a club for
Tsarist noblemen. The Red Square funeral of this most unloved of
late Soviet leaders was held on February 14th, 1984, Valentine's Day.
He was succeeded, however, by yet another dead hand: that of an
ageing Brezhnev acolyte, Konstantin Chernenko. If anything it was
a step backwards, but not one that looked like it would last long.
Chernenko needed an escalator to be built to get him to the top
of Lenin's Mausoleum for Andropov's send-off. He barely managed
to stammer his way through the eulogy in a wavering voice. He
had no sooner come to office than there were rumours that he was

hospitalised with pneumonia. The Soviet Union's supply of elderly leaders was gradually running out. Sooner or later – and the way things were going it looked like sooner – there would have to be a switch to a new generation.

Even so, there were still a few of the older generation lingering in the corridors of power hoping for a chance to step into the big office, if they didn't fall off their perch first. As a result every Kremlinologist in Moscow was constantly on the watch for changes in television programming – a switch from regular broadcasts to classical music was a surefire indicator someone big had snuffed it – or for Red Square being closed off at an unusual time (a preparation for a funeral). In November 1984 the defence minister Dmitry Ustinov, who had been in the job for eighteen years and was already in his mid-seventies, was added to the communal at-risk list after he failed to turn up at the annual Red Square parade to commemorate the 1917 revolution.

Just before Christmas – which was of course unmarked in the Soviet Union, except by Orthodox Christians who celebrated it according to the old calendar on January 7th – several of the streets around Red Square, including Gorky Street where the Hall of Columns was situated, were unexpectedly closed off. Our youngest trainee correspondent was sent down to nose around and see if she could find anything out. An hour later she came back bursting with excitement and declared that she had been definitively told Ustinov was dead and they were preparing a lying-in-state. The duty man at the office, a slightly more senior reporter, checked her source, thought for a minute, then turned to his green computer screen and banged out a brief 'urgent' one-liner to London: 'Soviet Defence Minister Dmitry Ustinov dead, reliable sources say,' it proclaimed in classic simple Reuterese.

Sure enough, however, before releasing this scoop to the world, the ever vigilant senior sub-editors on the World Desk in London came back on the internal telex with a service message: 'Please detail nature of sources.' In response back went a rewritten report: 'Soviet Defence Minister Dmitry Ustinov dead, a cleaning lady at the House of Columns said.'

Even as we watched the words chunter out on the teleprinter

– which was still how they were transmitted after leaving the computer screen – we could hear the roars of laughter from the old stagers in London. The trouble was that in Moscow terms, there could scarcely be a more reliable source for a scoop that didn't come from official announcements. Our young reporter who spoke excellent Russian – and had the advantage in this rare case of being female – had gone up to one of the dumpy babushkas with mops and buckets schlepping in and out of the grandiose old building which was, as everyone knew, the traditional venue for the lying-in-state of senior party members and asked, 'Who is it this time?' As a result, we had a genuine scoop. After ten tedious minutes of exchanging teleprinter messages with London, it was agreed that the report should be issued with the original – less specific – wording.

With Ustinov down, the list of geriatric power-seekers was shrinking. One of the few remaining was Nikolai Tikhonov, who despite being nearly ninety could not be discounted as the next short-term incumbent of the top job. He was currently prime minister, a job to which in the past Western correspondents (and government leaders) had mistakenly attributed more power than was due. Because in the Soviet system the Communist Party had made itself the sole power in the state, real power derived from being head of the party – its general secretary – rather than any office of state. It was only towards the end of the Brezhnev era that the Soviets themselves had realised it was easier to make this clear by giving the general secretary the courtesy title of President of the Supreme Soviet, which was in theory just the speaker of the rubber stamp parliament but it meant that the Americans could refer to Mr President. The Russians felt (correctly) that this would make things easier for them to understand.

Tikhonov himself was, however, also rumoured to be ill. By March 1985 Chernenko had not been seen in public for months. But nor had Tikhonov. As fate would have it, the bureau chief was on a trip to Geneva to see his girlfriend and I was the most senior of our little team when a rare telephone call came through from London in the middle of the night. It was, inevitably, one of the Princes of Darkness. His message was that the BBC's monitoring station at Caversham in Berkshire had picked up a change to classical music on most mainstream Soviet radio programmes. We talked over the situation and as one of his former protégés I was entrusted with both an honour and a burden: he would set up the codes so that if and when an announcement was made, instead of my report going first to the World Desk in London, it would go out live. To the world. This might, just might, give us an advantage over our rivals, the American Associated Press and the French Agence-France-Presse. That way it would be Reuters who 'told the world the news'. On such tiny things did the reputation of news agencies depend.

There was, of course, one other thing: accuracy. I was on no account to get it wrong! Staggering downstairs in my dressing gown – in the claustrophobic atmosphere in which we all lived the office was just one floor below our flat – I turned on the radio (it was still too early in the morning for television) and was treated to a never-ending sequence of Tchaikovsky piano recitals. The boys and girls at Caversham had hit the nail on the head. Something was up. But with the weight of my direct filing powers lying heavy on my hands, could I be absolutely certain what it was. It certainly had all the hall-marks of a death, but was it Chernenko's or Tikhonov's. Or what about the third possibility – much discussed amongst the Krem-linologists of late – that Chernenko would simply step down citing ill health and pass on the mantle to one of the relatively unknown younger men? That would hardly merit the solemn music, would it? Could I be sure? There was no precedent.

As a result I sat down at the computer screen and tapped out three alternative one-line reports, each of which properly 'topped and tailed' with the required codes so that if I chose it, it and it alone would go out to the world.

The first had a UU priority (urgent) and said simply: 'Soviet Prime Minister Nikolai Tikhonov dead – official.' There was no way I was pressing the button on this occasion unless it was official.

The second had an RR code (a rush) and was accompanied by three little bell symbols which mean bells would actually sound on the teleprinter alerting chief subs on newspapers, radio and televi-sion stations that something rather important had just happened. It read: 'Soviet leader Konstantin Chernenko resigns – official.'

The third – the biggie – had an SS priority, which stood for Snap, and was accompanied by a signal six bells, said: 'Soviet leader Konstantin Chernenko dead – official.'

That was it. All I had to do now was hunker down with the cup of strong coffee my wife had brewed to wake me up, and a snifter of Irish whiskey to steady my nerves, and settle in for a long morning of Tchaikovsky recitals.

It was nearly lunchtime before anything else happened. From about nine a.m. when television broadcasts had started for the day, both channels had shown only a red curtain and played similar programmes of Russian classical music. The TV men showed a slight preference for Rachmaninov. I thought I identified a snatch from his tone poem 'Isle of the Dead'. But that might just have been wishful thinking.

Then, virtually on the stroke of midday, the television went silent, as did the radio. The teleprinter which relayed to our office reports from the official government news agency TASS had ominously already stopped chuntering out its fill-in diet of agricultural reports and sports results more than twenty minutes ago. Suddenly it sprang into life, the printer key humming at the beginning of a line as my knees bounced with nervous tension under the desk waiting for whatever it was about to spring on me.

And then it began to move. I watched as the little print head crawling along the paper spelled out the tidings, Cyrillic letter by Cyrillic letter, and most agonisingly of all with every bit of the tortuous bureaucratic pompous language in which all important Soviet official statements were couched. It was as if they were teasing me ...

M-E-S-S-A-G-E_F-R-O-M

Clunk, and the teleprinter head shoots back as the paper whirrs and shunts up half a centimetre to start a new line:

T-H-E_C-E-N-T-R-A-L_C-O-M-M-I-T-T-E-E_
O-F_T-H-E_C-O-M-M-U-N-I-S-T_P-A-R-T-Y_O-F_
T-H-E_U-S-S-R

Clunk, whirr ...

T-H-E_P-R-E-S-I-D-I-U-M_O-F_T-H-E_
S-U-P-R-E-M-E_S-O-V-I-E-T_O-F_T-H-E_U-S-S-R

Clunk, whirr …

I-T_I-S_W-I-T-H_G-R-E-A-T_S-O-R-R-O-W …

My fingers flashed over the computer keyboard and deleted the Chernenko resignation option from the green screen. Sorrow was not an emotion reserved for resignations.

T-H-A-T_W-E_A-N-N-O-U-N-C-E_T-H-E_
D-E-A-T-H_A-T_1-9-2-0_O-N_T-H-E_
E-V-E-N-I-N-G_O-F_M-A-R-C-H_1-0 …

Yes, yes, yes, get on with it, I was almost shouting, taking in at the same time that whichever of them was dead had been dead for nearly eighteen hours before the authorities had got their act together to announce it.

…1-9-8-5_O-F_T-H-E_E-S-T-E-E-M-E-D_K-

Zap! K, not N, Konstanin Chernenko, and not Nikolai Tikhonov. My heart in my mouth – and my life in my hands – I hit the key that sent the 'Chernenko dead – official' flash around the world. And immediately covered my eyes. It wasn't Chernenko, all of a sudden I knew it wasn't. It was going to be somebody completely different, Karl Marx, Kemal Ataturk, Klaud Rains, Kary Grant.

But it wasn't. I turned back to the teleprinter which had just finished spelling K-O-N-S-T-AN-T-I-N_U-S-T-I-N-O-V-I-C-H_C-H-E-R-N-E-N-K-O, the full version of his name including patronymic and was now going on to list his titles. I breathed out a huge sigh of relief. I wasn't out of a job. In fact, if I was lucky I might even be in for a herogram.

It came through an hour later, by which time the bureau chief was winging his way back from Geneva in a flap while the three of us in the office were busy sending over full-length round-ups, including runners and riders for yet another succession race. It was character-istically terse and factual, but we knew that meant it was all the more genuine: 'Congratulations Moscow Office, 45 seconds lead over AP'.

Forty-five seconds! We were ecstatic. In the world most people inhabit, forty-five seconds is next to no time at all, but in the intense competition between international news agencies it was almost as big a result as Michael Schumacher winning a Grand Prix by a similar margin. Most importantly for me, despite the fact that almost all the papers the next day would run stories from their own correspondents and analysts, almost all of them would carry the little rough-edged image that we called a 'rag-out' of 'how the world heard the news'. And at the end of it would be a simple sign-off: REUTER PYM. Not exactly fame at last, but one of the biggest adrenalin highs of my career. I was bouncing off the walls for hours.

In fact I had only just about stopped bouncing, in time to get a cup of tea to sustain my energy levels – I had by now been in the office since three thirty a.m., having had barely three hours sleep before I had been awakened by the phone call from London – when the next shock hit us.

My colleague Tony Barber was still working on a lengthy piece about the possible succession candidates, and the likely date of an announcement. Nobody really knew exactly how the so-called 'elec-tion' procedure at the top of the Soviet hierarchy was conducted, except that everyone was pretty sure that democracy played little part in it. Officially the Central Committee which numbered some 300 members would convene in a special session to choose its general secretary but effectively one of the dozen or so members of its executive, the politburo, had already stitched it up. Nonetheless we expected procedures to be followed and an announcement of a new leader in about two days' time.

So it was shock enough to have me spill my tea when Robert, our Armenian office assistant who had been studying every tic of the TASS teleprinter, suddenly ripped off a short three-line despatch which had just come up and waved it excitedly under my nose. I had already leapt to the computer to enter the same Snap codes as before – without asking London for fresh authorisation – with Robert still babbling excitedly in my ear: '*Eto Gorbachev*, Peter, *Eto Gorbachev*!!'

It's Gorbachev! It was too. But even as I typed the six bells and the brief formulaic line: 'Mikhail Gorbachev elected Soviet leader – official', I had no idea how important those six words were going to prove. Nor had the rest of the world.

8

Back to Blighty, Back to Berlin

The Gorbachev effect was still no more than two hazily understood words – *glasnost* and *perestroika* – by the time my spell in Moscow came to a truncated end. It was truncated at my own instigation, though as things turned out it was unlikely to have lasted much longer anyhow.

I had finally done what I had been wanting to do for years: thrown myself off the Reuters treadmill of never-ending news cycles, feeding bare-bones stories into the maw of the global media machine. It was true we got to spread our wings occasionally – I had travelled into deepest Siberia to do a feature on the coldest inhabited place on Earth, and I had driven from Moscow to Tbilisi over the Georgian Military Highway through the Caucasus Mountains – but as far as writing was concerned we were always strapped into the straitjacket of the terse Reuters house style.

In the summer of 1985, I got an interview for the foreign desk of the *Daily Telegraph* through a word from my friend, their Moscow correspondent Nigel Wade. The man across the desk in the *Telegraph*'s grand but poky offices on Fleet Street was Peter Eastwood, the paper's infamously tyrannical managing editor. The actual editor was a former minor Tory minister called Bill Deedes, who was something of a Fleet Street legend, partly because he was suspected of being the model for Boot of the Beast in Evelyn Waugh's splendid satire *Scoop*, partly because he was the supposed recipient of the fictional letters from Margaret Thatcher's husband Denis published in *Private Eye*, and largely because he would go on churning out wry, if rather inconsequential, eye-witness journalism until well into his nineties. But there was one thing that by common accord he was absolutely no good at, and that was being an editor. As a result the hard-headed, domineering Eastwood had taken the throne from beneath him and controlled every aspect of the *Telegraph* except for a couple of columnists and the editorials.

To my surprise he seemed less interested in my journalistic credentials or ambitions than my place of education – Oxford was fine – my recommendation from Wade, and strangely, perhaps most significantly of all: what my father had done in the war. In fact he had been a mechanic in the RAF, which I doubt was what Eastwood was looking for, but it was my immense good fortune that he had been shot down over Burma. Burma was all Eastwood cared about. That's where he had been.

'What happened to him?'

'They bailed out over the jungle,' I said hesitantly, trying to remember all those stories my dad had told that I'd never paid enough attention to, 'and joined up with the Chindits.'

Eastwood's eyes both sparkled and glazed over at the same time. 'Ahhh, Orde Wingate's bunch. Magnificent men.'

For the next ten minutes or so he waxed lyrical about derring-do in the jungle, attacks on railway lines, carriages behind them exploding, carriages in front of them exploding. I smiled. Under the circumstances it wasn't hard.

'Father still alive, is he?'

'Yes, keeping well, thanks.'

I got the job. Unfortunately, it wasn't quite the job I was expecting it to be. The *Telegraph* was stuck in a time warp in more ways than one. For the past three years in Moscow I had been using computers – albeit primitive, green-screen models that were little more than electronic word processors linked to a telex line. At the *Telegraph* they were still using typewriters, and not even electric ones. News stories were typed on paper that looked and felt recycled but was probably just unprocessed – cheapness rather than concern for the environment being the overriding consideration – with three sheets and two layers of old-fashioned ink carbon in between so that a desk editor and sub-editor had their own copies. Every word was in any case eventually set in hot metal type by members of the print unions, typesetters and compositors who assembled the pages in mirror image out of shapes – words, pictures, adverts – all cast in lead alloy metal. It was a technology not light years removed from that which produced the Gutenberg Bible in the fifteenth century. It was not unrelated that each of the print trade unions in a newspaper was known as a chapel, headed by a Father of the Chapel. The official who presided over the whole lot was known as the Imperial Father of the Chapel.

Some of the machinery still in use in 1985 had been made in the late nineteenth century, and there were two brand new lino-type machines that had been delivered in the 1930s but were still in their packing cases because management and print unions had never reached agreement on terms for their introduction. Things were changing but Rupert Murdoch had yet to unleash the Wapping whirlwind that would change the industry for ever. On my first day foreign editor Ricky Marsh had to almost rugby tackle me to prevent me from stepping over a white line painted on the floor, which was the strict demarcation between journalists and 'the print'. Had I crossed it, even accidentally, the brothers could have walked out and there would have been no paper the next day. On evening shifts, when the giant presses in the bowels of the building began to run, you could feel the floors tremble, while going along the juddering elevated walkway that led to the canteen felt like a stroll above the engine room of a supertanker.

But even that had at least a frisson of excitement attached to it: of being at the heart of an industrial machine that was actually producing the newspapers to be delivered to breakfast tables all across the country. The same could not be said of the foreign desk. The *Daily Telegraph* foreign desk in the summer of 1985 looked and felt as if it hadn't changed since 1955. This was almost certainly because it hadn't. Apart from Marsh, there was old Tom Hughes, a genial, well-meaning elderly buffer who sounded and acted a bit like Corporal Jones from *Dad's Army*. Tom was the oldest member of the foreign desk but the others were to my youthful eyes not much better: a troika of tie-wearing gentlemen who looked more like clerks than journalists. Called Readman, Mossman and Dudman, their names alone were enough to fill me with silent dread. There had been a low-budget British TV movie I'd seen as a child called *Unman, Wittering and Zygo* about a teacher who dies for messing his public-school pupils' routine. Despite the reversal in the age spectrum, I feared something similar.

Marsh was a bright, rotund little man, perpetually fizzing with energy, forever bustling in and out of the Foreign Room, which for me rapidly began to rhyme with tomb. The only time of the day when I had to try hard to suppress a smile was mid-morning when the buzzer on the intercom linked to Eastwood's office sounded, and Ricky would actually stand up to answer it with a brisk, 'Yes, Peter.' And then he would bustle off to morning editorial conference.

The low point was when Tom painstakingly instructed me that, 'here in the Foreign Room we have a special way of using paperclips to make sure the copy stays together better', and showed me how rather than just sliding the paper in he bent the inside loop back to create 'tension'. I could have cried. The 'copy' in question, to boot, was usually Reuters, torn off into individual 'takes' – the classic 200-word Reuter 'page' which I had been so eager to escape – by the final member of our happy little team, Paul, who actually was a clerk and therefore a member of one of the print unions, which – in those days just before the Murdoch revolution – meant he probably earned more than most of us and certainly a lot more than me.

What the foreign desk did, I was learning to my horror, was not so much write or even edit copy as to order it up, in much the same way as we ordered milky tea from the lady who brought the tea trolley round. The *Telegraph* liked to maintain the impression that it had its 'own correspondents' in every corner of the globe. In reality most of these were just stringers, local journalists who would knock something together on demand for the *Telegraph* in exchange for a token annual retainer. This meant the *Telegraph* could continue to give the impression it still had its 'own man' in, say, Srinagar, the Kashmiri old summer capital of the Indian Raj. On the odd occasion that something cropped up in Srinagar or Darwin, Australia, or Durban, South Africa – far-flung outposts of Empire were firm favourites – the *Telegraph* wanted their man's byline on it. Or at the very least, 'from our own correspondent'.

The trouble was that some of these blokes whiling away their days in the outposts of empire were semi-retired, and even others who might work in local newspapers, often had less access to what was going on in their area than we had with the resources of Reuters, the AP and AFP feeding us news. As a result, it was often the task of the

Telegraph foreign desk man to ring up the local stringer and read him the Reuters copy. He would then take notes over the phone, go off, type out his own version, ring up the *Telegraph* copytakers and dictate it to them, and they would type it up on carbon triplicates, one of which would arrive back up in the foreign desk. Occasionally it was better, written in less-stilted style than that of the agency copy and with maybe a little more local background thrown in, but more often than not it was just a bastardised version of what I or someone else had read to him, with no infrequent occurrence of the 'send three and fourpence, we're going to a dance' syndrome. It was soul-destroying.

The only entertainment came, as it always did for journalists in those days, in the pub. The pub in question was the King and Keys, a dreadful shabby watering hole run by a southern Irishman called Andy, who might have got the job from Central Casting, as he spoke in a loud stage brogue, usually slurred, and routinely insulted all his customers. Luckily most of them never noticed and those who did couldn't care less, sometimes because they were beyond doing so. There was an interesting patch on the raised flock wallpaper near the door which had been worn smooth, just about head-height, because of the number of heads which over the years had taken an extended rest there on their way out the door. The K'n'K had the one saving grace that it was right next door to the paper and so could be nipped down to quickly for a short 'refresher' – often while the refreshee's jacket was left hanging over the back of his chair – and could also be got back from equally quickly in an emergency, such as when a senior editor noticed that despite the omnipresent jacket the seat in question had been cold for some considerable time.

The *Telegraph* did have more than its quota of amiable eccentrics, all of whom were regulars in the K'n'K. There was the erudite if somewhat pedantic home reporter who invariably closed his eyes when talking – occasionally enabling the subjects of his erudition to slope off unnoticed – whose modest byline was R. Barry O'Brien, and was therefore universally known as 'Our Barry'. His diminutive, combed-over colleague A.J. McIlroy became (rather unfairly) A.J. Makeitup. There was the learned, acerbic and witty leader writer 'Blind Peter' Utley, whose obvious disability meant he required a permanent assistant, invariably in the attractive shape of young female Oxbridge graduettes, whose job description included not only taking his dictation but also taking him to the pub. Considering he was quite capable of making his way, by touch, along the flocked wallpaper, to the Gents', it was remarkable how often he would completely 'miss' his target when turning to tap them on the shoulder or pat them on the knee. And then there was Bill O'Hagan, the former South African police officer who had quit when his colleagues ridiculed his collection of Miles Davis and Count Basie jazz records as 'kaffir music'. Bill was the *Telegraph*'s 'late stop' which meant his main job was to sit in the newsroom every night until four a.m. in case the Queen Mother died. He was a genial, round, hard-drinking man with a bald head and a little moustache who looked remarkably like a children's comic butcher, which in order to give reality a lesson is what he ultimately became, when the sausages he made in his garage in Croydon became so popular with his colleagues he decided there might be a business in it. He subsequently bought a butcher shop and you can now savour O'Hagan's sausages in pubs up and down Britain. Bill famously spent the night in the King and Keys when he dozed off momentarily in the upstairs function room and Andy locked him in.

None of this conviviality, however, made up for the fact that my own job, having finally made it to the mainstream of Fleet Street newspapers, was deathly dull. Luckily an escape route presented itself, in the jovial, ever optimistic, prematurely white-haired form of Graham Paterson. I had known Graham slightly at university, even if I had been rather put off by his overt self-confidence, loud voice, obvious ambition and the fact that his father had been deputy editor of the *New Statesman*. When he went straight from university to work on the *Telegraph*'s Peterborough gossip column on a salary at least fifty per cent higher than mine at Reuters, I muttered to myself about nepotism. Yet he was to prove my salvation. The *Daily Telegraph*'s dull Sunday sister paper desperately needed a shot in the arm and the man chosen to give it one was the foppish but charming and self-consciously intellectual Peregrine Worsthorne, who prided himself on his wit, dandyish clothes and a claim to have been the first person to say 'fuck' on British television (in 1973 – he was actually the second; theatre critic Kenneth Tynan had beaten him by eight years). He had picked Graham to be his news editor, and Graham in turn persuaded foreign editor Peter Taylor that I was the man to cover Europe for him.

In fact, Paterson's inspired eccentricity was the prime motor in pulling together one of the most remarkably talented groups of journalists ever to work, drink and play together on Fleet Street. It included Bruce Anderson, Patrick Bishop, David Blundy, Walter Ellis, Simon O'Dwyer-Russell, Ronald Payne and Megan Tressider to name but a few. From a newspaper that up until then had read as almost an afterthought to the daily, a stolid but uninspired and pedestrian review of the week, the *Sunday Telegraph* became – for a brief few years – an anarchic mix of radical opinion, fired by Worsthorne's erratic and often outrageous leaders, off-beat news stories, and lovingly-crafted, semi-literary, in-depth focus pieces. With far more limited resources it attempted to tackle the market-leading *Sunday Times* head-on. From 1985 to 1988, it was one hell of a place to work: we worked hard, played hard and lunched hard, doing our best to maintain Fleet Street standards of alcohol-fuelled eccentricity even as we were forced to migrate from the fabled Street of Shame itself to the more sterile surroundings of the then still near empty docklands around Canary Wharf.

But at last I was able to write the sort of longer, more thoughtful stories about a Europe that was changing faster than many people in Britain noticed or cared to notice. For someone who had spent years watching Eastern Europe in particular, there were definite early signs of rust on the Iron Curtain. Martial law in Poland had come to an end in 1983 but there were still severe restrictions on political rights and although Solidarity was still not the force it had once been, there were fresh rustlings in the undergrowth. These were encouraged by the award to Lech Walesa, recently released from prison, of the Nobel Peace Prize, even though he sent his wife Danuta to collect it, fearing that if he left the country himself the government might not let him return.

In the other two Eastern bloc states that had tried and failed in the past to shake off the crypto-colonial dead hand of Moscow, Czecho-slovakia and Hungary, eyes were still watchfully trained on events in Poland. In Prague, Czech dissident playwright Václav Havel had just been released after a four-year spell of imprisonment, though he was still under surveillance and subject to harassment. In Hungary, the communist leader János Kádár had sought to soften the blows inflicted in 1956 by a relatively liberal attitude to economic reform and less active harassment of political dissidents who did not make a nuisance of themselves. He had replaced the old hardline slogan of 'He who is not with us is against us', with 'He who is not against us is with us'. It was the kind of subtle difference – uncannily famil- iar to the Bush and Obama regimes in Washington – that has to be understood to get a grasp of what came to be known as 'goulash communism'. In short, the Hungarian party allowed a degree of political discussion and economic activity (including a flourishing black market in agricultural products which meant far better sup- plies) as long as lip service was paid to communist supremacy and the country's membership of the Warsaw Pact. The important thing was to play the game softly softly and make sure that Moscow either didn't notice or didn't care. It had worked for nearly two decades. Then along came Gorbachev. He did notice; in fact, he was rather impressed.

In Moscow itself, it was becoming clear that *perestroika* was not just another empty slogan: Gorbachev really did intend reform of the hidebound Soviet economy. There was a story told by a French diplomat that under Chernenko, when Gorbachev had been put in charge of the agricultural sector, he had arrived late for a state dinner with visiting French President François Mitterrand. When Chernenko asked what was wrong he said, 'Nothing works prop- erly'. 'How long has this been going on?' asked Chernenko, shocked by the revelation. 'Since 1917', Gorbachev replied. Apocryphal or not, the anecdote was certainly prophetic.

Similarly if *glasnost* did not yet mean the total transparency it proclaimed, there was at least a reduction in the climate of paranoid secrecy. And a more human face on display to the world. Gorbachev had retired foreign minister Andrei Gromyko, the dour face of the Soviet Union abroad for nearly three decades and nicknamed Mr Nyet. He had suspended the deployment of SS-20 missiles in East Germany and Czechoslovakia, and preparations were apace for him to meet Ronald Reagan at a summit in Reykjavik. Britain's Iron Lady Margaret Thatcher had said he was a man she could 'do business with'.

But the horizon was not without clouds. There were more disconcerting ripples of change running through Yugoslavia, the self-appointed leader of the 'non-aligned' movement that in the Soviet bloc was regarded by ordinary people as a soft semi-capitalist paradise and in the West as a cheap holiday destination 'sort of' behind the Iron Curtain. The 'neither fish nor fowl' state that was an amalgam of Balkan mini-nationalities with a history of bloody rivalry and vendetta, had been held together by two factors. One was the iron fist of Josip Tito, for whom communism was not so much an ideology as a means of clamping down on dissent which he believed would lead to a revival of old nationalisms and inevitable fragmentation. He was right.

After Tito had died in 1980, a 'collective presidency' had been established comprising representatives of each of the six constituent republics as well as from Serbia's two 'autonomous provinces', Kosovo and Vojvodina, which had respectively large Albanian and Hungarian-speaking populations. At first it seemed to work well: in 1984, Sarajevo, the capital of the racially- and ethnically-mixed republic of Bosnia-Herzegovina, had hosted the Winter Olympics. But then for the moment the other crucial factor in holding Yugoslavia together was still in place: the pressure of the mutually hostile blocs that flanked it on either side. The Cold War had become a guarantor of the status quo. This theory implied that ending it could cause the pressure cooker to explode. But it was only a theory. Europe's ideological divide was laid down in concrete: the physical concrete all too evident in the Berlin Wall. And no one was about to change that. It was as unimaginable as the idea that the beautiful old city that hosted the Winter Olympics would become a battlefield and its main thoroughfare earn the nickname Snipers' Alley.

I persuaded Worsthorne to let me style myself Central Europe Correspondent, thereby not just inventing a job but revitalising a term – Central Europe – that had been current for centuries but dormant since the onset of the Cold War and the continent's split down an ideological fault line. Central Europe prior to 1945 had been essentially everything north of the Alps from Germany's Western border to the Polish frontier with Russia, dipping down to include the Balkans. It was, in effect what had been the German and Austro-Hungarian empires. It would be nice to portray my new title as a prophetic glimpse of the new world order about to break through, and in truth there was just a hint of intuition if only that changing a name sometimes encourages people to look at things differently. The usual newspaper title of 'Eastern European correspondent' was, I felt, de facto collaboration with the existence of the Iron Curtain, which although it showed no likelihood of disappearing, was once again becoming just ever so slightly more permeable.

For three years I flitted across Europe, covering stories that were sometimes related to the Cold War, sometimes not. From time to time they overlapped in a way that made the reality of that unnatural divide stand out more clearly than ever. Rudolf Hess, the last prisoner in Spandau, whose demise I had so frequently anticipated when posted to Berlin, finally died, in dubious circumstances that suggested suicide or even foul play (he was found with an electrical extension cord twisted around his neck). I was gutted to miss the story, being on a family holiday in Spain at the time. As soon as I got back to the office I was expecting to be sent off to his funeral, particularly as there was widespread anticipation of neo-Nazi trouble. But his son Wolf-Rüdiger buried him secretly in a night-time ceremony in the little north Bavarian town of Wunsiedel where the old man's parents were buried.

I could not resist the opportunity to go and see the grave – if only for closure on the longest 'death watch' I had ever undertaken, the next time I was in the area. As it turned out the chance presented itself quite soon with a protest by small farmers in Germany against new EU agricultural rules. Always keen to have a poke at 'Europe' (a little Britain enthusiasm I hardly shared) Worsthorne sent me to cover the story. As fate had it one of the groups of protesters, whose action involved lighting bonfires on high ground in their fields at night, were farmers near the Bavarian town of Marktredwitz, not far from Wunsiedel. The Hess grave was as unremarkable as I might have expected, but the visit to Marktredwitz gave me a new insight into the aftermath of the Second World War, of which the Cold War was in all but name an indirect and less bloody continuation.

Just down the hill from where the farmers lit their bonfire we could see the outline of an old medieval town. 'That's Eger,' said one of them. 'We used to farm a lot of land round there.' 'Used to?' I asked. 'Yes,' he turned to me as if I was an idiot. That's the Sudeten. They threw everybody out in 1945, millions of us. They call that town Cheb now, but it's still Eger. Always will be.' I kept quiet. I knew that the 1945 universal expulsion of Germans from the Sudetenland they had always lived in had been cruel. But they might have reflected on that in 1938 before so enthusiastically rejoicing at being 'reunited' with the Reich they had never belonged to. Even so, I could see the wicked logic of the Iron Curtain when they pointed out that the main road north ran straight through 'Eger', not that it would have done them any good: when it returned to what was now German soil a few kilometres further on, it was East German soil. These people, these simple farmers with all their old gripes and prejudices had gone from living in the centre of the continent to living at the edge of the world.

It was inevitably – as things would turn out – Gorbachev who took me back to East Berlin, in May 1987, when he chaired a meeting of the Warsaw Pact leaders there, held in honour of the city's 750th anniversary. It was an anniversary that the East decided belonged solely to them because nothing now in the West had been part of tiny thirteenth-century Berlin. The East Germans rounded up the usual crowds of impressed citizens to line the route, but for once they need not have bothered: large numbers turned out unprompted. East Berliners, glued to West German news on their televisions, were curious to see the man from the hated empire to the East in whom Westerners were all of a sudden placing such hopes. A few wondered if they dared entrust him with their own, though most decided that on balance they would not.

If several thousand East Berliners had genuinely turned out to watch the motorcades flash by, they were still outnumbered by the plainclothes Stasi goons who fronted the lines, pumping their fists into the air and shouting 'Hoch! Hoch! Hoch!', the traditional, militarised old Prussian version of 'Hip, Hip, Hooray!' The East German and Soviet leaders still greeted each other on arrival and departure with the old comrades' kiss – just as they had done in Brezhnev's day – even if those of us who considered Soviet kisses another branch of

Kremlinology couldn't help but notice that Gorbachev puckered up as if kissing a lemon.

Only a week later US President Ronald Reagan visited West Berlin and delivered a challenge to the Soviet leader that would, more than two years later, seem like a prophetic demand: 'General Secretary Gorbachev, if you seek peace, if you seek prosperity for the Soviet Union and Eastern Europe, if you seek liberalisation, come here to this gate. Mr Gorbachev, open this gate. Mr Gorbachev, tear down this wall!' Reagan's speech has since been hailed as a decisive factor, if only because Gorbachev's actions – or rather inaction – were key to the events of 1989. At the time, it just seemed Reagan was trying to compete with the ghost of John F. Kennedy. There were many in the White House who advised him to leave it out, rather than embarrass a relatively new Soviet leader with whom he was getting on remarkably well.

West German President Richard von Weizsäcker visited Moscow a month later and raised the 'German Question' more as a traditional tease than with any real hope of an encouraging answer. Gorbachev's reply was slightly more encouraging than that of any of his predecessors, but only slightly. History would decide, he said, 'what will happen in the next 100 years'. Back in Berlin Honecker was smiling: centuries were the sort of time frame he had in mind for the Wall he boasted as his own.

After all he had only just cemented his position, hadn't he? In September Honecker made the first ever visit by an East German leader to West Germany. To many West Germans it was an uncomfortably alien sight to see the flag of the German Democratic Republic – which many still felt stood for a part of their country under alien occupation – flying over the Bonn chancellery: the way a naturally conservative Englishman might react to seeing a version of the Union Jack with a hammer and sickle on it flying over Westminster. (Or emblazoned with a swastika for an earlier generation.)

Honecker, who had been born in West Germany's Saarland, strutted and preened on the Bonn stage like a diminutive monochrome peacock alongside the overlarge Humpty Dumpty figure of West German chancellor Helmut Kohl. For Kohl it was a chance to parade as a statesman, to show that he was ready to match Gorbachev's expressions of goodwill with a show of at least superficial cordiality towards the Kremlin's puppet state on German soil. There was a bit of stage-managed humble pie for Honecker too. For several years the West German rock star Udo Lindenberg had been on a blacklist of performers not allowed to cross the Wall and perform in the East. In revenge he had penned a bestselling hit, a rock ballad to the tune of Chatanooga Choo Choo, which included the lines: '*Honi, ich weiss… bist du heimlich auch ein Rocker, du ziehst dir ganz heimlich auch gerne mal die Lederjacke an, schliesst dich ein auf das Kloh und hörst Westradio.*'('Honi, I know…/That you are secretly a rocker./At home on your own, you quietly put your leather jacket on,/ lock yourself in the loo and listen to West radio.')

Now at a contrived 'spontaneous' meeting, Lindenberg 'surprised' Honecker by seemingly emerging from the crowd – there was too much security on the trip for any genuinely unexpected event – to give him a signed guitar as a present. It was nothing more than a piece of theatre for the television cameras that would play well on both sides of the Wall. It was nonetheless a sign of the times that it happened at all. At the end of Lindenberg's 'choo choo' ballad, a sonorous voice was to be heard intoning in Russian: '*Myezhdu prochim, tovarishch Erich, Vyerkhovniy Soviet nye imyehet nichevo protiv gastroli gospodina Lindenberga v GDR*' ('As it happens, comrade Erich, the Supreme Soviet has no objections to Mr Lindenberg doing a concert in the GDR'). The concert duly took place, a few months afterwards, even if the audience was stuffed with the teenage children of loyal party members.

Of course, nobody knew what the Supreme Soviet really thought, least of all its members, who were accustomed to having their thinking done for them by the man at the head of the politburo. And he was proving an enigma inside a riddle all of his own. Gorbachev brought me back to East Berlin again that December when he stopped off on his way back from his first summit with Reagan in Washington. By now the number of East Berliners who had begun to see in him perhaps a real chance of at least some reform – a lessening of East Germany's draconian political repression was all even the boldest dared hope for – and some twenty of the old Swords to Ploughshares dared to mark Human Rights' Day by handing a petition to the Pact leaders asking if they could have some. They were summarily arrested on the street.

A burly uniformed policeman, overweight and puffing in his Soviet-style imitation fur hat, grabbed me by the collar as I watched the demonstrators being hustled away and demanded identification. I put my hand in my pocket and on a whim, took out my old, out-of-date Soviet press pass. He looked at it in near shock for a few seconds, then stood back and handed it over to me with a snappy salute. East German police were taught to recognise and respect Russian, very few of them could read or understand it.

I washed the politics down, as usual, with a few beers around the *Stammtisch* in Metzer Eck, seeing old faces, picking up on local gossip as much as anything else. But Gorbachev was becoming gossip. 'What do you think of him?' Alex asked me. I shrugged. Mrs Thatcher might have decided she could do business with him, but he wasn't going to affect life in Britain. 'I think he's genuinely different, but how different, I don't know,' I replied. There was a general nodding around the table, and Alex lifted his glass and proposed one of his favourite old toasts, which roughly translated ran: 'Who else can get so much pleasure from drink, than those of us who fear the Russian clink!' And we lifted our glasses and drank. To the ethics of survival in a world that could never change.

We were wrong. In just about every imaginable way. For a start back in Fleet Street, which like post-war Poland had been literally lifted up and moved, in this case East: to Wapping and Docklands, there was also a whiff of counter-revolution in the air. The Telegraph Group's chief executive Andrew Knight had for one of those reasons that remain forever obscure to those most affected by them – almost certainly as the result of an accountant-inspired 'cost-saving rationalisation' – announced that from now on the *Sunday Telegraph* and the *Daily Telegraph* would be run as a single seven-day operation. This is one of those accountants-versus-journalists conflicts that keeps on recurring over the years: it has the obvious bean-counting merit of needing, in theory, just one set of executives: one home news editor, one foreign editor, one features editor, one picture editor and so on. But it totally misses the essential point about British Sunday Journalism which is that the 'Sundays' had a different agenda, were more geared to scoop-breaking, to literary writing and in-depth analysis than the papers that appeared every day. The 'Sunday Papers', as the format-leading *The Sunday Times* never ceased to remind us, were a concept all of their own. This has changed to some extent with the development of the 'Saturdays' as a Sunday-paper-challenging 'weekend package', but in the eighties the old differentiation still held true.

The *Sunday Telegraph* in particular had, under Worsthorne and the 'crazy gang' evolved from a drab, dull old Tory seventh day seat-warmer into an eccentric, vivacious and often controversial newspaper with its own identity. Knight's bean-counter-inspired announcement sounded to those of us who heard it very much like a death knell. Several of us began to look elsewhere. My fellow foreign reporter David Blundy had been offered a job on the new *Sunday Correspondent*, a start-up that flew directly in the face of the *Telegraph*'s new seven-day concept. He had been unsure about moving to a new paper with an uncertain future. Now he took it.*

In the meantime I had also received a phone call from an old Reuters chum, John Witherow, the one who had in his interview for the job cited 'ratlike cunning' as the key attribute for a journalist. He had since moved to *The Times* and then *The Sunday Times*, where he was now deputy foreign editor. I knew there was no danger of a seven-day operation being introduced there: *The Sunday Times* had originally not even had the same owners as *The Times* (bizarrely it had been founded by the Telegraph Group but subsequently sold on). Both were now owned by Rupert Murdoch, but I was well aware that *The Sunday Times* was a major brand in its own right (that advert '*The Sunday Times* is the Sunday papers' was simply an expression of how most of the middle classes thought) and highly profitable, which its 'sister paper' was not.

John suggested I have lunch with him and his then boss (John has since gone on to become *The Sunday Times*'s most successful editor)

---

* Sadly the 'Corrie' did not last long, but even more sadly it outlived David. A week after the Berlin Wall came down he was in El Salvador covering the guerrilla conflict, cursing himself and the world because he was not in Berlin, when he was hit by a ricochet sniper bullet and died on the operating table.

Bob Tyrer, the foreign editor, in a restaurant off Stamford Street near Waterloo. They made me an offer I couldn't refuse, that I should come and do for them what I had done for the Sunday 'Tel'. If the 'crazy gang' had not been disintegrating I might have hesitated, but *The Sunday Times* was the market leader, the 'big beast' of British journalism. Bob said, 'Come on board. You'll be in the right place at the right time.'

He wasn't wrong.

9

The Unhappy Birthday Party

While I was sitting in a restaurant in Stamford Street trying to make a decision about my future, there were men and women across Eastern Europe making far more important ones about theirs. This was particularly true in Poland, where martial law had been lifted and Solidarity's leaders released from jail, but widespread popular discontent still smouldered. The communist government was increasingly frustrated that social and economic conditions continued to decline, fuelled by runaway inflation, while popular resentment at the imposition of martial law – lifted in 1983 – and the continued ban on the free trade union lingered. It was as if the population had stubbornly decided to let the country go to the dogs rather than obey a government most of them detested. By late 1988 the interior minister had begun putting out clandestine feelers to Lech Walesa to see if the old shipyard militant might be willing to come on board and bring some of his big hitters with him.

The communists' real hope was that by giving token jobs in government to some of the old rebels they could bring them on board and create an illusion of greater democracy. Formal discussions, known as the Round Table Talks had begun in February 1989 and continued until April, by which time the communists would have discovered that what the old rebels wanted was not an illusion, but the real thing. Or at least as close an approximation as anyone thought possible. The compromise that was finally hammered out legalised Solidarity again and allowed for free elections to the Sejm (parliament), although initially at least to just one third of the seats. There would also be a new upper house of parliament, the senate, with no restrictions on candidates for election, and a new post of president. The presidency was the clever bit. Solidarity was satisfied because having an elected executive president would end the tradition that the country was effectively ruled by the general secretary of the Communist Party. The communists were satisfied because it was agreed that in the first instance at least, the only candidate on the ballot paper would be the general secretary of the Communist Party.

But nothing went quite as planned. When the elections were held on June 4th, Solidarity won every single seat up for election to the Sejm and nearly all the seats in the new upper house. To rub in the lesson, when all the members of parliament voted to elect the president, Jaruzelski, despite being the only candidate, won by only a single vote, helped by a few Solidarity members who felt obliged to honour the Round Table agreement. The rest of the summer would be spent in trying to settle the composition of a new government which would be led for the first time since 1945 by a non-communist.

Almost simultaneously things were moving equally fast in Hungary where 'goulash communism' had been taking the hard edges off the system for years. The old hardliner Janos Kadar had been replaced as Communist Party leader by the more reform-minded Imre Poszgay. As in Poland, trade unions had been legalised, while the ghosts of the bloody anti-Soviet uprising of 1956 had literally been buried – the body of Imre Nagy, executed in 1958, was removed from an obscure corner of the city cemetery and given a formal burial which attracted a crowd of 100,000.

There had also been a steady rapprochement with neutral Austria with which it had for so long prior to 1918 been united. On June 27th, barely three weeks after the elections in Poland turned old assumptions about the settled order in Eastern Europe on their head, the foreign ministers of the two neighbouring little countries together took the cutters to a section of barbed wire on the border. It was the first serious crack in the Iron Curtain. From now on, the Hungarians had declared they would no longer maintain a manned surveillance network along the frontier. It was a signal of how far things had already moved in Budapest that the Communist Party no longer feared its citizens would flee en masse. But then Hungarians did not have a wealthy big brother who spoke the same language waiting to embrace them.

On August 19th, at the instigation of several of the smaller new political parties being set up, and Otto von Habsburg, the then already septuagenarian son of the last Austro-Hungarian emperor, a 'pan-European picnic' was organised on the frontier between the two countries near the town of Sopron. The event was eventually given the blessing even of the communists. Although the frontier could theoretically be crossed only with valid passports at recognised border points, the rules were suspended for the day. The intention was for a joint Austrian and Hungarian celebration of the new warmth in their relationship with speeches by invited dignitaries, including Habsburg, talking warmly about a new vision of Europe's future.

But one group had a vision of Europe's present, and saw it in the open frontier: several hundred East Germans who had been on holiday in Hungary. Even as the first invited Austrian guests – local dignitaries, journalists and college students – were crossing the border, a large group of East Germans appeared in the background, walking determinedly towards the frontier. They only stopped walking when they got within metres of it; they started running instead. Within minutes several hundred of them were on Austrian soil, outside the Warsaw Pact, and there was no way – particularly in the current climate – that the Hungarians were going to bring them back. Or, as it turned out, stop any more. Although in theory they were obliged to check the passports of any non-Hungarian or non-Austrian crossing the border, it simply became impracticable for them to do so. As the day progressed more and more East Germans turned up, some singly, some in families, some in larger groups. The Hungarians, busy with their pre-arranged event, found the East Germans simply pushing past them. By the end of the day the little wine-growing village of St Margarethen on the Austrian side of the frontier was swamped by fellow German-speakers with the long unheard accents of Saxony and Brandenburg.

The quick-thinking mayor organised accommodation and phoned the West German Embassy in Vienna, and within hours the West German Embassy in Budapest had sent passports by bus for the new citizens. The Berlin Wall was still standing and according to Erich Honecker, would 'stand for a hundred years', but all of a sudden the rusty Iron Curtain had started to crack. By September any semblance of communist solidarity disappeared when the Hungarians simply announced that as far as they were concerned, the border to Austria was open to anyone who cared to cross. East Germans did so in their thousands. Honecker put pressure on Prague to prevent East Germans crossing into Hungary and then, as the West German Embassy there filled to overflowing with would-be refugees, he closed the border to Czechoslovakia. East Germany was now truly the world's largest prison camp for its own citizens. But it was too much, much too late. West German estimates were that nearly 40,000 inhabitants of the GDR had opted for a one-way ticket to the West. And those that were left could only fume at their rulers.

The hectic pace of events during that summer had taken its toll on foreign correspondents too. Over the course of four months I spent only the occasional weekend with my wife and young family, as I flitted from one Eastern European country to another. Events on the other side of the world weighed heavily on my mind. After the bloody crackdown on dissident protesters in Beijing's Tiananmen Square, how long could it be before the Soviet Army did what it had done every previous time – East Berlin 1953, Budapest 1956, Prague 1968 and surely Warsaw 1981 had the Poles not jumped in first and done it for them? Except instead of the old men in the Forbidden Palace, we had the new man in the Kremlin. But was that really cause enough for hope? And would the knives come out in the politburo first?

June saw me in Warsaw and Moscow, then on Gorbachev's tail for his tour of West Germany – where he was treated like a film star rather than the leader of a supposedly hostile nation. In July I was back in Warsaw for the aftermath of the elections, then in Yugoslavia where an upstart politician called Slobodan Milosevic was threatening the country's fragile racial mix by inciting hatred of the majority Albanians in the Serb province of Kosovo. Then back to Poland, to Warsaw and Gdansk, and on to Hungary with US President George Bush (the first) promising US dollars in return for reform that would undermine communism terminally, in the setting of Budapest's Karl Marx University.

In a summer that was an endless succession of filing deadlines, airport departure lounges and improbable events on the ground, I had frequent reason to bless a minor Western revolution: in computers. Instead of a portable typewriter – which were never that portable – or scribbled longhand notes that had then to be read to copytakers back in London, which could lead to the sort of error that once saw the Warsaw Pact become the Walsall Pact – there was the Tandy 200. A clunky but functional 'portable computer' that was effectively little more than an electronic typewriter with an LCD black-on-green display, the Tandy was the journalist's lifesaver. It had a full-sized QWERTY keyboard and was powered by four AA batteries, the sort you could buy just about anywhere in the world, even behind the Iron Curtain. There was also the benefit of being able to send your copy directly into the newspaper's own computer systems.

The miracle of written words transformed into electronic signals and transmitted over the ether is so common now that it seems antique to remember that just twenty years ago, the most successful way to do it was to affix two 'crocodile clips' from the Tandy's output directly to telephone wires. This occasioned many a travelling correspondent being banned from the world's top hotels after being found taking a hammer to gain access to the telephone sockets in his (or her) room. The less destructive way was to attach something known as acoustic couplers – two foam pads with elastic tape and Velcro fasteners – to the telephone handset. This had the advantage that it could even be used from a public call box. But it had the disadvantage that the aural transmission was more liable to corrupt, resulting in garbled text. There was also the fact that to the general public it looked pretty stupid. I vividly remember standing with my finger to my lips in a West Berlin phone box on a wet night while frustrated and angry would-be callers rapped on the glass, wondering why the man inside was not using the phone but instead had a grey box with wires coming from it attached to the receiver clamped in his armpit.

By the beginning of October my trusty Tandy and I had taken up residence in the ancient university city of Leipzig where a liberal nexus of students and the arts community had begun regular marches around the Nikolaikirche, once again the Protestant churches acting as not so much the provocateur of dissent as an alternative focal point for those who dared to differ from the party line. These had graduated into weekly events attracting ever larger numbers, unprecedented outpourings of public dissent, carrying banners with what was for the regime – if only they had recognised it – a message that should have been even more threatening than those conveyed by the people who had voted with their feet: 'We are the people,' they declared, in pointed contrast to the 'People's Police' and other organs of state which had the attribute stuck on them as if the word alone somehow exempted them from democratic scrutiny. And more pertinently still: 'We're staying here.' When they chanted that on the doorsteps of the local Stasi headquarters there were those inside who for the first time began to wonder what it meant for them.

The marches were peaceful but brooding and watched by massed numbers of policemen in uniform and out of it. Afterwards I drove uneasily but deliberately past Soviet bases on the outskirts of the city, a weather eye watching – while pretending not to – for any signs of imminent mobilisation. If the tanks rolled, surely they would start here. But the tanks stayed where they were.

By the end of September things had gone so far that I wrote a double-page spread for *The Sunday Times* which now seems remarkably prophetic, but which then, I freely admit even I thought, was literally pushing the boundaries of the possible. Headed, 'One People. One Germany?' I declared: 'The scenario for reunification is complicated but not unimaginable.' My scenario was not followed to the letter, but then I had committed the mistake of assuming politics and logic would fuel the progress of history, instead of more potent human factors: emotion and accident.

It was an unnaturally balmy evening when I drove my rented BMW round the familiar corner from Schönhauser Allee into Metzer Strasse, parked and strolled over to the pub, only to see Bärbel leaning out of the window as if it were a summer's night. The weather was mild, but hardly warm. She looked flushed. I waved up and asked it there was something the matter. She dabbed at her eye and tried to answer but her voice was all choked up and she just shook her head.

Inside, Horst, who had long since finished his military service, was working behind the bar with his young wife Sylvia. He dried his hands, wet from wiping tables, shook mine and gave a cautionary glance around the pub. He motioned to Sylvia to pour me a beer as he took me to one side and said the words which explained everything: 'Kerstin's done a runner, gone West.' As I swallowed the bombshell, he dropped another: 'Mother's upstairs. She's a bit upset, in a mixed-up sort of way. We've just seen them on television.'

Bärbel's first indication that her eldest daughter was about to vanish from her life had come on Tuesday. The news was just beginning to sink in that East Germany's communist rulers had closed the border to Czechoslovakia. Kerstin called her mother and said in meaningful tones that she and her common-law husband, Andreas, had decided they would, after all, take that holiday in Poland. She would leave the keys to the flat with her father-in-law. And then the fateful phrase: 'He'll know what to do with the furniture.'

The exodus of young East Germans to the West had touched the lives of everyone who remained, leaving empty spaces at dinner tables and silent toasts to absent friends in corner bars. I still found it a shock to experience it first-hand. I had seen Kerstin grow from a chubby schoolgirl to a sophisticated woman of twenty-two who took a coquettish pride in her resemblance to the young Shirley MacLaine. She had everything to stay for. Kerstin had begun living with Andreas, eight years older and divorced, the previous year. She worked as a waitress in a bowling alley while Andreas was manager of a state-run bar in the relatively pleasant East Berlin suburb of Köpenick. They got a flat near his work and friends and family showered gifts on them, as if they had got married. By East German standards, they had everything: a colour television, new furniture, crystal glassware and even – this was one advantage of Andreas's age – straight from the production works at Eisenach, the Wartburg car that he had applied to buy thirteen years earlier. It had cost 33,000 Marks, a small fortune. But it seemed this relative affluence had only made them envy all the more the consumerist paradise of the West, suddenly – so unexpectedly – so near. And yet maybe about to become once again as far away as ever.

On Tuesday afternoon they packed only as many clothes as they could reasonably be expected to need for a two-week holiday and headed out on the last sure route to the West: East. They were taking the risk of a lifetime, saying farewell to family and friends in the full expectation that they might never see them again. The Poles had made it clear that East Germans were being allowed to leave the country for the West only if they had entered legally in the first place. And that was not as easy as people in the West assumed. Citizens of the countries behind the Iron Curtain needed not just passports but visas even to visit another communist state. And visas required an invitation. By chance Andreas and Kerstin had a Polish friend who had invited them months ago to visit for a holiday, but they had had a busy summer and Andreas's visa had expired. He was entitled in theory to an automatic extension, but it had required a visit to a police station, at tense experience in the current climate. But it had been granted.

I went upstairs to the flat and found Bärbel sprawled back on the sofa next to Alex, her eyes brimming. She had feared they would be found out or turned back at the border on some technicality. She had feared even more that they would not be, and then who knew when or if she would ever see them again? And then that evening, less than an hour before I had turned up as she and Alex had sat around their little black-and-white television watching the news on the West German channel ARD, they suddenly caught sight of Kerstin and Andreas grinning happily in the crowd in the grounds of the West German Embassy. Bärbel had burst into tears immediately.

Then as we sat there, still trying to take in what was happening, and what it all meant, the phone rang. It was Andreas, calling from Warsaw. He couldn't talk long – international phone lines were hard to get hold of – just to say they were registered at the embassy and had been given bed and breakfast privately until their fate was decided. But the main thing was they had been given assurances that they would not be sent back.

Bärbel fell back onto the sofa and lit up a cigarette in relief, tears welling again in her eyes. Alex had a quick word before putting the phone down and then turned to us with an expression of angry exasperation on his face: 'You won't believe it? That thickhead has sold the car to a Polish policeman. What did he get for it? A lousy one hundred American dollars. It won't be enough to buy him breakfast in West Berlin!' But he was grinning broadly. Seconds later the phone rang again. It was Renate calling from West Berlin; she had seen the TV, too, and thought she recognised Kerstin. 'It's wonderful, isn't it? But I know, awful for you. I must go shopping to cook them a big meal when they get here. They can stay with me as long as they like.' It was one of those conversations that highlighted the surreal situation: Renate lived barely three kilometres away as the crow flies. But in Berlin crows had a freedom Bärbel couldn't imagine.

'But Renate, they're still in Warsaw. We don't know how long it will be before they're allowed out.' Barely a few weeks earlier, people had been careful what they said on the phone to the West, worried about who was listening. Now it didn't seem to matter any more. In fact, it was barely twenty-four hours before Andreas and Kerstin were on their way west.

The previous week an agreement had been reached between the East and West German governments which must have had Erich Honecker gritting his teeth as he signed it, to transport west several thousand East Germans crammed into the embassy in Prague in increasingly intolerable conditions. It was a deal substantially brokered by Bonn's foreign minister Hans-Dietrich Genscher (who had been born in the East but fled West in 1952). The calendar helped: Honecker wanted the whole embarrassing episode closed before October 7th, when he would be hosting his fellow Warsaw Pact leaders, including Gorbachev, for a giant jamboree to mark East Germany's fortieth birthday. The East German official media described it as a humanitarian gesture towards deluded ungrateful wretches who were no longer worthy of their citizenship. The refugees would be 'expelled' from East Germany. It turned into a fiasco that should have been an omen for what would happen at the upcoming 'birthday party'.

The asylum seekers – or 'illegal occupiers' in East German government parlance – were to board East German trains, a significant concession to East Berlin's nominal sovereignty (they could have simply travelled West across the Czech-West German frontier), and travel across East German territory. This allowed Honecker to claim that rather than his citizens fleeing, he was expelling them. A gesture that was as pathetic as it was legalistic, and one that also backfired. Spectacularly.

In Dresden, the main East German city on the route the trains had to take, thousands of people stormed the tracks and the station, hoping to 'hitch' a lift. Police had to use dogs and water cannon to disperse them, under a hail of cobblestones and railway ballast. The trains were held in Prague and it was the dead of night before they finally rumbled through a Dresden station ringed off by armed police.

Now, for what Honecker hoped would be the end of the embarrassment – and to avoid a repetition of the chaos caused by the trains from Prague – the stations would be evacuated and sealed off well before the trains from Warsaw to the West passed through. Ironically the route they had to take skirted Berlin itself before reaching the border crossing point at Helmstedt, some ninety miles west of West Berlin. Even at a moment like this the old 'Berlin equation' still came into play: the deal had been done with West Germany, and West Berlin was not legally part of West Germany. The train was sealed and didn't stop from the moment it crossed the Polish border until it reached West German soil.

We all sat late into the night at the *Stammtisch* over beer, the last of the Hungarian wine and token Czech apricot schnapps, drinking the health of the fraternal republics who had turned out to be brothers after all. Between the tears, they hoped against hope and joked. 'Why is the socialist hell better than the capitalist hell? Because they keep running out of boiling oil and hot coals.' The next night Alex and Bärbel slept fitfully, aware that somewhere out there in the dark, Kerstin and Andreas were passing through a darkened, police-ringed Köpenick station, just a few hundred yards from the home they had so recently abandoned.

I promised to see Kerstin next time I was in West Berlin. 'Give her my love and tell her to send a photo.' Bärbel had no idea when she would see her daughter again. Least of all did she – or any of us – imagine it would be in a mere couple of weeks, in circumstances none of us – and nobody anywhere else in Washington, Bonn, London or even Moscow imagined.

Yet the signs were there for all to see. Gorbachev's urbane, intelligent and highly fluent chief spokesman Gennady Gerasimov appeared on the US talk show *Good Morning America* – in itself something not long before totally unimaginable. Faced with the practical fait accompli of a new order in Eastern Europe, he was asked about the future of the Brezhnev Doctrine, which had laid down that the satellite states did what Moscow told them. With a smile he replied: 'What we have now is the Sinatra Doctrine. He has a song: "I Did it My Way". The world gasped.

Barely four days later the weather had turned and I was stomping my feet to keep out the cold as I stood opposite the tribune erected on Unter den Linden waiting for the display of military might to mark the East German state's fortieth birthday. From my position on the steps of the State Opera I had a good view of the stony-faced troopers at the old Prussian royal guard-house – since 1945 renamed as the Monument to the Victims of Fascism and Militarism – performing their military ballet, stamping and pirouetting in their jackboots. The troops of the honour guard of the National People's Army paraded as usual in their ceremonial uniforms of grey with white braid, their jodhpur-clad legs kicking high in the rigid march invented by the Prussian General Yorck to strengthen soldiers' legs. In German it is called the Yorckmarsch after him; everywhere else it is known as the goose step. Tongues of orange flame licked into the night air, as they carried their torches high, as deliberately blind as ever to their parody of the immense spectacles organised by Hitler against this same backdrop of neoclassical Prussian palaces.

After them came the organised display of the FDJ, the Free German Youth, regiments of young people dragooned into this political version of Boy Scouts or Girl Guides and officially referred to as the 'Vanguard of the party'. They wore their uniform blue shirts over black jumpers to keep warm and waved their own, smaller, firebrands with the jovial enthusiasm of any group of provincial adolescents on a night out in the capital, even if it had been organised by their elders. Most had been brought in buses from Cottbus or Rostock, bleak industrial cities whose inhabitants' view of the world was even then still shaped by an awareness of being on the edge of communism rather than in the middle of Europe. Yet the authorities were tense. Almost every East German in the preceding months had seen a brother or sister, friend or neighbour leave forever. In Leipzig particularly, there had been problems; in the classrooms, indoctrination had been replaced by argument; some of those chosen to join the great birthday parade refused. In Berlin, Alex and Bärbel told their daughter Alexandra, fifteen, not to go even though she was a member of the FDJ. Their prohibition was issued more out of parental care than politics. They knew the organs of repression that had been ever-present throughout their adult lives were flexing their muscles, waiting for the slightest sign of domestic dissent on this of all evenings. Given the chance, they intended to crush it once and for all.

While Honecker feted his brother communists with a formal dinner on a scale none of their populations could ever enjoy, on the streets of East Berlin there were at first only flickering signs of resentment. Literally flickering: candles impaled on railings outside an old redbrick Lutheran church in Prenzlauer Berg, just a few streets from Metzer Eck. The Swords to Ploughshares campaign had faded from visibility but the loose bond between the church and disaffected youth had remained. The Gethsemane Church had opened its doors as a venue for peaceful demonstrations of solidarity for those imprisoned after the weekly marches in Leipzig.

The crowd inside was mostly the usual ragtag band of East Berlin's disenchanted young people, the ones who had outgrown or deliberately rejected the conformity of the FDJ. Their uniforms were spiky punk hairdos and denims bought with saved-up D-Marks at the hard currency shops. Their politics were those of disaffection, not revolution. Many of them sat on the floor, hand-rolling cigarettes, dozens hung leaning over the upstairs balconies. This was a congregation born out of the church's support for the dissident 'peaceniks'. But among them there were a growing number of more respectable 'middle class' kids into whose lives the unrest of the summer had already blown a chill wind.

One by one eighteen- and nineteen-year-olds came up to the pulpit to give a personal 'testimony'. One young girl with long dark hair looked teary-eyed at the crowd and said simply, 'Pray for my boyfriend, in jail since July.' After each testimony the church choir sang a brief, 'Kyrie Eleison': 'Lord have mercy.' They were not expecting much mercy from the state. That much was made clear by the attitude of the watchers outside, tough men in plain clothes that were in themselves as good as a uniform: hooded anoraks and dark, neatly-pressed trousers.

To me, of course, it was all good 'colour'. I made notes on the folded sheets of A4 paper that too often took the place of a proper notebook. In my head I had already composed the guts of my story for the next day's paper: it was to be a neat counterpoint to the pompous official celebration set against these scenes of quiet angry repression rounded off with the curious codicil that these days it was the presence of a Soviet leader that gave a glimmer of hope to Germans on the wrong side of the Berlin Wall. As it was a Saturday, time was running out fast for a Sunday newspaper man; I would have to get it across to the foreign desk by four p.m. at the latest to make the paper which would be running off the printing presses by six thirty p.m. I was hoping to get the lead story position on one of the foreign pages. If I was lucky, I might even get a line or two on the front, cross-referring to the inside piece, but with a big row brewing about MPs not having to pay the controversial poll tax on their second homes, and interest rates rising to fifteen per cent threatening to put the British economy into recession, frankly I doubted it.

All I needed for the finishing touches was to dash down to the official press centre to catch a briefing by Gorbachev's official spokesman Gennady Gerasimov. On the way, however, my hired car broke down. For no obvious reason, it just lost power. Whether it was a terminal transmission problem or maybe – not impossibly – I just ran out of petrol I shall never know. Right there and then, it didn't matter. The story came first. I coasted to the side of the road, got out and made it the rest of the way on foot. Gerasimov's briefing made little difference to the story I bashed out on my faithful Tandy 200, and sent down the line to London.

On the way back to retrieve my car I noticed several hundred young East Berliners shouting the by now familiar 'Gor-by, Gor-by' outside the Palace of the Republic where the Warsaw Pact leaders were saying their goodbyes. To all extents and purposes they were still leaders of one of the world's most powerful military and political alliances, celebrating the anniversary of one of their most important keystone members. It was unimaginable that in a year's time that keystone would be gone, the German Democratic Republic would no longer exist, the pact itself would be in its death throes, the Soviet Union on the verge of disintegration, and one of them, Nicolae Ceausescu, long dead, overthrown and executed by his own people just ten weeks after that October meeting.

It was unimaginable to me too. At that precise moment I was more concerned about the whereabouts of my rented Beamer. It was gone. There, at the bottom of Prenzlauer Allee, where I had left it, illegally parked but not dangerously so, by the side of the kerb on a main road, there was a glaring absence of BMW. I was dismayed but not wholly surprised. There was the possibility, of course, that it had been stolen. A new BMW would have been worth a large fortune in anybody's money in East Germany. But probably more money than possessed by anyone who didn't already have access to the West and therefore the possibility of buying one over there cheaper. Also crime rates in the GDR were low – in countries with a large number of political prisoners, there are often fewer 'ordinary' offenders – and it would have been nigh-on impossible for even most inspired crooks to get hold of a replacement key.

The more likely – even obvious – answer was that it had been towed away by the police. Particularly given the security paranoia surrounding the 'birthday party'. I decided to go and ask them. The nearest police station was Berlin's most famous – or infamous – *Polizeirevier Berlin Mitte*. Infamous, because it had once been the headquarters of the Gestapo. Not the actual building of course. Not much around there had survived the war intact. But it was the same site. And the name still had resonance. The East German 'People's Police' hadn't gone out of their way to dent that. Not least in the less than welcoming presence the entrance offered to the public: a closed and apparently locked door of ribbed steel.

I had been banging on it for several minutes before a buzzer sounded, it opened and an unseen voice ordered me in to an even less welcoming sight: a corridor sealed off with an iron-barred gate. The token human presence was a harassed and angry-looking policemen staring at me from behind a grille to the left. 'What do you want? How dare you make a noise here.' I explained that my car was missing and that I feared it had been towed away and that coming to report it to the police didn't seem that unreasonable. Which just went to show how much of everyday life in the 'people's republic' I had forgotten. He glared at me as if I was an idiot – and in retrospect he might have had a point – said bluntly that no, he had not the faintest idea – or interest – where my car might be. My very presence there, he indicated clearly, after demanding and inspecting my identity papers, was precisely the sort of 'provocation' to be expected from the malicious Western press, 'especially under the circumstances'.

I was about to ask him which particular circumstances he had in mind, when all of a sudden I came face to face with them: marching up in double file to the other side of the iron-barred gate in front of me was a small army of baton-wielding *Bereitschaftspolizei*, the People's Police paramilitary wing about to indulge in some less than popular policing. I took my cue and retreated through the steel door just as the iron-barred gate opened and they followed me.

Out on the wide pavements the crowds shouting 'Gor-by, Gor-by' were spilling into the centre of the road. The *Bereitschaftspolizei* decided to help them on their way, spreading into broad lines in an attempt to push them across the road and coral them, a technique known as *einkesseln*, (in a *Kessel* is how Germans described the situation of their trapped army at Stalingrad). Over-literally translated into English as 'kettling' it has since been adopted over-enthusiastically by London's Metropolitan Police, even if they don't boast about where they got the idea.

It didn't work. For one thing the crowd was too large and too fluid, this was not an organised demonstration, just a huge bunch of people who had coalesced rather than gathered. The few hundred who had been milling around earlier had now swollen to several thousand and more were joining them by the minute. The police's kettling attempt was not helped by the vindictive and highly aggressive policy of their plainclothes cousins: snatch squads of young men in imitation leather coats with scarves around their mouths – Stasi shock troops – had begun dashing into the crowd to pick up anyone they suspected might be a 'ringleader'. By now I had become part of the crowd, close enough to one Stasi snatch to see a teenage girl throw herself at the gang trying to drag her boyfriend away.

Within seconds one of them had produced an evil-looking sprung steel baton and used it whip-like to cut her legs from beneath her.

As the police piled forwards, the crowd pulled back, onto the tram lines now, as suddenly a familiar shrill bell split the night: a tram was coming. For a few tense moments both police and protesters edged back as the tram forced its way through the melee. Then with the tram still moving, the police surged forward again. The tram stopped dead. One young girl, little more than a child, was all of a sudden lifted up and passed through an open tram window to the relative safety inside. The tram driver rang his bell again and as the crowd in his path parted he accelerated away. By now we were right across the road from Alexanderplatz, at the foot of the long broad streets that led uphill to Prenzlauer Berg. And still the crowd kept somehow growing. I estimated there were maybe as many as 10,000 East Berliners now on the streets confronting their 'own' police. The last time such a thing had happened had been during a short-lived workers' strike in June 1953, following the death of Stalin. They had been crushed by Soviet tanks. Now once again on this cold autumn night a fresh breath of springtime seemed too much to hope for. The tanks were still not far away. East Berlin was ringed by Soviet bases.

As the crowds flowed up the hill, the police followed. From time to time the Stasi snatch squads still made their rapid incursions. But they were less confident now. Dilapidated Prenzlauer Berg was home ground for most of the crowd. They melted into the ill-lit side streets and re-emerged on main streets a block further on. The police formed lines across the streets to follow us, but a *Kessel* was harder to create in a network of back streets with the courtyards and stairwells of the six-storey 'rental barracks' to retreat into. The kettle leaked. In one interlude of pure farce, the police charged from both ends of a street, but the demonstrators disappeared into doorways to scuttle through backyards and reappear, hooting with laughter behind the two lines of scowling People's Police left facing each other with raised truncheons.

It was like a scene from *Les Misérables*: a red banner was snatched from a lamp post and waved against the police: '*We* are the people,' they chanted. And then, to rub it in they sang – we sang – that great revolutionary hymn, the 'Internationale', the communist anthem flung in the communists' faces. *We* sang? What about the 'Prime Directive', I hear you say! To hell with the 'Prime Directive', I was working for a paper now, not a neutral news agency. Making a difference was part of the plot. Anyhow, this was no 'strange new world', this was home, or as good as. This was my struggle too. *Wir sind das Volk*, we chanted. We are the people. And I meant it as much as any of them.

As we swarmed down the side streets, like an army of ants amidst a canyon of tenement buildings, illuminated only by lights turned on in upper-floor windows, there was a sudden outbreak of laughter, cheering and police confusion. From the sixth-floor flats old ladies had opened their windows and were dropping precious eggs onto the heads of the police. As ever I cursed myself for not having a proper notebook and scrawled semi-legible notes on the only piece of paper I could find (which in stark contrast to the popular revolution going on around me, turned out to be an old American Express statement).

As the ebb and flow of people and police moved deeper into the heart of Prenzlauer Berg I let myself slip into a doorway for a moment, out of the main body of protesters. Metzer Eck was only a street away. It was not that I desperately needed a beer – although I did – it was that I desperately needed that implement that all those years ago Terry Williams had advised me to tell the interviewers at Reuters would be the first thing on my mind in a crisis: a telephone. It was nearly seven p.m., just six p.m. in London, and already too late for the first edition of *The Sunday Times*, but the colour I had gleaned from the streets would freshen up the story I had already filed. Especially the eggs. They would love the eggs. I was still pushing for a place on the front page. And the way things were going, it was looking more likely every moment. If only I'd known.

In Metzer Eck, however, it was business as normal. Horst was behind the bar and the *Stammtisch* was full of the usual gang: Manne, Busch and Alex deep as ever in joke-swapping political repartee. They had heard the noise outside but looked out too late. The revolution was passing them by. Like many others that night, they assumed it was a flash in the pan, a youthful exuberance that would have vanished by the morning. They were surprised to hear that the marchers were still assembled in a body only a few streets away. Alex handed me the phone, in itself a sign of how things were changing: a few years earlier I would not have risked compromising him by filing a report to a British newspaper over an East German citizen's phone line. But we both knew that right now the Stasi had other priorities. Squinting at my scribbled notes I gabbled the additions to my story to the deputy foreign editor in London. I was right about the eggs. He loved them.

Then I downed the beer Horst had pushed into my hand and said I would be back soon. I thought I would be. Surely it was all over bar the shouting, and even I thought there would not be much more of that. I knew where I would catch up with whatever was left of the protest crowd: the Gethsemane Church. When I got there I found the momentum had stalled. The crowds were still in their thousands, not so much running scared as exhilarated at their moment of glory, but here, for the first time, they wavered. Some wanted to continue, but did not know where to go. The church offered a prime opportunity for someone to address the crowds; they called for speakers, but nobody came forward. In the streets they had chanted 'New Forum', the most broadly based of the new, still illegal, embryonic political groupings, but no spokesman appeared. A figure with a sense of occasion and minimal rhetorical ability could have moulded them to his whim, sent them where he wanted, turned them into a mob and directed them to the Central Committee buildings, to the Brandenburg Gate where the crowds from the West would gather on that fateful night just a few weeks distant yet still totally unimaginable, where they would have forced themselves before the television cameras and into the living rooms of the world. But the cameramen were still blindly intent on the official 'birthday party' and oblivious to the fact that the celebration was fast becoming the prelude to a wake.

But the one thing on everyone's mind was that their own East German government had been the first to endorse the massacre in Tiananmen Square. A few wandered into the church to be told by Berlin bishop Gottfried Forck that it was time to go home. His words were met with sour grumbles that turning the other cheek invited crucifixion. But nobody had a better idea. Except of course, the police. Their pride had been dented. They wanted revenge. An orderly dispersal would have implied those who had dared confront them had got away with it. And what would that lead to? Next thing you knew they'd be demanding the right to peaceful protest. Or free speech! They weren't having it.

They went for the *Kessel* again, driving the crowds away from the church – too much like a safe refuge – towards the relatively open space of broad Schönhauser Allee. It was only when we got to the entrance to the S-Bahn station, that a brave group of young people sat on the ground, refusing to move and began to chant '*Volkspolizei, steh dem Volke bei*' (People's Police, stand by the people). But by now the People's Police weren't standing by anyone; they had had enough of standing by: it was time to get their toys out. Water cannon drew up and police with attack dogs emerged from vans. The demonstrators got the message, and got up and ran, into a side street. On the right were high fences and railway tracks, on the left tenement blocks. Everyone knew that if the police kept pushing them, in the end they would have their backs against the Wall. Literally. We were just 300 metres from the 'state border'. For anyone in that crowd the idea of climbing it was synonymous with instant death.

Then, from the other end of the street, a line of truncheon-wielding police began to advance, the classic sandwich manoeuvre: closing the 'kettle'. Behind them we could see empty military trucks with bars on the windows. We had a grim suspicion of what they might be for. Three young women, aged eighteen to twenty, went up to the grey line of young men their own age and pleaded: 'What are you doing this for? We're all in this shit together.' And then the empty trucks began to back into the street, rear doors gaping like jaws, the advancing line of police ready to feed them. The three young women were the first victims, snatched by plainclothes Stasi thugs before they could get back to the safety of the masses. Not that it mattered. Within minutes a blanket operation had seized almost everyone in the street, myself included. '*Warte mal!*' ('Hang on a minute!') I shouted, about to brandish my press card. But I shouted it in a broad Berlin accent, so they bunged me in with the rest and slammed the doors.

There were forty of us with seats for thirty, caged in like chickens behind wire. Two armed police beyond the wire guarded the doors. The engine growled into life and bumped off over the cobblestones. We had no idea where we were heading, but no one was in a hurry to get there. A couple in a car at traffic lights looked aghast at a truckload of incarcerated fellow citizens. The boy next to me in the truck held up his fingers to the barred window in a victory sign. The woman in the Lada behind us bit her lip, looked at her husband and then made the same sign back. The police looked away, embarrassed.

Rattling through the night in a prison van, under armed guard with sirens screaming in the distance, we could have been forgiven for being gripped with despair. But Berliners are a tough lot. Instead there was Berliner Schnauze (literally 'Berlin snout' but a lot more easily understood if you think of it as 'Cockney lip'; the two have a lot in common). Martha, a fifty-year-old bar landlady, nagged the two young policemen: 'A fine way to behave, this is. I suppose you'd do the same to your own mothers. You need your rear ends spanked.' 'I'll tell you one thing, I think I'll take the day off work tomorrow.' 'Don't you worry, they'll claim their fortieth anniversary record production figures without you.' 'Oh, we're slowing down – do you think that means the cops have to economise on petrol too.' As the truck passed the district police station, we showed them what we were worth: a rousing chorus of the 'Internationale' again. They had taught them well in school '*Völker, hört die Signale, auf zum letzten Gefecht, die Internationa-a-a-le erkämpft das Menschen-recht*' (the German version was particularly suited to our situation: 'People, hear the call, march on to the final fight, the Internationale will win our human rights).

After twenty minutes we pulled into a brick courtyard and stopped in a line of other trucks. And waited. And waited. It was an hour of suspense laced with working-class black humour: 'I wonder where that boy of mine is,' wondered Martha. 'I bet they've got him too.' We asked the police. They had. He was in the next truck. His disembodied but still sarcastic voice came through the night air: 'Hello Mum, got you too, did they?' We fell apart in nervous laughter. 'Hey mister, let me out,' called a bubble-gum-chewing girl from the back, 'I'm dying to go for a weewee.' 'I can't help that love. You'll have to hold on.' 'It's alright for you, big boy – I've got nothing to squeeze.' And then: 'Oh bollocks, I've just ruined my last pair of tights.'

Then we shunted off again into the dark, still in convoy. The cells were full, one policeman carelessly revealed. This time the laughter stopped when the truck did. The doors opened to reveal a high-walled, floodlit courtyard, ringed by People's Police in jackboots and jodhpurs, a scene from every nightmare about Germany that every German shares. They clasped lethally thin truncheons, the same as I had seen the Stasi man whip across the fallen girl's legs down on Alexanderplatz. Through the chicken wire that caged us inside the lorry, we faced a brightly lit room, like a carwash, with white-tiled ceiling, walls and floor. Around the edge of the floor ran gutters to take away urine and vomit. Young men stood spreadeagled, legs apart, hands high against the wall, quiet, subdued and sick. Anyone foolish enough to complain had his inside leg measured with a truncheon. Not many said anything after that.

The man squeezed next to me in the prison lorry sighed deeply in despair. The infectious collective euphoria that had survived our arrest evaporated into the cold night air that seemed to have swept in across the north German plain, straight from Siberia. This, one of my fellow prisoners recognised, was Marzahn police post, a forbidding fortress amid the drab tower blocks on the eastern edge of East Berlin. 'Out, one by one,' ordered a blond crew-cut officer, and pushed us to a neat bureaucratic desk where identity cards were taken away, the men separated from the women and shoved into the white room to join the miserable line. It looked like the party was over. Big time.

And no time for heroics. When it was my turn to present my identity card to the cold-faced clerk sorting humanity at his folding card table, I handed over my passport and my press card. So where was 'We are the people' now? I could argue that suffering the same fate as my fellow captives would not help them, whereas by getting released and spreading the news of what was happening, I just might. And in any case they would have found the passport when they searched me. But to be honest a far more simple principle had kicked in: the principle of self-preservation. The blond beast behind him snarled and shot bayonet glances at the two policemen who had been our guards. Their dragnet had caught a crab: the last thing anyone wanted here was the presence of a foreign reporter. East Germany wanted to do its dirty washing very much in private.

I was hustled away, out of the glare of the blinding white lights into a welcome darkness, then down a courtyard and into a drab administrative building. It could have been a 1960s school or local government office. The stern-faced sergeant accompanying me pressed a buzzer and the doors unlocked. He showed his pass and led me upstairs. I was apprehensive, but not as much as I would have been had I been standing spreadeagled against a wall in that white-tiled garage. The sergeant left and my interrogators arrived. They didn't look at all as I imagined they would. But then no one who has grown up on a diet of old World War II movies can entirely shake the image of stiff-faced Prussians with clipped accents saying, 'Ve are asking ze questions.'

Predictably there were two of them: the good cop and the bad cop, just like in the movies. They even said they were cops – 'Kripo', *Kriminalpolizei*, the German equivalent of CID – but then secret policemen aren't supposed to give their profession as secret police-men. And these two were Stasi. Nobody else was going to be allowed to grill a Western reporter caught up in a demonstration that challenged a totalitarian state. The 'bad cop' was short, with a dark-haired crew cut, and sneered a lot, particularly at my press card. The 'good cop' had shoulder-length blond hair, a leather bomber jacket and tight blue jeans. He could have been one of the crowd. He almost certainly had been. Neither would give me a name.

They wanted a statement. So I gave them one: a detailed description of my night's adventures from my missing car to the back of the police van, though I saw no need to let them know where I might have stopped off for a swift beer or to use the telephone. The lad in jeans, who was obviously in charge, took it all down, fairly, neatly and allowing me to see it in case I wanted to alter anything. My only suggestions were a few corrections to his grammar. I was feeling cheeky again. They took my documents away. Somewhere in a backroom in Normannenstrasse, somebody was checking through that thick file I would only uncover more than three years later. But I had no need to see it with my own eyes to believe in its existence, no doubt with additions courtesy of Moscow's much larger 'fraternal service', the Stasi's Big Brother. He went over the night's proceedings at least half a dozen times, checking for inconsistencies. At first I didn't know what he expected. Then he made it clear: had I joined in any of these 'anti-socialist protests'. 'Of course not,' I told him and handed out the old line remembered from my Reuters days: my mission was like Captain Kirk's: to boldly go but not to interfere in the native civilisation. It raised a chuckle for half a second. Thanks to the porous airwaves, even in East Germany there were Trekkies. It was a lie, of course. It is not every day that you get the chance to join in a revolution you believe in.

In the end they gave up on the interrogation and took me to a spartan little anteroom of some sort where the sergeant who had brought me in and the 'bad cop' took turns to guard me. Their main task, it seemed, was to stop me looking out of the curtained window into the courtyard below where they were still bringing in and unloading prison vans full of their fellow citizens. The sergeant looked tired. He lived nearby, he said, when I squeezed a few words out of him at last; in one of the tower blocks of Marzahn. He wanted to get home to his wife. He had little taste for the night's work, but blamed the 'rowdies'. Then he went silent, suspecting I was trying to provoke him.

After an hour or two, as the clock hand crept round and the sky edged towards a still distant autumn dawn, the 'hard man' grew more chatty. He was only twenty-nine, he said, a few years younger than me. He had been on duty almost continuously for three weeks. It was the first indication I had had as to how much the exodus, the anniversary and the Gorbachev visit had strained both the manpower of even East Germany's overstaffed police force, and its nerves. Close to, he looked exhausted. 'I have had only a few hours sleep this week,' he admitted. 'My wife has hardly seen me. I had only just got to bed two hours before I was hauled out again for this emergency. What sort of characters are they out there anyway? Hooligans, I'll bet.'

I said they seemed to me to be just ordinary people, decent Berliners who were fed up with their lot and had thought things might be changing enough for them to shout about it on the streets without being locked up and beaten. He looked offended, shocked, suspicious, then just tired again. '*Na ja, gut,* perhaps they are right.' It was a thought he instantly regretted having uttered. He turned on me, the hard man and the soft all at once: 'This is just chitchat, right, between us? I mean, you being a reporter and all? You wouldn't publish this in some West rag just to get me into trouble? If you did, I'd run into you again some time you know.' It was meant as a threat but it sounded desperate; a year later some of the Stasi men who had been sent out that night to mingle with and spy on the demonstrators claimed it had changed their lives. It was easy to be wise after the event. Enough people had had the same experience in 1945.

By six thirty a.m. we were both restless. His denim-clad colleague came back. They were, he said, trying to locate my car. They might have been, for all I know; they never found it. That was left to the hire firm who, although I reported the inconvenience to them, did not get too worried for a couple of weeks, then sent their own man to find it and sent *The Sunday Times* a thumping bill. I was more worried at the time in case the delay had been to allow the Stasi to search my hotel room. What concerned me most was that they might find a carrier bag in which I had left social security papers Alex had asked me to take to Kerstin and Andreas in West Berlin. These papers proved they had made full contributions towards the East German state pension scheme (not that they had any choice). West Germany would honour refugees' contributions made in the East, but, being German, they insisted on seeing the paperwork.

My worry at that precise moment, however, was less about helping them deal with bureaucracy, but that if the Stasi found them they could accuse me – quite rightly – of smuggling documents belonging to the East German state. It was still on my mind as shortly after seven a.m. I was driven by police through streets that were now conspicuously empty, the pale autumn sun reflecting in puddles left from the use of water cannon. I had been given until midday to leave the GDR. We pulled up at the Grand Hotel and my suspicions deepened when the reception said they could not find my key. I asked for the floor manager to open my room, expecting the worst, particularly when I heard hurried grunts and movements inside. I edged open the door not knowing what to expect, but a sudden, unmistakeably female squeal made me suspect it wasn't the Stasi after all.

It wasn't. Poking their heads out from under the bedclothes were an American correspondent, who for obvious reasons shall remain nameless – he is today a senior consultant for an international communications company – and a young British reporter. They had, he explained as he hurried into his trousers under the gaze of my bemused police minder, spotted me being herded into the back of the police truck, and reckoned I wouldn't be needing my bed for the night. Oh, and by the way, she – also necessarily nameless – added by way of excuse: she had rung *The Sunday Times* to tell them I had been arrested. She thought they'd put it on the front page.

They had. Late, of course, so late in fact that it had only made a very final edition which got little further than central London. (I only saw it days later.) But I had got my front page. The 'splash' no less. My story as updated over the phone from Metzer Eck beneath the headline: 'Gorby, Help Us!' Alongside was a full-length picture of a snarling, baton-wielding People's Policeman. To the left: my picture byline, and the brief statement saying '*The Sunday Times* Central Europe correspondent Peter Millar was arrested last night during the demonstrations in East Berlin'. Right now the East Germans were no longer arresting me, they were expelling me: I was given until noon to leave the country (i.e. cross into West Berlin), and was unsure when or if I would be allowed back.

'I called your wife,' Bob, the foreign editor said in his usual laidback laconic manner when I checked in to say I was on my way back. 'She didn't seem too worried. I expect it's the sort of thing that happens to you all the time.'

'Not exactly.'

'Well, hurry back,' he added. 'I've got another story for you. A change of scenery.'

Neither of us, even then, realised the big one was waiting just around the corner.

10

9/11/1989: All Fall Down

'It's a big story, it really is, you should hang on until at least the end of next week.' Italian Photographer Dario Mitidieri was at his most persuasive. We were sitting over sundowners in the bar of the Kalahari Sands Hotel in Windhoek, Namibia.

In a week's time – between November 7th and 11th, 1989 – the former Southwest Africa was to have its first democratic elections, the first area administered by the apartheid regime in Pretoria to concede the vote to the black population. I was there to do a 'curtainraiser': an advance feature to whet the public's appetite. It was Bob's idea of a 'break'. Admittedly it was a bit of a change from Warsaw and Berlin. 'I dunno, Dario,' I said as we nursed our drinks in the tropical heat, 'I have a feeling I should get back to Berlin'. Luckily, Bob agreed. No matter how exotic the Namibian jungles and desert might be, I would have felt seven kinds of idiot if I had still been sitting there on November 9th. It was Dario who ended up kicking himself.

With hindsight it seems improbable in the extreme that barely a week before the Berlin Wall came down, a journalist who had spent years living there, and even covering the remarkable events happening in Eastern Europe over the previous months, had no idea it would happen. But then you have to take into account that nor did the CIA, MI6, nor West Germany's intelligence service the BND* nor even the KGB. Nor was it in the pipedreams of any civil rights campaigner or even in the wildest drunken fantasies of anyone in the pubs and bars of Berlin (East or West). The best anyone hoped for was change: gradual, creeping reform that would make the dictatorship in East Berlin just that tiny bit less dictatorial, more

---

* The Bundesnachrichtendienst (Federal Intelligence Service)

responsive to public opinion, more open to economic reforms that could benefit the population. And then maybe – just maybe – one day, when things had improved, a more liberal visa regime would be introduced that would make movement between the two German states easier, in both directions. To have said that the borders would be open within a week and German unity a done deed within a year would have sounded like rampant insanity.

It was not that there were no signs of progress. There were. Bigger ones than had been expected. The demonstrations that ruined the planned fortieth birthday party had taken their toll on morale within the East German politburo. Barely ten days later, on October 18th, the geriatrics who for years had fawned on their little auto-cratic leader, Erich Honecker, turned and stabbed him in the back. His successor was an apparatchik some twenty years younger who had been waiting in the wings for years, a man Honecker had hand-picked because he was no threat. His name was Egon Krenz, but to most East Germans he was known simply as Horseface. For obvious reasons. He was the last man who expected to inherit a crisis and the least capable of coping with it.

This surprise development had meant that barely two weeks after my expulsion from the GDR, I touched down once again at Tegel in West Berlin. Exhausted I found myself a hotel in the West, flopped on the bed and turned on the television, then decided – true to the old rule – I had better check in with the desk back in London. The duty staffer on the foreign desk came on and asked, rather shrilly, what I was doing in West Berlin: 'Shouldn't you be in the East?' I humoured her as best as I could without shouting. It was ten thirty at night and the only really sensible thing for me to be doing if I was to hit the ground running the next day was to take in the West German news coverage on television and in the press. That way I would know what was going on in the big picture before I started focusing again on the details. There was also the serious possibility that I would not be allowed back into East Berlin.

In the meantime I planned to have a quick meeting with Kerstin so I would be able to pass first-hand information to Bärbel and Alex if and when I crossed into the East. We met at Cafe Kranzler, a pave-ment cafe on the corner of the Ku'damm which for three decades had been the place to see and be seen in West Berlin. Kerstin and her husband Andreas had been out of East Germany barely two weeks and spent part of that time as refugees in Poland, but looked as if they had emerged from a glossy fashion catalogue rather than the drab world beyond the Wall. Both were sporting what for Germans, East and West, was the symbol of the good life: leather blouson designer jackets. Kerstin combined satin-pink lipstick with a spiky-slick hairdo and tight tapering trousers. Andreas's fashionably faded new blue jeans offset exactly his pastel-green leathers.

The waitress smiled politely as she took our order; nobody was treated like a refugee in those heady weeks, provided, of course, that they looked as if they could pay the bill. After all, Cafe Kranzler was itself a *Flüchtling*. In its pre-war days when it was frequented by the young Marlene Dietrich it had stood in the city centre, on the corner of Friedrichstrasse and Unter den Linden, now just across the Wall. Kerstin giggled. 'It's all so colourful,' she said. 'Such consumerism,' Andreas sighed happily. These were not young idealists, delighting in the freedom of expression offered by life in the West; they were young materialists delighted by the shopping. What had most impressed the pair was the food hall at *KaDewe* (an acronym for *Kaufhaus des Westens*: Shop of the West), West Berlin's most exclusive store. It was the first stop for West Berliners showing off the riches of capitalism to relatives from the East. Kerstin and Andreas went there with Aunt Renate.

Their smart clothes were bought with money scraped together by Andreas's father before they left East Berlin. Kerstin had already found herself a job as a waitress at the Argentinian Steak House on the Ku'damm at twice the salary she earned at the bowling alley in the East. In D-Marks too! Andreas was toying between taking up an offer of a waiter's job in the Wienerwald fast-food chain or a trial as a *maitre d'* at the Old Nuremberg Bavarian sausage restaurant in the basement of the Europa Centre, directly beneath the skyscraper with the symbol of capitalism: the Mercedes star itself. 'They have only offered me a three-month contract to see how I do, but that sounds fair enough,' he said. Their biggest problem was finding a flat. Andreas was hopeful. 'It all works through strings, you know,' he confided with a grin, 'just like *drüben*, over there,' he laughed, jerking his thumb in the manner East Berliners always used to indicate the West, but now meaning the East. They had settled into a new world with disconcerting speed, almost as if they had only moved a few miles across town. Which was, of course, precisely what they had done. But could the East German system's imprint on its citizens really be so fragile? It seemed it could.

In fact West Berlin had seen fewer of the new refugees settle there than most of the rest of West Germany. Many of those who had fled came from the East German provinces with no real roots in Berlin, while even some of the East Berliners who had got out felt that to move to the enclave of West Berlin was moving back into the bear's den. On the other hand there were some who, like Kerstin and Andreas, couldn't properly feel at home in West Germany, which they regarded as too provincial and where people spoke with funny, unfamiliar accents. At one of the welcome centres set up over the previous weeks I had met Petra, a twenty-two-year-old dentist who had fled via Prague, Budapest and finally Bavaria. She was friendless and jobless but still could live nowhere but Berlin: 'I had to come back to Berlin, at least to understand the mentality, the accent, the sense of humour. Bavaria was beautiful but more foreign than I'd imagined. It would be very hard to fit in there. The only problem here is that I love the landscape but access to it is still restricted by the bloody Wall. It's hard to see the rest of one's past so near, yet so far.' She had been warned by the West Berlin authorities not to use transit routes through East Germany, nor the few U-Bahn underground railway lines which, run by the West, passed under East Berlin streets and therefore were for a few miles nominally under communist jurisdiction.

I introduced her to Günter, my old opera-singing beer-drinking actor chum from the East Berlin Volksbühne. He had been in the West for over three years, and was working at several theatres. Life as an actor in the West was a lot less certain than in the state-sponsored East German arts world, but he had little good to say about the regime on the other side. He had asked on several occasions for permission to visit West Berlin for the birthday of his ageing mother and been refused without reason. When she died, they let him out for the funeral. He did not go back: 'Their stupidity is matched only by their thoughtlessness. But it's the friends I still miss most. Last month I became a granddad (he was only forty-four) but I cannot visit my grandchildren. They would let me move back permanently, which I don't want to do, but not for a visit. It's funny, you know; there I felt locked in, unable even to go to Poland without a visa. Now I can travel wherever I want in the world, but the one thing I'd really like to do is get on a train and nip up to Alex's place for a drink.' He had no idea how soon his wish would be fulfilled.

Only the day before, Kerstin had been on her way to work at the steakhouse when she noticed the dramatic news on the electronic billboard at the Ku'damm Eck crossroads. It displayed a giant electronic picture of an elderly man in glasses. The picture was familiar, the disrespectful text that ran underneath it was not: 'Bye bye, Honey.' Erich the red had gone, pushed out by his own crown prince. Giggling with malice, she told me that by some delicious mischance the announcement of his appointment as the new leader of East Germany had interrupted a television programme on state-run television called *Everyone Dreams of a Horse*.

With swept-back iron-grey hair and curling lips that revealed a mouthful of sharp teeth, Krenz at fifty-two had the sort of 'kindly uncle' leering smile that makes adults cringe and grab their children tightly by the hand. Back in my hotel, I watched a rerun of his first televised address as ruler of East Germany: he sat hunched over his script, reading slowly, his head moving from left to right as he followed the words, looking into the camera with sunken but penetrating eyes at the end of each paragraph. His assumption of power reassured nobody. Wolf Biermann, the satirical singer-songwriter expelled from East Germany in 1976, described Krenz as the 'nastiest possible candidate'. Several thousand East Berliners had already shocked the new regime by briefly forming a human chain across Alexanderplatz to express their scepticism about the promise of a more human face.

That news in itself was enough to set me hurrying in my hire car along the old familiar rat run that went along side streets, across main thoroughfares blocked by the Wall and ended up, as always, at the one checkpoint where 'non-German foreigners' (a nice expression which in itself expressed East Germany's hard-to-shake schizophrenia) could cross into the East. Although I had not been formally told when I was expelled that I was henceforward *persona non grata*, I was aware that I was still by no means sure that I would be allowed across. But I had a card to play I thought just might come up trumps: I had two passports. Amongst journalists it was a not uncommon phenomenon, for many reasons. To cite but one: the Israelis insisted on stamping those of all visitors, and anyone with an Israeli stamp in their passport was then automatically barred from most Arab countries.

But I had an additional advantage: being born in Northern Ireland, I was entitled to both a British and an Irish passport. Most people back home chose one or another, depending on their religion and/ or attitude towards the sectarian divide. As a journalist, I thought I was obliged to see both sides of every question so I opted for one of each. There was also the fact that we were not long past the days of airline hijacks – usually by pro-Palestinian groups – who would take hostages and threaten to shoot them. They routinely started with the Israelis, but then soon went on to the Americans, and because of the sort of poodle politics Britain had played over recent decades, eventually moved onto the Brits. I hoped we Irish 'sons of the revolution, begorrah' were a sight further down the firing line.

I had been travelling on my British passport two weeks earlier when I had been arrested – even if bizarrely it had been my Irish passport I pulled out of my pocket to separate me from the crowd of other detainees at the interrogation centre. But on balance I decided that if they had banned me it was more likely to be the British passport that had gone on the blacklist, and therefore the Irish card was the one to play now. As it happened the border guard on duty was my burly old acquaintance I had nicknamed the Bear. He said simply, 'Not surprised to see you back,' which was as close to a political comment I ever heard him make, and stamped my visa. I was in. First stop, obviously: Metzer Eck. Where better to take the pulse? Alex and Bärbel were delighted by my news from Kerstin and Andreas and my first-hand impressions of how well they were doing in their new lives. But most of the discussion in the pub centred on what was happening on their side of the Wall. Michy, a new Metzer Eck regular who was a cabaret artiste from the *Reiz'zwecken* (Tin

Tacks) cabaret troupe lamented that popular wit was outstripping their scriptwriters. They had just rehearsed a new sketch with Krenz as the wolf in a version of *Little Red Riding Hood* when he saw a banner on the street showing the new leader's face with pointed ears and the caption: 'My, grandma, what big teeth you have.' 'They don't laugh any more,' Michy despaired. 'We used to have to fight the censor for every bloody comma. Now we can't even keep up with the jokes on the streets.' Alex laughed and poured him another beer.

The feeling of change in the air was palpable. Although nobody seemed very sure what form it might take. Reforms that only a few weeks earlier were deemed unnecessary were suddenly declared ripe for discussion. Krenz acknowledged that the tide of emigration was an 'open wound'. Busch told me, behind his hand, that rumours emerging from the communist ranks said Krenz had been given only until the party congress – May at the latest. Talk was already of Hans Modrow, the Dresden party boss, a self-billed Gorbachev fan, taking over, despite the violence which had occurred in his city when the refugee trains passed through. There was a new 'citizens'' body called *Neues Forum* (New Forum) largely made up of people who had been active in the old Swords to Ploughshares movement. One of its guiding lights was a woman called Bärbel Bohley, yet another disillusioned former communist. She lived just around the corner so I went to see her and took copies of her 'charter', a document she said they were asking people to sign to petition the government for a 'new dialogue', though she was adamant they were not trying to organise themselves as a formal political party: 'We're thinking of getting people together to have a march, or something, just a show of numbers really.' I nodded. It was much the same as had been happening in Leipzig where we had at one stage feared the Soviet tanks would roll, but now seemed the beginnings of a push for some sort of social and economic reform as had already happened in Poland and Hungary. We all knew that the big problem was the border. But to question that was to question the integrity of the country itself. And that was not on the cards.

I filed my copy, a report of the interview with Bohley, her hopes and aspirations, a sense of the 'deadline' hanging over the Krenz regime and – as everyone was saying – a feeling that there was more to come. But maybe not until the spring. I flew back to London, spent the weekend with my family, and got on the plane to Namibia. It didn't seem anywhere near as daft as it sounds. Honestly.

It certainly seemed daft by the time I got back. 1989 was to be the *annus mirabilis* in the history of the post-Second World War world, with the democratisation of much of Southern Africa no less a cause for celebration than the demise of the Iron Curtain. It was a big story. It just wasn't my story.

I was frustrated that while I had been away, there had been the biggest demonstration ever seen in the centre of East Berlin. Bärbel Bohley and her New Forum people had managed to enthuse not just thousands but hundreds of thousands, almost half a million in total, to converge on the Red City Hall carrying banners similar to those up until now seen only in Leipzig: 'We are the people'. And this time there were a hell of a lot of them. Even Alex and Bärbel, who had been content to leave the 'revolution' to the kids, had joined in.

'Why not,' said Bärbel over a ciggy and a schnapps in Metzer Eck. 'At least we can show them we're not afraid.' And there was the rub: the fear had faded. The assumption that brutal force would be deployed had faded with the assumption that it would work. It was as if a sinister spell that had for decades held a population in thrall had suddenly been revealed as a piece of bogus hocus pocus. Almost a Sleeping Beauty moment. But if the long sleep was over nobody knew exactly what the world would look like when they finally rubbed the dust from their eyes.

As far as I was concerned, looking for a focus on a Wednesday afternoon for a story that I would write on Friday for that week's Sunday paper, it seemed the best chance would be another demonstration, this time up in Rostock, on the Baltic coast. It was unlikely to be a big demonstration on the scale of Leipzig or the previous week's huge gathering in Berlin, but it would be a further sign of unrest spreading across the country, and Rostock, an old and once pretty Hanseatic trading city going slowly to the dogs under the moribund Comecon economic grouping, would provide a little more unusual background colour.

It was on my way back, with little more than that colour under my belt and still wondering what was going to be the 'intro' on my story for the week, that I turned on the car radio. And almost fainted. I felt for a surreal moment as if I had crossed into an alternative universe. It was RIAS Berlin *(Radio im Amerikanischen Sektor)*, usually a reliable mix of music and news. They had abandoned the music. In a gabbling chatter rather than the usual sober tones, the news anchor was saying, 'It appears now that a second crossing point on the Wall has opened. As I speak thousands of East Berliners are pouring into the West.'

Stunned and horrified – I was still more than an hour and a half away – I did the only thing I could: put my foot to the floor. And discovered, to my exquisite anguish, that Mercedes had already joined the green lobby and my rented shiny black metallic M-190 for all its boasts about low fuel consumption and low emissions (this was back in 1989, remember!) had the acceleration of a donkey cart. For the best part of ninety minutes I tried to push my foot through the chassis as I willed the car back to East Berlin, accelerating to over 170 kph, my ear glued to the radio all the way. What had happened was less than clear-cut: at an unheralded news conference in East Berlin, politburo member Günter Schabowski had said that it was the government's intention to 'normalise' the frontier with West Germany and West Berlin and in general relax travel restrictions. He was obviously not completely up to speed with what had actually been decided, but he had been heard to say it would be possible for 'every citizen of the German Democratic Republic to leave the GDR through any of the border crossings'. Asked when this would come into effect, he had fumbled through his papers and said, uncertainly, 'Immediately, from now'. The press conference had been broadcast live on East German television too and within half an hour there were crowds at the checkpoints demanding to be let through and eventually some – and then more and more – were. Exactly what the formalities were, and how long this would last, nobody knew.

Once within the city limits I headed straight for the Wall. At the Invalidenstrasse checkpoint there were already thousands. I spoke to the border guard on charge who would give no details about the apparent dramatic change in attitude other than to confirm that they were letting GDR citizens through. But he would not let me through. As a foreigner, I would have to go to Checkpoint Charlie. Cursing Prussian pedantry to the last, I ran back to the car and drove the kilometre or so distance, taking with me, piled into the Merc, a group of East Berliners who had despaired of the Invalidenstrasse queue.

There it was every bit as chaotic. I drove into the middle of the wide expanse of the East German control area. I was delighted to see that one of the obviously harassed border guards on duty was the Bear. He grimaced at me, gave an approving look at the car – surprised when I told him it had rubbish acceleration – and said: 'It's chaos over there'. He and his colleagues did their best to complete my formalities in a few minutes, but would not let the East Germans come with me in the car. They had to go on foot. 'There's no point in trying to drive that through tonight. It's a madhouse,' said the Bear.

I could see what he meant about the 'madhouse'. Some twenty metres away on the other side of the checkpoint's customs sheds, was a vast and obviously drunk throng of West Berliners. From the Eastern side it genuinely looked like an angry drunken mob. The other side of the checkpoint here was Kreuzberg, home of West Berlin's disaffected squatters and anarchists, and some in the crowd were hurling abusive insults and beer cans at the border troops, seen close up for the first time, suddenly transformed from sinister armed silhouettes behind searchlights into a close-up human enemy (any uniform was a target for some Kreuzberg characters). The control area between the barriers had meanwhile filled with cars. One party of Third World diplomats, completely uncaring about the history unfolding before them and more concerned about getting to their favourite West Berlin nightclub, fumed at the helpless troops for not opening the gates which, although pedestrians were passing through, remained closed against the teeming throng.

Frenetic, confused, at last the East German guards opened the gates. My car was first in the line. 'Go on then if you want to tackle that lot,' shouted one, now angry, lieutenant. I didn't. I was not sure if the crowds dancing in the gap ahead of me were angry or happy, but I knew one thing: I did not want to be responsible for the first casualty of the night by running over someone. It would be much later that night, when the mood of celebration had been firmly established, before the first fibreglass Trabants began to trundle through and the curious welcome custom of 'Trabby-bouncing' – lifting the little cars up and down as if giving them 'the bumps' could be created. At that moment, I made my own decision; I turned the car round and drove East, leaving the diplomats fuming as the troops closed the gates again to stop an influx of partying drunks set on invading East Berlin.

'Tell you what,' said the Bear. 'Stick the motor over there,' pointing at a normally out of bounds patch of land just to the left of the Checkpoint Charlie barrier. 'We'll look after it. That is, if you're serious about going through.'

'It's my job,' I told him. And he shrugged. He understood. After all, he was just doing his.

Right up at the Western barrier, East German guards with megaphones ran to and fro, shouting preposterously at photographers to stop taking pictures as families streaming tears kissed and hugged and Western revellers climbed onto the electrically-controlled metal barriers. I didn't know it at the time but the same uncontrollable mob only half a mile away were already clambering onto the Western section of the Wall before the Brandenburg Gate and, egged on by Western media snappers, tearing at it with pickaxes in front of totally confused and conflicted border guards who only a few weeks earlier would have shot them.

Going through the pedestrian gate I had used a thousand times before was a strange and unforgettable experience. I had my hair ruffled by a forest of outstretched hands, was kissed at random by unseen lips and found a can of beer thrust into my hand with the emotional cry '*Herzlich Wilkommen in die Freiheit*' (Welcome to freedom!). Dazed, and probably looking as emotional as if I had indeed set foot for the first time in West Berlin, I muttered '*Danke*' and stumbled on through the crowd who were already embracing the next arrival.

I went to the Adler Bar, recently opened in a building just a few yards beyond Checkpoint Charlie. For years the building in a road to nowhere had lain derelict and empty. Now it was heaving, the bar at the centre of the turning world. I found their call box and phoned Alex in Metzer Eck. To my astonishment, he told me he was not going to come over: 'Guess who has just turned up? Günter. He says it was only the other week he was telling you his one wish was to be able to drink in Metzer Eck. Well, now he can. There's progress for you.' For Alex, it was every bit as important that his friend could come back as that he could leave.

He said he did not know about Bärbel, but Horst and Sylvia had gone and would probably, he guessed, turn up at Renate's. For the next hour or so I hung around Checkpoint Charlie, drinking in a scene I had thought impossible and cursing the fact that it was a Thursday night – too late to get much in the Friday editions but the Saturdays would hoover it up. Hoover what up? Nobody was still exactly sure what was happening, how or why and how long it would last. I talked at random to some of those who had just come over. Most had their hearts in their mouths. Petra Lorenz, a dumpy, middle-aged mother-of-two, had travelled two hours by bus and tram from her flat in Marzahn, leaving her husband to look after their children. 'Don't be daft, it's a lie,' he had said. She wandered in a trance for twenty minutes on the Western side of Checkpoint Charlie but was scared to go further in case they slammed the door and she would be cut off from her family forever. Nothing seemed impossible. She took back a newspaper as a souvenir from a dream.

The burning question in everyone's mind was answered by a bus driver from the East, smiling with a crisp certainty as he downed the beer from the can pressed into his hand as he pushed through the crowds and into the West: 'Can they take back their decision? Close the wall again? Never. We'll see them sink in ashes first.' I scribbled his words down in my notebook. In my head I was already preparing the big double-page spread I knew I would be required to produce for Sunday, whether it was 'Flash in a Pan' or 'End of an Era'. The analysis could come later, tomorrow, in the cold light of day and in the wake of whatever happened over the next few hours. Right now what I wanted was colour. And raw emotion. And there was no shortage of either.

It was time to go to the Ku'damm, the centre of West Berlin nightlife, where it seemed likely most of the more adventurous would head. But it made sense to take some East Berliners with me. The obvious candidates soon presented themselves. Running through a cheering gauntlet of beery West Berliners dancing on the Wall came a ready-made party. These three young waitresses from the Hotel Stadt Berlin, who came whooping through the Wall, spraying *Rotkäppchen* (Little Red Riding Hood), the fizzy party plonk of the East, at grinning policemen, were ready-made feel-good copy. I grabbed a taxi and offered them a lift to the Ku'damm in exchange for the story of their evening.

In the taxi as we rushed through streets full of drunk pedestrians and cars honking their horns, Christiane, Janna and Andrea told me how it had been a routine boring evening serving the usual unappetising East German institutional food to sour-faced Russian tourists. When the news came through that the Wall was open they had bitten their lips and looked at each other. But *deutsche Gründlichkeit* (German thoroughness) was in their genes: there might have been a revolution going on all around them, but they could hardly join in until they had finished their shift. It had gone midnight before Andrea turned to the others, giggling, and suggested: 'Anyone for the Ku'damm?' And now we were there. When we piled out of the taxi in the middle of the carnival that had spread across the centre of West Berlin, Andrea looked longingly at a telephone box that would work only with the Western cash she did not have. I handed her a few D-Marks and she woke her parents in the East: '*Mutti*, I'm on the Ku'damm. It's mad. It's marvellous. Oh, don't be cross. I'm coming back.' Then they gave another delirious whoop of delight. And were off into the melee.

I let them go. They had given me the 'human element' my copy needed. Now it was time to fill in the rest. Despite trying to keep a clear head for detail, I was as intoxicated as any Berliner on the pure champagne atmosphere of a city that couldn't quite believe what was happening to it. Watching the little apple-green and baby-blue fibreglass Trabbies with their two-stroke engines tootle by amidst the Mercs and Beamers on the Ku'damm – giggling lunatics waving from the windows – was like watching one of those Hollywood films where cartoon characters merge with real life: think Roger Rabbit in a Cold War context. The sky was ablaze with fireworks, total strangers embraced in the streets. Bars spilled out onto the streets and the streets flooded into the bars.

For a while I just stood there watching in stunned amazement only to be startled when I was suddenly grabbed round the neck by a tall man in a leather jacket with cropped hair. It was Andreas, an improbable *deus ex machina*, but profoundly welcome. He had just met Kerstin after work and they were still reeling from the news. We dived into a phone box and called Renate to find out if she had heard from Horst and Sylvia. They were with her. We arranged to meet them as soon as they could manage it on the Ku'damm Eck, probably the most confused spot in Europe at that moment. But we managed it. 'We've ... uh, just popped over for a drink,' said Horst, looking exaggeratedly nonchalant before he whooped with joy and swung his sister into his arms.

By five thirty a.m. we were sitting over tall beers in a bar down Kantstrasse while Kerstin wept quietly with happiness. Horst was teasing the bar staff and West Berlin customers, touting for custom for Metzer Eck: 'Better pig's knuckles than any you get here,' he shouted. As we left, he asked the waitress if he could perhaps buy two of the tall, elegant Warsteiner beer glasses, just as a souvenir. She laughed and told him to take them and not ask silly questions. As an unimaginable dawn broke on the first day of a new Germany, we staggered off to bed, the East Berliners to Renate's West Berlin flat. Whatever happened, they were not missing the chance to spend a night in the West. Meanwhile I, the Westerner, wandered in a daze back East, to my hotel on Marx-Engels-Platz. The sun was coming up as I kicked my way through the broken bottles on the roadway next to Checkpoint Charlie and presented my passport to stunned-looking border guards. How long would I still need to do so, was the question neither asked nor answered.

The night the Berlin Wall came down was the ultimate vindication of the 'cock-up theory' of history. Over the years since, Krenz, Schabowski, even Gorbachev who more than anyone perhaps bears the indirect responsibility – or right to claim the credit – have told their own, differing stories about what happened and what was intended. The facts that emerged piecemeal in the days that followed, and subsequently in an endless series of interviews, many of them conducted under the aegis of my fellow Metzer Eck regular, film producer Axel Grote, allow the real jigsaw of that night to be pieced together.

Schabowski's ill-organised and incompetent press conference was merely the result of a Communist Party still reeling at its own boldness in sacking its leader. They were also under immense pressure from Prague where the sight of thousands of East Germans camped in the overflowing grounds of the West German Embassy was causing social and political unrest in a communist regime that, despite the changes in Poland and Hungary, was still only slightly less Stalinist than that in East Berlin. The Czechoslovaks were furious and had made clear to their comrades that something had to be done. At the same time the grey men in East Berlin realised they were sitting on a pressure cooker. They thought that by making concessions on travel to the West they would ease the pressure by letting off steam. What they didn't realise was that it was actually a bottle of champagne, and the cork, once out, would not go back in.

Schabowski's statements that night were worse than shambolic. Transcripts show that what he actually said revealed that the polit-buro had been working on new regulations for travel to the West but was worried about it: 'We are naturally concerned at the possibilities of this travel regulation – it's still not in effect, it's still only a draft'. He then immediately followed this up by saying that pressure from Prague had forced them to accelerate their thinking: 'This movement is taking place (um) across the territory of an allied state (um), which is not an easy burden for that state to bear.' As a result they were bringing forward 'a passage' from the planned new rules.

He then quickly read out the rules from a piece of paper: 'Applications for travel abroad by private individuals can now be made without the previously existing requirements (of demonstrating a need to travel or proving familial relationships). The travel authorisations will be issued within a short time. Grounds for denial will only be applied in particular exceptional cases. The responsible departments of passport and registration control in the People's Police district offices in the GDR are instructed to issue visas for permanent exit without delays and without presentation of the existing requirements for permanent exit.'

What was clearly intended was that East Germans, from the Friday morning, would have the right to go to their local police station and request a passport, which would be granted them automatically, within a few days at most, and that with this they would be able to travel to the West. The hope was that the refugee flood would stop immediately. They realised there would be a large number of visitors to the West in the coming weeks, but in numbers controlled through the bureaucracy needed to issue passports; of these, many would not come back. Most of the rest would taste the West but still come back; the scenario would then be open for a series of internal reforms in much the same way as had happened in Hungary. It would not be easy for the communists to cope with but at least it would not create difficulties on the international level. It was a stopgap policy.

All they were proposing to do was cut the red tape, not throw open the Berlin Wall. But all that remained in the minds of anyone listening was that one sentence: 'We have decided today (um) to implement a regulation that allows every citizen of the German Democratic Republic (um) to (um) leave the GDR through any of the border crossings,' and when it was to come into effect: 'Immediately, without delay.' In the background the foreign trade minister Gerhard Beil could be heard muttering: 'to be decided by the council of ministers.' But nobody was listening to him.

East Berliners living nearest the Wall were first to react. The commandant of the contingent of border guards at the Bornholmer Strasse crossing in Prenzlauer Berg was Manfred Sens. He was later to complain that he and his fellow guards felt betrayed: for years they had done a thankless, even despised task, only to have it made a mockery overnight for no clear reason and without proper explanation or clear orders. He had heard no instructions about any proposed change in border regulations other than that which came over the public radio, by which time he was facing several hundred East Berliners clamouring to be allowed to cross.

Sens had a veritable arsenal in his stores, allowing for every degree of retaliation to any attempt to force a passage: rubber bullets, gas grenades, water cannon and, of course, live ammunition. But he was reluctant to start an incident without orders from above, especially when everyone was telling him that to prevent them crossing would be against the orders he would shortly receive. But he hadn't had them yet. Sens sat on the telephone trying in vain to get a clear response, not least because Schabowski's fumbled presentation had confused everybody. Eventually he got through to the very top man Fritz Streletz, a former Second World War *Wehrmacht* soldier who was now chief of the National People's Army General Staff and the man in charge of all border fortifications. But Streletz couldn't give him a definitive answer either. All he did was to remind Sens that he had been chosen for his experience and must be aware of the importance of avoiding serious incidents at the country's frontiers, especially in these critical times.

Sens was not at all sure what his senior officer was suggesting. But time wore on and eventually he lifted the barrier and let the first of his whooping fellow citizens, on production only of their national identity card, cross into the West, a street away. They had no idea if they were letting people out for the night or for ever; at one stage the instruction came through to put the exit stamp across the photograph in the identity card – for identification purposes. But within twenty-four hours, tipsy teenagers coming back from West Berlin simply waved identity cards at bemused border guards who only weeks earlier might have shot them.

When the barrier first went up there was a rush for the door in the bar just a hundred yards away from the checkpoint. By coincidence, it happened to be run by Dieter Kanitz, Alex's former waiter in Metzer Eck. He and his wife Hannelore had set up on their own managing a state-run pub in the middle of a *Laubenkolonie*. These were basically allotments equipped with elaborate wooden sheds that keen gardeners fitted with curtains and beds and often spent the weekend in. The allotments abutted the railway tracks on one side and the Wall on the other. As his customers headed west, Dieter would have loved to go with them; but he had lost his identity card, and Hannelore sat with him. It turned out to be one of the best night's business they ever had as they poured beer into the early morning hours to those returning home for a drink at prices they could afford after the adventure of a lifetime. Just one street away.

At nine a.m. on Friday, November 10th, when KaDeWe, the Harrods of West Berlin, opened its doors, the East Berliners flooded in to stare at the electronic miracles on offer, at the mountainous meat and fruit display on the 'Gourmet Floor'. But with Western D-Marks like rare gold, most only window-shopped. Those who did buy something to take home made their purchases at the cheaper super-markets and discount electrical stores.

Alex and Bärbel came over in the afternoon and we all met at Renate's flat and went out for a celebratory Chinese meal. Bärbel had spent hours wandering the Ku'damm which she had last seen as a little girl, and caused laughter when she returned, still daydream-ing with the single comment: 'The streets don't seem as wide as I remember.' On the wall, the East German police and border guards had abandoned trying to understand what was really intended by the new border regulations. Their confusion only reflected that in the minds of their masters. But their masters were by now no more in control of the human tide washing across the frontier than King Canute on his throne on the beach. A media circus had flocked to Berlin from around the world, in most cases with little or no idea about what was happening other than the obvious delirious scenes against which well-groomed anchor men and women posed and talked twaddle. But the twaddle declared the Berlin Wall history, and millions of East Germans on the march – believing what they saw on television – had made it so.

On Friday, under fresh instruction from whatever still consti-tuted 'above', East German border guards were once again insisting on stamping documents and issuing visas, but of random validity from three days to six months. Manfred Sens would later testify that on November 14th, five days after the Wall 'came down', he received the order again to 'secure the frontier'. 'That was a joke,' he snorted. 'By that stage it was all we could do to ensure an orderly flow of traffic.' The stream of honking Eastern cars continued to flow down the Ku'damm, over the border and along Unter den Linden. The wall before the Brandenburg Gate looked more redundant than ever. Within weeks it would be breached in dozens of places, with souvenir hunters fighting over chunks – ideally with the best graf-fiti, and within seven months it would be consigned to historical archaeology.

Back at *The Sunday Times*, Bob the foreign editor had agreed that to keep me in position and my marriage together, he would do a deal on paying for my wife and two tiny sons to come out to Berlin for a few days. For Jackie it was a cathartic experience, coming back to the place where we had begun married life to see the impossible come true. For my two children – a five-year old and a toddler – it was 'a funny holiday'. But the pictures I have of them, one in a knitted jumper with pictures of penguins, the other in a down coat two sizes too big, both pushing their little hands into a crack in the Wall, remains a family treasure. As does the chunk of it in my desk drawer. It was our Wall too. And we were glad to see the end of it.

The significance of what had happened began to sink in fast. The Berlin Wall *was* the Iron Curtain, far more than any other Eastern European frontier. But the East German communists had played their last card, gambling on a scorched earth policy, yielding every demand in the hope of exhausting the enemy. It was one of the founding fathers of communism, a high deity in the crumbled East German pantheon, Friedrich Engels, who, a century earlier, had summed up how it happened: 'Everyone strives for his own interests, but in the end what emerges is something no one intended.'

11

The Domino Effect

It was, by a long chalk, the most off-the-wall overlong sentence ever to appear in a *Sunday Times* news story, let alone near the top of it. Twice it had been cut into easier-to-digest bite-sized nuggets by the sub-editors, and twice it had been restored, mostly at the hands of Bob Tyrer, foreign editor and literary connoisseur who recognised the vain (in every sense) attempts of his correspondents in the field to do more than just tell the news. On a freezing cold night in the Czech capital I had sat and tried to do almost literally poetic justice to the most exhilarating two days in my life since the fall of the Berlin Wall, though as that was only three weeks earlier, things were getting hard to keep track of.

I wrote it as I had experienced it, trying to give form in the limited vocabulary of journalism to a popular movement in the truest sense of the term, the cadences of the sentence matching the extraordinary celebration performed by the people of the Czechoslovak capital as communism crumbled:

'A hands-across-Prague protest designed as a human chain became instead a merry dance, a living tableau from a Brueghel painting, as laughing, skipping people in warm mufflers and long scarves formed an endless twisting snake around the trees, through the snowy park, up to the floodlit spires, the castle itself and the archbishop's palace, then helter-skelter slithered giggling down steep, slippery, narrow cobbled streets and, holding hands with exaggerated formality, like a pastiche mazurka, passed across the fifteenth-century Charles Bridge, watched by all the statues of all the saints, and on to Wenceslas Square.'

Over the top? Maybe. But as we stood in the square looking up at the magnificent old statue of Good King Wenceslas on his horse, we all felt it was going to be a truly magical Christmas across the whole of Eastern Europe. Even if it would be black magic in one particular godforsaken corner. True to my family-work ratio in this extraordinary, chaotic year, I managed two days back in Britain with my wife and children before returning to Berlin (already we were no longer saying 'East' and 'West'). Egon Krenz, the stopgap successor to Honecker had already gone, in his place Hans Modrow, the mayor of Dresden, tried to lead a 'reform coalition' but on the streets it was slowly becoming clear that the whole communist-led system had lost not only the credibility it never had, but the power to enforce its position. The open frontier was an open door to an increasingly – almost unbelievably – inevitable German unification. As long as there wasn't a Soviet veto. And that veto, for so long assumed to be automatic, did not seem to be forthcoming.

A Soviet spokesman billed the superpower summit about to take place in warships on the choppy seas off Valletta in early December as the progress of history 'from Yalta to Malta'. In effect Gorbachev was making it clear that Moscow no longer claimed the advantage Stalin had wrestled from Churchill and Roosevelt as they partitioned the world in the elegant drawing room of Livadia Palace in the Crimea in February 1945. But not in Washington, not in London, not in Paris, nor even Bonn – and least of all Brussels – was there a blueprint for Europe to replace the strategic certainties of the Cold War. Wolf Biermann was right: 'We had already half-swallowed the lie that the sun could never rise again in the East'. In Bonn, Chancellor Kohl prepared his 'ten-point-plan', a steady, long-term timetable for progress towards German unity. But in Washington, George Bush paid little more than lip service to the idea. US Secretary of State James Baker told reporters that talk about German reunification was premature. In London Margaret Thatcher was all but openly hostile, implying even consideration of such a topic was 'destabilising'. She had clearly not heard what Gorbachev had told Honecker that he (or she) 'who is too late will be punished by history.'

History on the ground was not about to wait for the men on the boats to tell it what to do. And it was not just happening in Berlin. After my by now customary one weekend in three at home, events in Prague summoned me back to the middle of a rapidly unfolding new map of Europe. In the wake of the euphoria in Berlin, Prague, which had until then been merely a backdrop for the East German drama, had been swept up in demonstrations in which one young man had died. Václav Havel, the playwright, who for two decades had been a thorn in the communist regime's side was a guiding light in the overnight foundation of Civic Forum, a citizens' group that was trying to assume the role of Poland's Solidarity union and the East German grass-roots protest movement in one go. It succeeded faster than they could have imagined. The Berlin Wall *was* the Iron Curtain, and its collapse was the crucial event that meant the domino effect would go all the way to the end. Even with a resounding thud that only came a year later, to the fall of the 'Evil Empire' itself.

Civic Forum was founded on November 19th, ten days after the Wall came down, and over the next three days it filled the streets of Prague with tens then hundreds of thousands of protesters. On November 23rd, in a wholly surreal moment, Havel appeared on a balcony on Wenceslas Square before a crowd of half a million, and by his side, Alexander Dubcek, the man who had led the ill-fated Prague Spring of 1968. The following night we were sitting in the *Laterna Magika* (Magic Lantern) theatre that had become the would-be revolutionaries' headquarters (where else for a rebellion led by a playwright) wondering what would happen next. We watched Havel sit on stage that Friday night, his legs crossed on a stool, for all the world like contemporary comedian Dave Allen about to tell a few yarns, when a student came rushing in with a tall tale that at first even Havel could not believe: the top members of the communist government had resigned en masse.

'I think it is time for champagne,' Havel said with a strange, disbelieving smile. 'I think it is time to be cautious and wait and see what tomorrow brings,' said the venerable Dubcek at his side. Tomorrow brought confirmation. But it was Sunday night before it dawned on all of Czechoslovakia that their 'Velvet Revolution' had worked and they had taken their celebration to that extraordinary gavotte around their beautiful medieval and baroque city that once again had escaped intact without a fight. The rumours of Soviet tanks massing on the outskirts had proved to be a canard. Gorbachev had not done it in East Germany, he would not do it here. The Sinatra Doctrine was for real. And *The Sunday Times* foreign editor's efforts to retrieve his wordy correspondent's literary artifice were to be rewarded too when historian Martin Gilbert, compiling his *History of the Twentieth Century* a decade later, included that preposterous piece of prose intact. I had achieved one ambition: I had genuinely become a footnote in history.

Within days the Czechoslovak Communist Party had removed the reference in the constitution to its own 'leading role' and committed the ultimate political sin of revisionism, declaring that the Soviet invasion of 1968 had after all been 'unjustified'. All over Europe, history was not just being written; it was being rewritten. The border to Austria was opened before the end of the week and a few days later travel restrictions to all other countries were abolished, the fortifications along the frontier with West Germany, from where I had looked over at the old Sudeten town of Eger, now Cheb, dismantled. Nobody in Prague feared their citizens all clamouring for union with another country; though nor had anyone yet realised that before long they would be clamouring for their own country to be split in two. By the end of the year Havel, the shy self-deprecating dramatist, was president. Democracy, installed overnight, would decide the rest.

I had my own eyes set on a family Christmas back in Britain, but not before at least one more trip back to East Berlin, where Erich Honecker, only two months earlier supreme dictator in his country and master of his party, was an ailing private pensioner about to be expelled by his former comrades. Yet even his going had something sinister about it, as if the communists were now fighting for their very existence as a political party. They had renounced their past, as though the Wall and forty years of repression behind it had never happened, and renamed themselves the Party of Democratic Socialism. They had done with Stalinism, yet they still forced their former leader to undergo a humiliation uncannily akin to a Stalinist show trial. From his sickbed – he was now revealed to have long been suffering from cancer – he was forced to recant his own mistakes, including losing touch with reality.

My friend Axel, the television producer from Metzer Eck, had already joined a new party called Demokratischer Aufbruch (Democratic Breakthrough) and was talking as its representative to West Berlin politicians about launching a full-scale campaign for German

unification. But in Bonn the physically larger-than-life but person-
ally underwhelming chancellor Helmut Kohl was about to seize the
appealing nettle offered to him: achieving German unity would be
a painful exercise, but it would give him a place in history beyond
anything he had ever dared imagine. But was the door to a brave
new world just waiting to be pushed? And if it was, could he be
sure what lay on the other side. The labels 'West' and 'East' Germany
were geographical tags not actual state entities. The men in Bonn,
with a pragmatism born of the years, had eventually recognised
the 'other Germany' as a state in its own right, but if the people of
the German Democratic Republic effectively voted their own state
out of existence, then the constitution of the Federal Republic of
Germany required that they be accepted within it. So far, so easy,
but East Germany was an economic basket case, home to seventeen million people whose currency was virtually valueless. Could
the West German economic miracle survive under the pressure of
taking in so many impoverished cousins?

But while the future of Germany looked like dominating my
New Year agenda, there was a bigger threat to my family Christmas
looming. The wind of change had suddenly struck another domino,
the Soviet Union's most maverick satellite and the most cruel and
repressive of all the communist dictatorships in what had once
been civilised Europe: Romania. Under their diminutive megalo-
maniac leader Nicolae Ceausescu, Romania was a country notoriously hard to report on, relentlessly hostile to foreign journalists. I
had been there only once before, several years previously, to write
features about life in a society that tried to keep its doors closed
to the outside world. Travelling as a tourist on my Irish passport
which at that stage gave my profession as a 'translator', I had gone
in by train from Budapest, on a rationale I hold still that long train
journeys offer a peek at a nation's underbelly.* Amongst those I met
there were the German-speaking farmers of Transylvania, descend-
ants of those warrior-peasants brought in by Wallachian princes
five hundred years earlier to help defend their lands against the

---

* See also Peter Millar's *All Gone to Look for America: Riding the Iron Horse Across
a Continent and Back*. London: Arcadia Books, 2008

Turks. They told me heart-rending stories of medieval villages razed because they were in the way of Ceausescu's insane plans to build vast agro-industrial collective farms, of families split up arbitrarily and members taken away for interrogation who never returned.

Now in this last most barbaric bastion of totalitarianism, the wind of change had turned into a hurricane. Only a couple of weeks earlier, as even Honecker was being ousted and the Czechoslovak communists were shaking in their boots, Ceausescu had been delivering a five-hour eulogy on the achievements of his own squalid rule to an audience of party placemen. During his endless peroration they had risen to their feet no fewer than sixty-seven times to interrupt him with applause. If Honecker had been 'losing touch with reality', Ceausescu was on a whole other planet. Most of the time he spent going over the plans for his vast *folies de grandeur*, notably his great House of the People, a vast marble palace at the end of a grandiose Boulevard of the Victory of Socialism, which he had bulldozed several whole districts of historic Bucharest to construct. He termed himself the *Conducator*, the leader – a direct throwback to the days when Franco styled himself *El Caudillo*, Mussolini *Il Duce*, Hitler *Der Führer* and Stalin *Vozhd*. The man who terrorised the peasant farmers of Transylvania was perceived by his entire population as a bloodsucker.

His wife Elena was a fitting Bride of Dracula. In a bid to increase the population of workers and peasants, in a state with chronic housing shortages made worse by their mad master's penchant for arbitrarily ripping down parts of the capital to create pleasure palaces, Elena posed as 'mother of the nation' and banned birth control. Romanians, many of whom lived in tiny one-bedroom flats or bedsits, were encouraged to have four children per couple. Their eldest son, Nicu, was a provincial Communist Party leader being groomed for the succession. But Elena used the dreaded Securitate – Romania's Stasi – to spy on her other two children. Their daughter Zoia's bedroom was bugged and fitted with hidden cameras so her mother could check up on her sexual activity. She and her husband disapproved of the marriage of their son Valentin, a nuclear physicist, to the daughter of a political rival and expelled her and their own grandchild to Canada.

Considering how they treated their own flesh and blood their attitude towards the rest of the population – patronisingly called 'our children' – was unsurprising. A strike in the city of Brasov in 1987 was brutally suppressed by the army, allegedly with several hundred dead. The ringleaders were treated to five-minute chest X-rays that gave them cancer. The national currency, the *lei*, was all but valueless; the consumer economy – such as it was – functioned as a black market in which goods were paid for in cigarettes, the 'gold standard' being curiously the American brand, Kent, which were worth twice as much as any other. In May 1988, the 'leader's' determination to ratchet up agricultural production to industrial levels led him to announce that up to 8,000 traditional villages would be wiped off the map, an announcement that even drew protest from HRH, the Prince of Wales. That was not quite so laughable an intervention as it might sound; Ceausescu frequently boasted of his experiences in 1978 when thanks to an invitation from the Labour government of Jim Callaghan, this odious dictator was the guest of the Queen at Buckingham Palace.

Now, at long last, even in downtrodden Romania there were fresh rumblings of discontent. A group of senior party figures purged by Ceausescu began to stir against him. In Transylvania, which until 1918 had been part of the Austro-Hungarian Empire, there was not just a German-speaking minority but a much larger Hungarian-speaking population which now, inspired by the sudden transformation of their 'mother country' began fleeing across the frontier. The regime moved to deport László Tökés, an ethnic Hungarian pastor considered to be a troublemaker and based in the town Hungarian-speakers called Temesvar and Romanians, Timisoara. When local people gathered around him, refusing to let the police pass, Ceausescu ordered in the troops backed up by the hated Securitate. What should have been nothing more than a tough exercise in crowd control turned into bloodshed. But instead of the brutality causing the trouble to abate, it escalated. Ever more people came out into the streets. Securitate ordered the troops to fire point blank into the crowds. Those few who refused were summarily executed.

In the midst of all this Ceausescu, thinking himself omnipotent, went on a three-day state visit to Iran, leaving his Securitate thugs to put down a crisis he refused to acknowledge. When he returned he was astounded to find the global condemnation of events in Timisoara included his erstwhile allies in Budapest, Warsaw and now even East Berlin. Ceausescu made a dramatic television speech blaming the trouble on 'hooligans' and 'external agitators', banned all foreigners from entering country, and declared a state of emergency.

Back in London, with reports pouring out from the few reporters, notably Reuters, permanently based in the country, nobody was watching the situation more anxiously than me. I had just returned from East Berlin yet again, watching the preparations for the ceremonial opening of a crossing point at that so symbolic focus of division, the spot where I had taken Jackie on her fist night in Berlin to point to our future home on the other side of the Wall: the Brandenburg Gate. I had made something like a hundred flights in the course of the past twelve months, spent far more time apart from my family than with them, and now, with only days to go to Christmas, and my parents coming to stay, I was determined to spend it home. So when the phone call came from the foreign desk, as I knew it must, I joined the crowds of those doing the unthinkable: I said no. Politely, but firmly, pleading for understanding. And I got it, up to a point: at least I got the reprieve. Another journalist, Walter Ellis, a friend of mine, but already divorced, was sent instead.

But the story would not wait for him to get there. I took my place on the foreign desk, watching the wires, monitoring the television broadcasts, putting in my own knowledge and analysis and pulling together a two-page special. The next day, Thursday, Ceausescu organised a demonstration of support outside the presidential palace. Suddenly his placemen realised they were outnumbered. His speech from the balcony, filled with the usual platitudes about 'the inevitable victory of the socialist revolution', suddenly encountered revolution. The planned applause was weak, and then came the unimaginable: heckling. Within minutes the demonstration designed to illustrate his power proved it had evaporated as the crowd below him began shouting 'Down with Ceausescu'. Within minutes, a big Securitate man motioned the confused 'great leader' back inside his palace. The army moved in against a crowd that had proved itself unfaithful and within minutes the square rang out with the sound of gunshots and tear gas filled the air. The Ceausescus fled, taking a helicopter from the palace courtyard to a nearby airport of Targoviste. When they landed they were informed that the army had closed all airspace and was not about to reopen it, even for their leader. The tide was beginning to turn, irrevocably.

That was as much as I, or anyone in the Western world, knew as I left *The Sunday Times* office in Wapping on Saturday night, December 23rd, 1989, and went home for a long-anticipated and much-needed family Christmas. There was no holiday however for the reporters on the ground, nor for the people of Romania. The Ceausescus, it turned out, had tried to continue their escape from the vengeance of their 'children' by car, a little red Dacia rustbucket rather than the armour-plated Mercedes limousines they were used to. But they did not get far. With revolution in the air across an entire country, the police were setting up roadblocks. Those outside Targoviste were astonished to find who they had stopped. The former ruling couple were arrested and held while the police listened to the radio to find out which way the tide was flowing. Then they made their decision: they handed them over to the army. And the army had already decided it was now behind the people instead of against them.

The Ceausescus were taken to a secret military base as prisoners. Amid rumours that loyalists were planning to rescue them and mount a counter-revolution, they were summarily tried on Christmas Day, on a confused multiplicity of charges, including genocide, then taken out immediately and shot. Elena allegedly turned on the soldiers to say, 'I was like a mother to you.' One replied without thinking, 'You murdered our mothers.' Within hours of the event the summary trial and the Ceausescus' execution were shown live on Romanian television, the station itself having been the scene of bloody battles between Securitate and the rebels. The broadcast effectively ended the battle for the old guard who had lost their figurehead. By that stage each and every one of them knew there was no point looking towards Moscow for backup. A message from Gorbachev's Kremlin advised Ceausescu loyalists to lay down their arms.

It was a cruel, nasty, but probably necessary codicil to a year of miraculous and largely peaceful revolutions. On New Year's Eve – I had managed almost a whole week with my family – we held a party at home that became a celebration of the end of the Cold War. It was a party already full of journalists when at five minutes to midnight – the mythical hour that the doom-mongers had warned us the Cold War had brought the human race to – the bell rang and in came a horde of revellers straight from the front line. ITV had chartered a plane to get their crew out of Romania in time for a New Year's celebration, and onto it had piled virtually every British correspondent who could fit. The all now tried to squeeze inside our kitchen, champagne mingling with vodka and *tuiça*, fiery Romanian plum brandy. Amongst the decorations strung across our living room that heady night was a string of bunting, bought in East Germany eight years earlier on the occasion of a Warsaw Pact summit, in the form of the flags of all the countries of the communist military alliance. Now, as the revolutions on the ground had done, I took a pair of scissors and cut out the communist symbols from each: last but not least, the 'Hammer and Compasses' from the flag of the German Democratic Republic. So modified, it alone became identical to the flag of one other country: the Federal Republic of Germany. That the two would become one now seemed inevitable. The only questions were how and when?

But before I could turn my attention back to the 'wrapping-up' of what had to be Germany's march to reunification, I needed – and the paper needed – a visit to the scene of the year of miracles' bloody ending. January 3rd, 1990, therefore found me sitting once again in the departure lounge at Heathrow Airport, waiting for the Tarom Romanian airlines flight to Bucharest. I would have preferred to travel by another airline – any other airline – but with the situation on the ground still uncertain, nobody else at all was flying into Romania. When, four hours late, the few of us foolish enough to want do so went out on the tarmac we were not exactly reassured. I had flown in many a Boeing 707 before, although by then the enduring workhorse of air transport was considered a relative antique. But never before had I flown in one streaked with mud. We were only allowed to get on board after they had unloaded stretchers bearing the injured. The flight was delayed because it had been diverted via Timisoara to pick up several seriously wounded civilians who needed urgent medical treatment only available in London.

As we tried to settle down in our threadbare seats I noticed one young couple almost in tears who had been on the flight and not disembarked. Gently I tried to coax them into conversation, only to find they spoke little English. They did, however, speak French, which was not unusual for Romanians, whose own language was Latin-derived. It turned out, however, that they were not Romanian at all, but Belgian, and on their way home from their honeymoon. Not in Timisoara – or even Bucharest – needless to say. They had got married in early December and booked a honeymoon in Thailand. Their only mistake had been to go for the absolute cheapest flights they could find, offered, unsurprisingly, by Tarom, itinerary Brussels-Bucharest-Bangkok. Lazing on the beaches of Koh Samui, they had heard nothing about the revolution in Romania and were horrified to land in the middle of a capital in chaos, then be diverted to Timisoara where they had picked up moaning bloodied bodies which were laid in stretchers in the aisles. They had been in the air already for more than twenty-four hours.

I wondered how they were going to get home, until the obvious truth dawned on me, a few moments after take-off. Take-off in itself was a hair-raising experience, not least because I was seated across the aisle from a British Airways ground agent I had known in Moscow. He was now on his way to Bucharest in the hope of discussing a better deal on routes and landing fees with the new regime (I had to admire the capitalist nerve). I made a few remarks on the state of the plane, but he laughed it off as 'mere cosmetics'; he had lived in Somalia for several years with experience of their national airline, never mind our mutual grim tales of Aeroflot. 'It'll be fine,' he said with a laugh. Which was why, when we lurched along the runway, heaved up into the air and then suddenly seemed to drop, and then maybe a few thousand feet above West London, did it again, that I looked across to him for moral support. Only to see that his face was every bit as white as mine, and his knuckles were if anything whiter as we both clutched our armrests as if they contained the controls to ejector seats. Barely an hour later we landed, as I had reluctantly come to anticipate, in Brussels. Though I could not help feeling relieved on behalf of our poor honeymooners who literally ran off the plane as if they feared it might at any moment take off again with them still on board.

I could all too easily understand their terror. It was not as if our aircrew exactly inspired confidence. Ever since our upsy-daisy take-off from Heathrow I had been waiting for them to bring round the booze to calm my nerves. In vain. Now, as we repeated the same antics to get airbound in Brussels – think of a small child playing with a model airliner, going 'Vrooom, vrooooom' – I was beginning to seriously look forward to a stiff gin and tonic. When the alcohol finally did emerge, however, it turned out all they apparently had was *tuiça*, that Romanian plum brandy which had spiced up our New Year's Eve cocktails. There was a bigger problem, however: the aircrew weren't offering it around. They were drinking it. For the next several hours we watched two lumpen air stewardesses standing in the aisle, leaning over the backs of empty seats – there were by now only a dozen passengers on board – and getting solidly pissed out of their minds, while puffing on endless cigarettes. Kent, of course. Not once were we even offered a drop – of anything – and when I made an attempt to ask, they waved a finger at me, as if I were a naughty schoolboy asking if I could leave the room during lessons.

This was bad enough but it seemed to be taking an unconscionably long time to get to Bucharest. I had expected the flight to take between three and a half and four hours. From London. Brussels was already part – admittedly a small part – of the way there. But after nearly five hours on board, I was beginning to wonder what the hell was going on, with vague visions of having become trapped in an episode of *The Twilight Zone*, possibly entitled 'Flight into Infinity', when the less than totally slurred voice of a male attendant (the captain?) asked us to fasten our seat belts, as we would be landing in ten minutes, 'in Constanta'. The BA man and I turned to one another, our mouths simultaneously making the expression, where? Not that we didn't know where: Constanta was Romania's biggest city on the Black Sea, and had for years been fighting a – relatively doomed – battle to make it into the catalogues of British packet tour operators.

'Why not Bucharest?' I tried getting something, in elementary

English, out of the *tuiça*-sodden stewardess. She did that finger-wagging thing again, and said, 'Not possible.'

'Why?' I tried, more in hope than expectation.

'*Tanki*,' she said, 'tanks. On the runway.'

'Oh,' I said, because it was, after all, not a bad explanation.

We piled off the aircraft, relieved at least to be back on *terra firma*, to find ourselves in an unheated waiting room with temperatures hovering around minus five degrees Centigrade. For half an hour we stood there, our teeth chattering, while they roused a customs and immigration man to stamp our visas. 'Tonight,' a bleary-eyed Tarom ground agent told us, 'you will stay in motel. Here. Then tomorrow, when we get clearance from Bucharest, we get back on plane. Okay?' The BA man and I looked at one another and thought the same thing: no, not okay. Not okay at all. Not only would we have to spend the night in some undoubtedly freezing, flea-ridden motel room, but the next day we would have to get on that damn plane again. We weren't doing it. Not if they threatened us with a firing squad, though under the circumstances we decided not to raise that option. 'No thanks,' we said together, firmly. 'We'll take a taxi.'

They looked at us as if we were mad, which was a bit rich coming from this shower, and shrugged. It was of course, fairly mad. It wasn't as if Bucharest was just down the road. It was almost 150 miles away, in a country with nothing that resembled motorways. Nonetheless, for an extortionate – in Romanian terms – couple of hundred US dollars we found a local driver willing to take us, and did our best to grab a few hours sleep – it was gone two a.m. – as we rattled across the Danube floodplain. We crawled into Bucharest in the last hour before dawn, as if entering the lowest level of Dante's inferno: a spectral city with belching, steaming industrial plants on its outskirts, shrunken, huddled figures trudging through the slush along the unlit roadside to begin their ten-hour shifts labouring for the Victory of Socialism. Even now, with military vehicles on every street corner and tanks at every intersection, people still had to earn a crust. And in Romania, a crust meant a crust.

I spent five days there, putting together an 'aftermath' and 'what next' piece, soaking up colour in a monochrome city where it seemed life itself, like the politics and the people, only came in shades of grey. Or occasionally black. Had this city once really been described as the 'Paris of the East?' I watched tramps sleeping rough in Ceausescu's still unfinished great folly, the House of the People, now given over to the people, who were lighting camp fires on its marble floors. I gingerly climbed four floors up a stairwell pock-marked with bullet holes to reach the television studios where the rebels had announced to the nation that the 'great leader' had fled, and from where they had broadcast the footage of his execution. And then I went home.

Over the next few months, markedly less hectic than those that had gone before, I returned repeatedly to East Germany, watching in wonder as the Wall vanished almost as rapidly as it was erected. Bulldozers dealt with most of it, though whole slabs – particularly those with the 'prettiest' graffiti on the Western side went for high prices at auction. Elsewhere people simply chipped away at it. East Germany's frontiers remained, but in little more than theory as all but the most rudimentary controls were removed. Driving south to Bavaria, through what had once been a rigorously controlled fron-tier with a single crossing point, watchtowers, automatic machine guns and series after series of high barbed wire fences, I decided – just to see what would happen – to try to take a back road, the sort that would have been regularly used by farm tractors or villag-ers going to market in the days before the country was divided. I fully expected to come across a 'road closed' sign at least, or maybe even still the barbed wire and tank traps. Instead I found the road open and in use, the frontier marked only by the presence of a little caravan, the sort English pensioners might drag behind their Austin Princesses for a weekend at the seaside, inhabited by a cheery-faced East German border guard who stamped my passport (not nec-essary for Germans) and leaned out smiling to be photographed, the now redundant watchtower looming in the background like an abandoned beach umbrella.

As the two Germanys moved inexorably towards union, my old friends Alex and Bärbel moved inexorably apart. The new situation brought new challenges as well as new opportunities, but above all it turned their old world upside down. Alex embraced capitalism wholeheartedly and wanted to set up a new bar, maybe more than one. Bärbel was just happy that her children were happy and that she was reunited with them and wanted nothing more than to keep Metzer Eck up and running, to see it flourish in a world where it would begin to face previously unimagined competition. Those were her prime goals, plus a holiday in Florida.

The mechanics of the process of German unification are too detailed, lengthy and cumbersome to be dealt with here. East Germany's first free elections, held in March 1990, produced a pro-unification coalition government headed by Christian Democrats led by Lothar de Maizière, a soft-spoken reluctant politician of distant French Huguenot origins (the French protestants had fled persecution in Catholic France for tolerant Prussia in the seventeenth century), whose prime job would be to see his country into oblivion.

The first big step was a monetary union between one of the strongest currencies in the world, the West German D-Mark, and one which had almost no value at all, the East German Mark. Eventually after a lot of hand-wringing and calculator button-pressing, a solution was reached that was a fusion of economic and political reality: East Germans up to the age of twenty-five would be able to exchange up to 2,000 Marks at 1:1. The figure for those between twenty-six and sixty would be 4,000 Marks, and 6,000 for those over sixty. Cash or assets above that level would be translated at 2:1. It was both generous and risky. Few East Germans had large savings from their paltry wages and the state had nationalised most businesses and a substantial amount of property. Bärbel for example ran Metzer Eck as a private business, inherited from her father, but the property itself was owned by the state, as was the flat upstairs in which she lived.

Rents were another matter that reunification had to deal with, as were repossessions. There were many people living in West Berlin and West Germany with claims on property nationalised by the communists in the East. Their claims would have to be examined, and where valid, the property either returned or compensation issued. But it was hardly practicable for private landlords to move in and overnight start charging ordinary East Berliners what they might consider to be a 'market rate'. As a result rents were fixed, with a long-term sliding scale for them to move to market levels. The same applied to prices of necessities. But salaries and benefits in the East were also put on a rising scale, a decision that inevitably sparked many people, particularly the young, to give up their guaranteed cheap rent for the chance to move west and make 'real money', even if they faced much higher living costs. It was a risk that not everyone was prepared to take but it would lead to substantial depopulation in some areas nonetheless. As did the inevitable collapse of some of East Germany's rust belt industries, particularly in the mining, chemical and heavy industrial sectors. A government agency, the *Treuhandanstalt* (roughly: transition trust), was set up to find buyers or backers for viable industries, but its work over the succeeding years was marred with allegations of corruption and dodgy deals. In the midst of all this was born the *Ossie* and *Wessie* syndrome of mutual suspicion that Lothar de Maizière famously said would not vanish, 'until the last person to be born under communism has died'.

But as June 1990 came to an end and the death of the East German Mark approached, there was only a mood of celebration in Metzer Eck. On the morning of July 1st people queued outside banks and specially opened exchange offices to hand in their old notes for new. Alex had by then moved out and opened his new bar with some 'business colleagues' (who would later turn out to be dodgy characters looking for ways to launder Stasi slush funds), but he still came back for the party. The date for the final act of union itself was no longer far away. At Potsdamer Platz, prior to 1939 the bustling heart of Berlin but since 1961 a wasteland between the walls under which lay the buried ruins of Hitler's Führerbunker, I bought from a kiosk set up by the West Berlin municipal government one of the multilingual hardboard signs that had been part of the Cold War landscape: '*Achtung! Sie verlassen jetzt den Amerikanischen Sektor*. Attention, you are now leaving the American sector.' It cost me DM5 (£2). I wish I had bought a dozen.

By the beginning of October, the last bits of the legalistic jigsaw puzzle finally fell into place. In effect the German Democratic Republic was ceasing to exist, and its component states – Brandenburg, Saxony, Saxony-Anhalt, Thuringia and Mecklenburg-Vorpommern – were joining the Federal Republic of Germany, as was Berlin, reunified and a city-state in its own right. The word officially used was not 'reunification' but 'unification', to avoid any worries in Warsaw that there might be some hidden agenda that would eventually include restoring to Germany the lands ceded to Poland in 1945. To emphasise the point, a law had been passed in the parliament in Bonn – which only now were politicians beginning to realise would inevitably have to move 'back' to Berlin – formally acknowledging the 'new' eastern border of the Federal Republic as definitive and permanent.

On October 2nd, the eve of formal unification, I met up with Alex on Unter den Linden and did a pub crawl that brought us at midnight to the Brandenburg Gate. On the steps of the Reichstag, a museum building since 1945 but which it was now clear would one day once again be the country's parliament, stood every dignitary in Germany. Chief among them were Chancellor Helmut Kohl, whose remit would now run over a country fifty per cent larger, and East Germany's last leader Lothar de Maizière. They presided over the midnight raising of the 'black-red-gold' flag – without hammers or compasses – that had formerly represented West Germany and now represented all of it. Unsurprisingly Kohl, who would go down in history as the 'unity chancellor' despite a less than dignified departure from office several years later, described it as 'the happiest day of my life'. The relatively nondescript De Maizière made the more memorable speech. He said: 'We are one people, we are become one state. It is an hour of great joy. It is the end of some illusions. It is a farewell without tears.'

In reality there were tears aplenty as the fireworks erupted in the night sky. Tears of happiness mostly, but not only: nobody believed unification would be a panacea for all ills, especially the now soaring unemployment rate in the East. Alex and I however embraced and drank a toast to the future, whatever it might bring. And then we continued the pub crawl. Our first stop was the Adler on Friedrichstrasse, the bar just on the Western side of Checkpoint Charlie where I had watched the crowd pour through on the night the Wall came down. To my surprise – and great delight – one of the men at the bar, still in uniform, was Yogi Bear, the East German border guard who had been a familiar face at the frontier for so many years. I bought him a beer, and we toasted one another. He told me his name was Uwe. Obviously he already knew mine: he had stamped my passport often enough. Putting a name for the first time to a face I had known for years was an odd and strangely poignant experience. I asked him what he was planning to do now. 'I don't know,' he said, gesturing towards the empty control posts and the red-and-white striped vehicle barrier, now raised permanently, pointing upwards into the sky like an old-fashioned barber's pole: 'I guess I'm unemployed.'

A month later, on the first anniversary of the Fall of the Wall, I came back to Checkpoint Charlie with a couple of other journalists writing 'one year on' pieces. We had driven from Hamburg taking in the creeping signs of Westernisation spreading across the former 'East'. On the outskirts of Berlin we had detoured around the perimeter of the old West Berlin boundary, tracing the route of the 'rural Wall'. I had climbed up an abandoned concrete watchtower and tried to imagine myself a guard looking out so see if I could spot one of my fellow countrymen trying to cross from one bit of countryside to another, knowing it was my duty to shoot to kill if I did. Now at Checkpoint Charlie, empty and abandoned and awaiting demolition, we wandered among the old customs sheds, passport control cabins and the 'holding rooms' where anyone detained for incorrect documentation might be sequestered. And we committed wanton vandalism: kicking in a few doors, smashing the occasional window. It was stupid, childish, futile and meaningless. But it didn't half feel good.

Brave New World

And with that, history came to an end.

I wish.

American political philosopher Francis Fukuyama's celebrated 1992 book, *The End of History and the Last Man*, arguing that the collapse of communism spelled the global triumph of Western liberal democracy could not have been more wrong. In early 1990, I described the tumultuous events of the previous year as a wave of revolutions that had finally ended a seventy-five-year European civil war. Round One, 1914–1918, had been a furious slugfest, with the heavyweight empires of the old world battling it out, ending with them all battered but one lot more bloodied than the rest. Round Two had been twenty years of dancing around one another, landing glancing blows here and there – Italy's grab for Ethiopia, Spain's internecine conflict, the rise of the dictators, Stalin's famine in Ukraine, and Hitler's clawing back of the Saarland, the aftermath of the punitive, self-defeating 1919 Versailles Peace Treaty. Round Three, 1939–45, was another no-holds-barred bloodbath, an orgy of unprecedented atrocity that blended almost seamlessly into: Round Four, the 'Cold War's' long slow potentially deadly dance of attrition, that had ended only when one side collapsed of exhaustion.

By the end of course, it was no longer a European war – the hands on the levers of power were in Washington and Moscow (and Russia has forever been a continent unto itself). When the counterweights that held the fragile balance slipped, rather than the world exploding, old Europe imploded, fell back into itself and reconstituted its constituent parts. Countries that, in a world divided into West and East, had been written off the mental as well as geographical map, rediscovered themselves and their place in history.

At the same time, one of the major players wrote itself out of history. Gorbachev's humane, logical and fundamentally decent liberalisation policies, famously summed up by his spokesman Gennady Gerasimov as the 'Sinatra Doctrine', were inevitably a step too far for some of the more recidivist hardliners in the Kremlin. With Moscow's Eastern European empire largely liberated, the pressure within the Soviet Union itself, and its fifteen nominally confederated constituent republics, began to build towards boiling point. In August 1991, while Gorbachev was on holiday at a government *dacha* outside Yalta in the Crimea, a 'gang of eight' back in Moscow used the opportunity to seize power. Gorbachev was placed under house arrest and a national state of emergency declared. Their plot ran aground on one man, a contrary, ambitious, hard-drinking rock of a man called Boris Yeltsin, who had himself been angling for power by becoming president of the Russian Federation, nominally just one of the fifteen republics under control of the Soviet president, but the one that constituted by far the greatest bulk of the country.

Yeltsin declared the 'state of emergency' to be an illegal coup and with his supporters barricaded himself inside the Russian Federation parliament building on the banks of the Moscow River. A huge building architecturally similar to the Shell Centre on the banks of the Thames in London, it was known to most Muscovites by its nickname, 'The White House'. The putschists sent the tanks in but the level of popular anger and the small army of volunteers, many of them armed, whom Yeltsin had gathered around him, determined to turn the White House into a fortress, convinced them that they could be facing a pitched battle with potentially major loss of life. They backed down, and Gorbachev came back. But it was the last straw for the Soviet Union as he resigned his role as general secretary of the Communist Party, and one by one the constituent republics, having seen that Moscow would not or could not restrain them, declared some degree of independence.

At the time of the coup, I was stuck in London with no possibility of getting into Moscow after all entry to and exit from the Soviet Union had been suspended under the state of emergency. With the quality of the copy we were getting out of Moscow less than up to the drama of the situation and the standards readers expected from the country's leading Sunday paper, I was called upon to do what Dave Goddard had taught me all those years previously on the night shift at

Reuters World Desk; re-imagine it. Wholly familiar with the *dramatis personae*, as well as the physical stage on which the tragedy was being played out, I sat down late on a Friday night – with a bottle of champagne in front of me supplied by the editor – to turn a series of dry, factual news reports into a gripping narrative of the events that led to the collapse of the world's second superpower. It was published as a pull-out tabloid insert in the main newspaper, entitled 'Red Sunset'.

The copy we received from Moscow said things like: 'Top Soviet leaders gathered for emergency talks in the Kremlin last night'. Not wrong, but I could hear old Dave's Dorset tones in my ear as I translated it: 'Convoys of Zil limousines … (*that's it boy, they didn't get there on foot, did they? You know what they drive, and never in ones or twos either!*) … sped over the glistening cobbles of Red Square … (*that's it, it was raining out there last night, weren't it, and that's not tarmac, is it? What do cobbles do in the rain? Load of old cobblers, mate, smashing stuff*) … and armed guards stood stiffly to attention … (*not got peashooters in their pockets and they'd hardly be slouching, would they?*) … while they passed through the Great Saviour's Gate … (*not the sort of lads to use the tradesmen's entrance, are they, and that name's good too, got resonance, that has – see, you just have to use what you know*) … into the medieval fortress at the heart of the world's second superpower. (*There you go, lad, you'll be getting the hang of this soon.*)

In fact, the disintegration of the Soviet Union happened more quickly than even we imagined that night. In Moscow statues of Felix Dzerzhinsky, founder of the KGB, and other luminaries of the communist era were pulled to the ground. Those few republics that did not declare outright independence loosened their bonds to Moscow in a new 'Commonwealth of Independent States'. On December 25th, Christmas Day – although not in the Russian church, which observes the Orthodox calendar – exactly two years after Ceausescu was shot, Gorbachev resigned as president of the Soviet Union. Two days later Yeltsin moved into his office as president of Russia. On New Year's Eve, two years after our party celebrating the collapse of the Wall and the end of the 'evil empire's' dominance in Eastern Europe, we held a smaller, black-tie dinner party at home, the highlight of which was the playing of the Soviet national anthem at midnight and lowering of the red flag. Tongue in cheek symbolism. And a bit of a laugh.

I for one was not celebrating Gorbachev's removal from power. More than anyone else he had been the sane force that had made 1989 a year of miracles rather than of bloodbaths. He was – and is – both a great and a tragic figure in world history. He tried to reform an empire and ended up overseeing its disintegration. At any stage he could have stepped in and halted that disintegration, though he would probably only have postponed it, and at incalculable cost in human life. The most remarkable thing I heard him say was several years after his resignation when he was asked who figured largest amongst his role models. His answer was not any icon from the pantheon of communist, or even historical Russian leaders. Instead he named a much more unlikely individual: King Juan Carlos of Spain. Asked why, he answered simply: 'Because he too inherited absolute power and chose to give it away.'

The end of the Soviet Union also opened the final chapter in the history of East Germany's long-time dictator. The ailing Erich Honecker and his wife Margot had taken refuge in a Soviet military hospital in East Berlin after the Wall came down. Fearing that he might be put on trial they subsequently fled to Moscow, claiming asylum. But with the Soviet Union no more, Russia's new master, Boris Yeltsin, sent him back to the now unified Germany. As he feared he was put under arrest and charged with responsibility for the deaths of a token 192 people shot trying to cross the Wall. But by the time his trial finally began in 1993, he was judged too ill and released on compassionate grounds. He moved to Chile where his daughter lived and died there of cancer a year later.

The former Soviet 'constituent republics' now suddenly reappeared on the stage of a world that had forgotten them. My children's school in south London set up a twinning programme with a school in Tallinn, capital of Estonia, a country that just ten years before would hardly have been mentioned even in geography lessons. The other Baltic republics, swallowed up by Stalin in his devil's pact with Hitler – Latvia and Lithuania – reappeared, complete with cultures and languages most Britons, perhaps the most insular of Europeans, barely knew existed. Today all of these countries are members of the European Union, which they see not as a bureaucracy imposing silly rules about the shape of bananas (tales mostly invented, exaggerated or misrepresented by London's sensation-seeking xenophobic tabloid press), but as a community of nations that for all its institutional flaws, is a guarantor of their freedom and independence. Nobody thinks the EU is perfect but there are many new members who have less than warm memories of the potential alternatives.

The events of 1989 changed not just the future but also perceptions of the past. In London the aged remnants of the Polish 'government-in-exile' which had fled to its ally in 1939, had for decades been snubbed and ignored by a 'pragmatic' Foreign Office that had reached a *Realpolitik* accommodation with the communist regime in Warsaw. Now all of a sudden here was Lech Walesa, the shipyard electrician become president of his country on a state visit at the invitation of the Queen, going down on his knees before these old men to accept from them the seal of legitimate government they had preserved since the Nazi invasion, and condemning the years between 1945 and 1989 as 'foreign occupation'.

Berlin today is a city reborn. The scar that for twenty-eight years ran through its heart has been removed with such a fervid haste that there is almost no trace of it left for history. It is not hard to understand: Berliners sometimes feel their city has over the past century had more than enough history, from Nazi capital of most of Europe to bombed and burnt-out rubble, then schizophrenic divided anomaly. They are more than happy for it to be 'normal' for a change. Yet history cannot be escaped. In the city centre they have now marked lines on the roads and pavements to indicate where the wall once ran and preserved a tiny section on Bernauer Strasse as a 'Wall Park'. Perhaps most telling however, is the section on Niederkirchnerstrasse, formerly Prinz-Albrecht-Strasse, where beneath the surviving fragments of the Wall lie the excavated traces of an older monstrosity: the basement cells of the long-gone Gestapo headquarters. A permanent exhibition there is justly entitled 'Topography of Terror'.

Just a few hundred yards north the Reichstag building, burnt out as Hitler's pretext for abolishing democracy, stands restored by British architect Norman Foster as the new home of one of the most flourishing democracies in Europe. Between the two lies the monolithic monument to those who died in the Holocaust.

If the rip through the heart of Berlin has been healed, the

stitching in many places is all too evident: the rash of vast modernist skyscrapers around long abandoned Potsdamer Platz: now home to such temples of capitalism as the Sony Centre and Grand Hyatt hotels. Oranienburger Strasse where the Lutheran church ran its information office for the Swords to Ploughshares movement now also boasts one of the most splendid and ornate synagogues in Europe, while there is another in Prenzlauer Berg. Trabants, if they are to be found, are now lovingly preserved collectors' items, or, more often, turned into novelty seats in trendy nightclubs. The speedy abandonment of everything 'DDR' was regretted in the mid-nineties and replaced by a wave of 'Ostalgie' (nostalgia for the East). But that too has now receded as history melds memory and reality, and a new generation emerges.

For too many people in Britain particularly, an offshore island on the literal and psychological fringes of Europe, still belatedly, and not always coherently coming to terms over the lifetime of a generation with the fact that it is no longer a global power, the miracles of 1989 became all too quickly just last year's entertainment on television. A country that prides itself on not having been successfully invaded by a foreign power since 1066 too readily forgets on how many occasions that has been a close-run thing, prevented only by the existence of a twenty-one-mile strip of water. As a result we have far too little empathy for countries that have for decades lived under alien occupation. We glibly pretend that an upsurge in Polish plumbers is much the same thing. Believe me, it isn't.

In reunited Germany the sour taste of the years of partition not only failed to disappear overnight but continued to come back over the years like reflux after an indigestible meal. As hundreds and thousands of people did what I did and asked to see their Stasi files, one after another prominent figure from the worlds of politics, sport and culture had their reputation tainted as having been an IM, an 'informal collaborator'. If the Stasi, with its tens of thousands of operatives, and tens of thousands more 'fellow travellers' had a long arm in its prime, it also cast a long shadow in its passing.

I have never sought out Lieutenant Weichelt or Colonel Lehmann or any other of the Stasi officers' names in my file. There was no point. What would we say? In 1997, however, I did go back to Berlin to meet a much bigger fish from the Stasi rock pool. Markus Wolf was born in south-west Germany in 1923 into a communist-voting family of Jewish origin which unsurprisingly decided in 1933 when Hitler came to power that they would be better off in Russia. He grew up bilingual and returned to Germany only in 1945 with a group of other exiled German communists to take command of the Soviet sector. He became a founding member of the Stasi's foreign intelligence service which he headed until his retirement in 1986. When the Wall fell he tried to claim political asylum in the Soviet Union, only to be turned down. By 1997 he had been convicted of treason by a Düsseldorf court. He appealed on the grounds that he had loyally served the German Democratic Republic, the country of which he was then a citizen, and therefore could not have committed treason against the Federal Republic, as he was, by default, not its citizen. He won.

An urbane, sophisticated, cultured and highly intelligent man, the reason I was interviewing him in 1997 was that he had just published his first cookbook: a highly readable nostalgic collection of Russian recipes and childhood reminiscences. There was something more than slightly surreal about sitting at one of the new pavement cafés outside the redbrick *Rotes Rathaus*, now once again City Hall for reunited Berlin, chatting to a man credited with being the Soviet bloc's most successful spymaster. It was Wolf who had infiltrated one of his own agents into the heart of the Bonn government, a coup which when belatedly discovered led to the fall of Chancellor Willy Brandt's government. He chose to regale me with far more entertaining stories, notably about how difficult it was to organise security when Fidel Castro paid a state visit to East Berlin, because instead of sticking to his schedule and keeping within sight of his Stasi-appointed bodyguards the Cuban dictator lived up to his reputation by climbing out of hotel room windows to visit whorehouses. Before we parted I had the chance, however, to pull a surprise on Wolf: I produced from my bag the thick lever-arch bound copy of my Stasi file and asked him to comment. He looked uncomfortable for a bit, then shrugged and said that after all, his responsibility had been gathering foreign intelligence, not domestic surveillance. But he signed it for me, anyhow, adding the comment: 'As a bit of fun.'

But as he knew, as I know, as anyone who ever lived in a totalitarian society will testify, a state that practises constant surveillance of its citizens is no laughing matter. George Orwell, whose mould-breaking novel 1984 was published sixty years ago this year, gave us neologisms that are not only still with us, but expand their resonance year on year: doublethink, newspeak, Room 101, and above all, Big Brother. Orwell described a world in which three competing alliances – Oceania, Eurasia and Eastasia – are forever at war with one another, a war which necessitates their near-total control over their own citizens' lives; a war of which occasionally maverick citizens doubt the necessity – or reality – but which is convenient for the authorities who rule over them.

Orwell may not have got it exactly right – the power blocs of today may not be absolutely identical in number or geography – but he came a lot closer than is comfortable. His concept of Britain redesignated 'Airstrip One', an unsinkable aircraft carrier and unquestioning ally of an American-based power bloc, appeared horribly near the knuckle during the uncomfortable unequal alliance entered into by former prime minister Tony Blair with US president George Bush. For decades we were told that the Cold War was a standoff that threatened humanity, that the clock stood at five minutes to midnight. Life seemed perpetually under threat. Having grown up in Northern Ireland and used to the perennial IRA threat, to being forever on the lookout for suspect packages, to being searched going into shops, the respite after the Good Friday agreement seemed wonderful. Yet no sooner had both decades-old threats been lifted than along came the 'clash of civilisations' and the 'war on terror' to take their place. Our politicians abhor a vacuum of terror. A climate of fear gives them a greater mandate over the lives of their citizens.

What could be more Orwellian an example of doublethink and newspeak than the daily announcement on the London Underground that it is 'important to be watchful at all times during this period of heightened security'? What they mean is 'heightened insecurity', but to say so would be to reduce the impression that 'they' are in control, especially when – as the shooting of innocent Brazilian electrician Jean-Charles de Menezes at Stockwell Tube station showed – they often are not. At the very least, 'they' are not as in control as they would like to be. But living as we do in a nation-state with more security cameras per head of population than any other on earth (London alone has more than many whole countries) – compare any German, or even Russian, airport; their experience of Big Brother is too recent – the 'security situation' is a convenient excuse for almost every organ of government, from Whitehall to your local council refuse collection department, to 'collect evidence' about 'miscreant behaviour'. To those who say 'if you have done nothing, you have nothing to fear', I would ask only who defines 'nothing', and how do you know when – or why – that definition may change?

I am not saying there are no terrorists or no threat. The attacks on New York and the London Underground proved that. What lacks proof is that the risks always inherent in a free society justify curtailing that freedom: measures such as locking up citizens for three months without trial or even charge, investigating the contents of rubbish bins or keeping a database of every phone call made, email sent or website looked at, all of which have in recent years been proposed by the government of a country that likes to boast of its people's freedom and democracy. Recent press exposés of the corruption endemic in the British parliament have only proved how important it is for the press to be free, for journalists to be able to report what they see, for the public to have the power to censure governments, rather than governments have the power to censor what the public may see, or do.

I would not have thought, in East Germany in 1989 as we rejoiced at the crumbling of the Berlin Wall and the collapse of corrupt governments who thought their power over their populations was total, backed up by policemen – secret or otherwise – who considered themselves unanswerable to the public, that twenty years later, Britain would be a country where politicians tried to use the law to prevent revelation of how they twisted the rules to their own profit, or where policemen would wear masks and illegally cover up their identifying numbers to lash out at legitimate demonstrators. No, we are not a worse country today than East Germany was before the Wall came down. But we are not always so very much better as we like to imagine.

The lesson of '1989 and all that' is that history is not something that happens around us. It is something we are part of. For richer, for poorer, for better or worse.